TIME TEAM 99

THE SITE REPORTS

Written by
TIM TAYLOR
Series Producer

Archaeological
Consultant
MICK ASTON

The TIME TEAM cast and crew at the end of filming at Beauport Park *Chris Bennett*

THE TIME TEAM

Tony Robinson, the series presenter, is probably best known for his role as Baldrick in *Blackadder* and as the Sheriff of Nottingham in *Maid Marian and Her Merry Men*, which he also wrote. He has a keen interest in history and archaeology – he is president of the Young Archaeologists' Club – and is particularly fascinated by ancient Greece and the biblical lands of the Middle East.

Professor Mick Aston, the team leader, has been involved with archaeology for more than 30 years, and is currently Professor of Landscape Archaeology at the University of Bristol. He has written numerous articles and books, including *Interpreting the Landscape*, the standard work on landscape archaeology. To date, he has appeared in seven series on archaeology for Channel 4.

Phil Harding works as a field archaeologist with Wessex Archaeology, and has been involved in a project listing and plotting all known Palaeolithic sites in Britain. He has also completed a number of excavation reports – including some for TIME TEAM – on sites ranging from the Palaeolithic to the Industrial Revolution. He continues to demonstrate flint knapping at craft shows and to local societies.

Carenza Lewis has been with the Royal Commission on the Historical Monuments of England (RCHME) since 1985. A specialist in the medieval period and in historic landscapes, she worked extensively as a field archaeologist in Wessex and co-edited a collection of essays on the medieval landscape of this part of England. Her book on the medieval landscape of the East Midlands – *Village, Hamlet and Field* – was published in 1997.

Stewart Ainsworth trained as a surveyor before moving into the archaeology section of the Ordnance Survey as an investigator, working in Britain on archaeological sites and monuments and, on secondment, on a mapping project on the Caribbean islands of St Kitts and Nevis. In 1985, he joined the RCHME as an archaeological investigator and is now head of the field archaeology office for the West Midlands.

Victor Ambrus, who arrived in Britain from Hungary in 1956, is a freelance illustrator with almost 300 books to his credit. Winner of the World Wildlife Award and twice winner of the Kate Greenaway gold medal for the best illustrated book of the year, his recent work includes illustrated editions of *The Iliad* and *Moby Dick* and illustrations for a book on the Anglo-Saxon ship burials at Sutton Hoo. He is a Fellow of the Royal Society of Arts and the Royal Society of Engravers.

Robin Bush, formerly deputy county archivist for Somerset, is a freelance lecturer, historian and broad-caster. An expert in genealogy and on the history of early emigration to the United States, he is author of numerous books on local history, including a definitive guide to Somerset.

CREATIVE TV, responsible for TIME TEAM's computer graphics: **Sue Francis** worked with the BBC for two years and then as a freelance designer before, in 1989, setting up Creative TV Facilities where she is chief designer. **Steve Breeze** was signed to RCA Publishing as a singer/songwriter before joining Creative TV where he creates 3D visualisations.

Dr Chris Gaffney has worked in geophysics since 1983, including extensive site-based experience in the UK, Greece and the former Yugoslavia. In 1989, he formed a partnership with John Gater at GSB Prospection. He, is an associate editor of the *Journal of Archaeological Prospection.*

John Gater has been involved in archaeological geophysics for almost 20 years, working for British Gas, the Ancient Monuments Laboratory (English Heritage) and Bradford University Research. In 1986, he set up GSB Prospection, an independent consultancy in geophysics for archaeology. He is associate editor of the *Journal of Archaeological Prospection.*

Bernard Thomason is head of Technical Survey for Archaeology at the RCHME with responsibility for keeping its survey teams up to date with equipment and techniques. For the last three years, he has concentrated on applying surveying techniques using the global positioning system (GPS) of satellites to archaeology, both at work and for TIME TEAM.

Victor Ambrus's impressions of some members of the TIME TEAM: *(from left)* Carenza Lewis, Mick Aston, Phil Harding, Robin Bush, Tony Robinson.

One of the impressive trenches at Bawsey St James. *Mick Aston*

CONTENTS

All terms printed in **bold** are defined in the 'Archaeological methods' section.

PAPCASTLE

CUMBRIA

WHAT MIGHT HAVE HAPPENED

Finally, at this outpost of the empire, they would have some buildings worthy of Rome. The new structures would last – the best builders had been appointed and the new foundations were deep and solid and of a classic mould.

The massive stones had been wedged against each other to create an immovable base for the finely carved structures that would stand on top.

Now those who had followed the soldiers to this frontier could at last give some thought to ordering the decorations of the interior and the supplies of pottery that would grace the tables.

Despite its northern location, the fort had been well positioned, looking across the beautiful valley and protected by the hills and fortifications.

The new buildings were just what were needed to give it an edge over the other provincial settlements.

Victor's reconstruction of the substantial Roman building, the remains of which were found in the Buckinghams' garden.

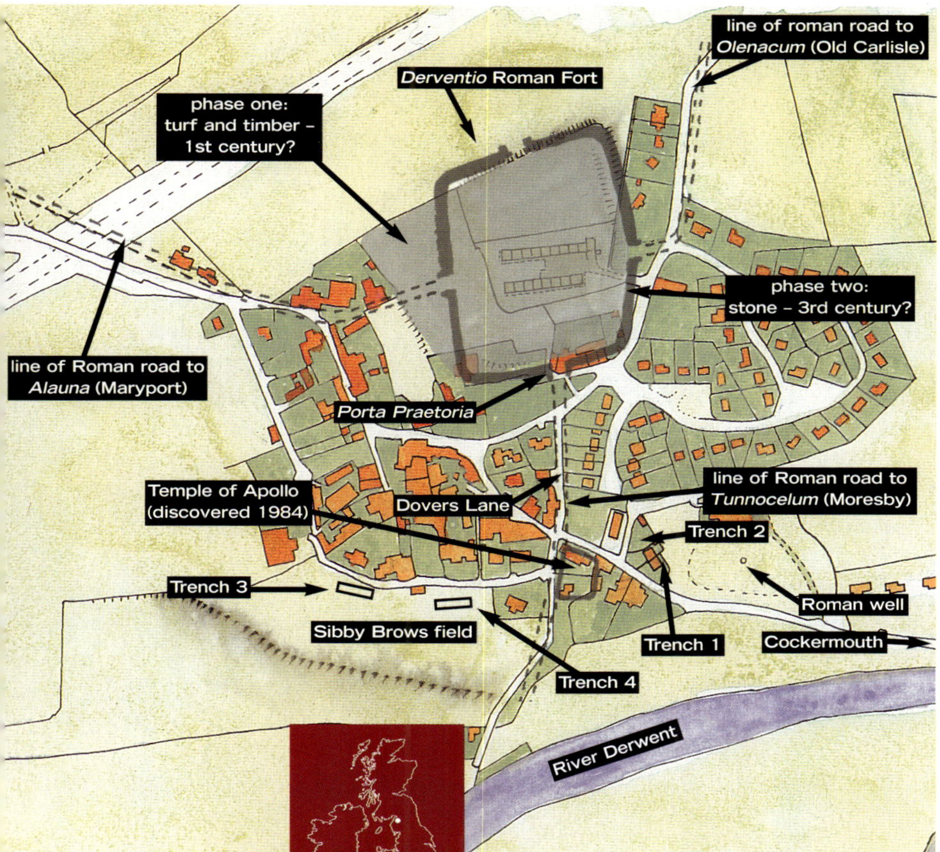

WHY WE WENT THERE

In AD 43, the Roman emperor Claudius ordered the invasion of Britain, partly because of rumours of mineral wealth there (gold, silver and lead), but primarily to boost his own political status. Eventually about 10% of the Roman army was on British soil – the most heavily militarised part of the empire. Within four decades or so, a pattern of military occupation had been established: major strategic centres (Caerleon, Chester and York) with a network of auxiliary forts in between. The latter, usually with an area of 1.2–2.4 hectares (3–6 acres), were placed about a day's march apart (14–20 miles) and were connected by roads. Hadrian's Wall, begun in AD 122, was intended to protect against invasion from Scottish tribes as well as to regulate who entered and left the Roman province. In addition, coastal forts were erected along both east and west coasts as well as, later, along the 'Saxon Shore' of the south-east, to repel sea-borne invaders.

TIME TEAM's interest in this era of British history became focused on Papcastle, a village to the west of

Cockermouth in Cumbria, by a letter from Ray Buckingham. In the course of moving about 30 tons of earth to build an extension to his house and construct a patio, he had come across a huge number of Roman finds – including Samian pottery and jewellery – and what appeared to be a Roman building in his back garden.

The existence of a Roman fort at Papcastle has been known for a long time. It occupied a strategic position at a major crossing point of the River Derwent – which took its name from Papcastle's Latin one: *Derventio* – where the hills and mountains of the Lake District meet the north Cumbrian coastal plain. It is believed to have been established in relation to coastal defences – the forts at Maryport *(Alauna)* and Moresby *(Tunnocelum)* about 5–10 miles away – and was at the crossroads of at least two Roman roads: Moresby to Old Carlisle *(Olenacum)* and Maryport to Keswick.

An area of the village close to the fort was excavated in 1984 by Adrian Olivier of English Heritage. He found massive wall foundations forming the corner of a substantial enclosure, probably dating from the 3rd century, inside of which were a series of clay floors. Further down the hill, he also unearthed a substantial sandstone slab, which may have been the foundation for an altar in a temple. This interpretation was strengthened by a large number of finds, including some of eastern origin, which may in turn indicate the presence at the fort of Sarmatian cavalry from south-western Russia. Also found was a unique statuette of the satyr Marsyas, which suggests that the temple may have been dedicated to Apollo. It appears that the fort as a whole was abandoned or destroyed towards the end of the 3rd century.

Other than Olivier's work and some 'rescue' archaeology carried out during the 1960s, Papcastle has been somewhat

(Above) Emperor Claudius, the leader of the Roman invasion of Britain. *Mary Evans Picture Library*
(Above right) Walltown Crags on Hadrian's Wall. *Mick Aston*

overlooked by the archaeological establishment. But there are some clues that point to a site of greater than usual importance. The fort itself covers 2.8 hectares (6.9 acres), an untypically large size, and its *vicus* – the civilian settlement that would have grown up around the fort – appeared to be 9 hectares (22.2 acres) in extent, much greater than the usual 5 hectares (12.4 acres).

At the invitation of Ray and his wife Helen and their three children Zoë, Thomas and Hannah, TIME TEAM went to Papcastle and invaded the Buckinghams' cottage and garden, down the hill from the fort. We were going to try to identify their finds and find out what the Romans were doing here almost 2,000 years ago.

Day One

Our first day dawned clear but with a stiff wind off the sea five miles away. In the incident room, set up in the local village reading room, Bernard investigated the Landmark historical map database on CD-ROM for details of Papcastle. Later he would be using the Ordnance Survey database to plot all the Roman finds discovered by Ray and his neighbours in the village, as well as any results from the **field survey** that Stewart had already begun.

In another room, Victor began working with Gilbert Burroughes to make a Roman Samian ware bowl. Gilbert had been involved with TIME TEAM before, at Lavenham in Suffolk where he had helped to make Roman glass. A farmer by profession, he is also a skilled potter and is, as far as we know, the only person in the UK to have managed to reproduce figured Samian ware successfully.

At the Buckinghams' cottage, the top layer of the area that would some day be a patio had been cleaned down to what appeared to be the start of the archaeology – a brown loam with charcoal flecks. After this was drawn and photographed, a grid covering virtually the entire area was marked out and our first trench was begun by Phil and diggers Melanie and Jenni. They soon found a cobbled yard and more large dressed stones to add to those uncovered by Ray, which completed one line of a possible building extending under the corner of the house.

Ray showed Mick, Tony and Mike McCarthy, director of the Carlisle Archaeological Unit, some of the stones he had incorporated into the retaining wall outside his back door. Mick thought that one of them might be a voussoir, a shaped stone once part of an arch, and there was also a sharpening stone, roofing tiles, querns (grain grinding stones) and a fragment of a Roman brick, complete with a paw print.

All the surfaces in the cottage's living room were covered with the vast number of finds that had already emerged from the Buckingham's garden. Lindsay Allason-Jones, archaeological museums officer at the University of Newcastle, was helping Helen to sort through them. She identified a great many pieces of pottery: Samian tableware from the 1st century, domestic cooking pots from the 2nd and 3rd centuries, amphorae (large jugs that carried wine or oil) from Spain as well as the ubiquitous mortaria, flat dishes on which various food ingredients were crushed. In addition, there was a fragment of a *Dea nutrix* figurine made of pipe clay and executed in Gaul in the 2nd century. The entire piece, which had religious significance, would have shown a woman sitting in a basket chair while suckling a pair of babies. The great variety and large range in ages of all these fragments suggest that this layer of the site was where rubbish had been tipped over the centuries.

After lunch, some of the residents of the village arrived at the incident room with possible Roman finds from their own properties. By far the best pieces were brought in by artist Peter Skillen, who is a metal detectorist in his spare time. From various builders' spoil heaps in the area, he had been able to find a Cupid figure, a bronze handle that may have come from a jug in the shape of a baby's head, the lid from a stein-like jug, and a silver *denarius*, a coin from the Roman Republic of the 1st century AD. Most interesting of all was a bronze coin dating from the time of Faustina Junior (175–146 BC), which would have been quite old even at the time of the Roman conquest of Britain. However, its presence near a Roman fort in northern Britain was not that unusual since it is likely that a high-status coin such as this would have been used as currency for quite a long time. Peter was dubbed an honorary member of TIME TEAM and carried out the metal detecting of our spoil heaps for the rest of the weekend.

Mick, Carenza and Roman expert Guy de la Bédoyère looked at the map evidence. Ray's cottage was between the fort and the river, and so could very well have been within the fort's *vicus*. Not only was the possible temple found by Adrian Olivier nearby, but the remains of a Roman well were in the grounds of Derwent Lodge, which abutted Ray's property (and to which we had been unsuccessful in gaining access).

From the Roman road map that Sue

(Top left) The earthworks of the Roman fort on top of the hill at Papcastle. *Mick Aston*
(Above left) Behind the Buckinghams' cottage where trenches have been dug where the stone building was found *(upper left)* and over the location of the GPR anomaly. *Mick Aston*

had created on computer, it was immediately apparent that there had been extensive Roman occupation in this part of Britain. The roads that criss-crossed it and the forts 10–20 miles apart meant that there would have been a large Roman military and civilian population here.

While the Romans had initially come to the north-west to control the local Celtic tribe, the Brigantes, there is no specific evidence to show that the later militarisation of the region was due to a need to control insurgents from the north. Instead, it now appears that the reason for all this building and activity was the mining of lead and a mineral sometimes associated with it: silver.

Silver was fundamental to the Roman economy, used for currency and, especially, to pay the soldiers. According to Mick, 'lead was the Romans' plastic', used for waterproofing and piping among many other things. It is, then, hardly surprising that the Roman authorities felt a need to control and protect this natural resource.

Back at Trench 1 in the Buckinghams' patio, over 100 horses' teeth and what appeared to be a horse's jaw had been found. There was a cult of the horse in Roman times, but equally such evidence could indicate the site of a butcher specialising in horse meat. At *Vindolanda* (Chesterholm) on Hadrian's Wall, archaeologists had found the remains of a shop probably devoted to horsemeat sausages since the bones discovered there showed evidence of the meat having been scraped off, not sliced or cut.

John Gater's geophysics team had carried out a **resistivity** survey in the Buckinghams' garden, but because of the relatively great depth of deposits (if any), the results were poor. This was the moment for **ground-penetrating radar** (GPR) to retrieve its reputation, after its less-than-successful TIME TEAM debut on the very first programme, at Much Wenlock; it had also failed to make the grade at the Birmingham dig in 1996. Geophysicists Jesper Emilsson of the Swedish company MALA GeoScience, which provided the machine, and Sue Overton from John's company GSB Prospection only had time for a couple of traverses, but they did come up with anomalies that might prove to be something interesting a little over 1.5 m (5 ft) down. It was decided to dig Trench 2 here, and a JCB mini-digger was brought in to create a 1 x 3.5 m (3.3 x 11.5 ft) hole.

Stewart arrived back from his hike around the area, having as his mission the discovery of the wider context of Roman Papcastle. He had looked at the existing earthworks, mainly to establish the complete location of the fort. From excavations, there seem to have been two forts, built at different times. The first was built in a strange quadrilateral shape to fit the topography of the hill. The later one was constructed on top of this, but was smaller, being a standard 2 hectare (5 acre) auxiliary fort. Previous excavation had revealed the west and east gates, and now Stewart was confident that he had found the south gate, which appeared to align with present-day Dovers Lane, which may have been a settlement road around which the *vicus* had arisen. The Buckinghams' property was on a road parallel to this.

To determine the limits of the settlement, Stewart had also looked at the earthworks down at Sibby Brows Field, a short walk from the Buckinghams' cottage, at the top of a hill overlooking the River Derwent. There was a strong feature running north–south, a ridge running east–west along the hill and slight undulations on its side. He believed that what lay

beneath the grass could be a remnant of another fort, striphouses (relatively long buildings in which a multiplicity of activities would have been carried out) or even a bath house with compartments. In addition, the footpath next to the field, running down the hill towards the river, could be seen as an extension of Dovers Lane. With all these clues, opening another trench here was a distinct possibility.

A geophysical survey had also been carried out on Sibby Brows Field. John's excitement at the results from here was palpable – 'This is juicy archaeology,' he enthused. In the early 1740s, the antiquarian Routh had found a pavement here 'curiously laid with large stones three-quarters of a yard square and two or three inches thick' on a base of 'coarse strong cement'; there had also been two walls running east–west, '7 yards [6.4 m] apart'. Now John and his colleague Claire Stephens had found high-resistance linear features stretching right across the field. Geophysics had no way of dating these anomalies, but they could mean that the *vicus* extended right down to the river.

One of the local residents who had come to see us at work told an interesting story. It is said that when, in the winter of 1134, Waltheof of Dunbar came to build the castle in nearby Cockermouth, stones from the Roman fort at Papcastle were rolled down to the river via the road that is now Dovers Lane and the footpath next to Sibby

(Above left) Sue Francis's reconstruction of the *Dea nutrix* figurine.
(Above right) Swedish visitor Jesper Emilsson puzzles over his GPR results. *Mick Aston*

Brows Field. When they reached the frozen river, the stones were slid down to Cockermouth to the castle site!

At the end of the day, Ray left to travel to Sellafield, where he works as an engineer. British Nuclear Fuels Ltd (BNFL) had agreed to provide facilties for TIME TEAM to X-ray two of the coins he had found in the patio area.

Day Two

The good weather was still holding – as long as we kept out of the wind, which still had enough force to chill us to the bone. Everyone working on the site was in a good mood, looking forward to discovering what the tantalising signs in the ground we had encountered the day before would turn out to be.

The owner of Sibby Brows Field, farmer Edmund Jackson, was discovered in his barn delivering lambs and agreed to TIME TEAM digging up his field as long as everything was made good afterwards. A large JCB removed the first few inches of grass and top soil of what was designated Trench 3 and then Carenza and some diggers from Mike's unit in Carlisle got to work. Meanwhile, the geophysics team began surveying the field to the east of this.

In the Buckinghams' garden, Ian, one of the diggers, got out of the ground and into the mini-digger to excavate Trench 2. However, when he had removed earth to a depth of 1.5 m (5 ft), we were surprised by the complete lack of finds. Then Ray told us that, when the cellars of Derwent Lodge had been dug in the 19th century, all the earth from there had been dumped into an area that included his garden. And as we looked more closely, we could see that the depth of this trench had not reached the same level as Trench 1, where so much had been and was being found but where none of the spoil from the lodge cellars had been deposited.

There were fears that, if Trench 2 was dug any deeper, the sides would begin to fall in. It was decided to bring in a bigger JCB to enlarge the trench and make a square, but not to dig down so far in the new areas, thus creating a 'stepped' trench that would be much safer.

Finds were still emerging from Trench 1 in the patio, and now that we had definitely reached the archaeology (rather than any casually dumped detritus), these confirmed that the structure we were uncovering was definitely Roman. The prize find was a bronze mirror from the 1st or 2nd century, which was lying directly on a floor surface. It would have been highly polished on one side (with silver or tin), and may once have had a single handle. However, its large diameter – 17 cm (6.7 in) – suggested that it might have had two handles on the back so that it could be held up by a servant.

As well as the mirror, a 3rd-century bronze cosmetic spoon – a long, narrow tool that would have been used for scooping out ointment – was also found, and together, they were positive evidence of the presence of women in the Roman settlement. Roman soldiers were not allowed to marry until the reign of Septimius Severus (AD 193–211), but before then, many may have been accompanied by mothers, sisters or common-law wives. However, the mirror and spoon appear to be of a higher status than a soldier's family.

Back in the incident room, Victor and Gilbert had completed the mould for the Samian ware bowl. Gilbert had created the basic shape on his wheel, and Victor had decorated the inside by cutting out figures to represent the Buckingham *ménage:* a man (Ray), a woman (Helen), three children, a dog and a rabbit, all running round the side of the mould. This was first placed in the family's oven to slow dry; then it was put in a kiln set up at the local Walkers factory, where it would remain until noon the next day.

Bernard continued to update the site map, registering finds unearthed by TIME TEAM or brought in by residents. Among the latter was a gold *aureus* coin struck late in the reign of Nero (AD 54–68) and found on a spoil heap when the Walkers factory was built in the early 1970s. There was also a bronze *centenionalis* coin dating from the reign of Constans I (AD 340–50), who had crossed the Channel and made peace with the united Scots and Picts in 343. The reverse showed the emperor dragging a captive from beneath a tree and had the inscription FEL TEMP REPARATIO (To the Restoration of Happy Times). One of the villagers, David Johnson, contributed some Roman quern stones and some burned grain, which he had found in the fort as a boy when the retirement homes were being built there. Except for the stones used in Ray's garden wall, very little reused Roman material was found in village buildings.

Once the large JCB had finished creating the stepped trench in the garden, Mike climbed down into the bottom and – while the rest of us watched with bated breath (especially our Swedish visitor Jesper) – hand dug down a few inches to see if he could find what had caused the 'blip' on the GPR. Right on target, his trowel scraped against a hard flat surface, and a cheer went up. Ian re-entered the trench to take over the heavy work of excavating what turned out to be four large dressed stones. When John heard of this very satisfactory geophysics result, he said that it just showed that GPR, when used in the proper circumstances, could come up with the goods.

But were these stones Roman? All the experts were unsure, and Mick even said that they might be part of a drain. (Producer Tim Taylor told him that he was not allowed to use the 'D word'!) Then Helen pointed out that the line of stones in this trench appeared to be at

The remains of the bronze mirror found in Trench 1. *Mick Aston*

the same level as and aligned with the ones in Trench 1.

All the Trench 2 stones were more regular on one side. In Roman times, the smoother surface would almost invariably have been on the outside, so this might tell us on which side was the interior of the building. But before any more work could be done here, health and safety considerations had to be addressed. Yet again, the depth of Trench 2 was causing concern; if we were to dig any deeper all round, we would have to make the trench larger (but we had used up almost all of the Buckinghams' garden) or shore up the sides (expensive and time-consuming). In the end, it was decided to dig a 75 cm (30 in) slot trench up to the smoother side of the stones.

back to Papcastle. Coming in from the west, the stepped nature of the hill was very clear: the Roman fort would have been at the top, then the *vicus* on the next level and finally the river flood plain below.

The excavation in Trench 3 was perhaps even more promising than in Trenches 1 and 2. Just under the surface, the diggers had found a cobbled surface with walls on either side. It was the regularity of these structures that greatly surprised the archaeologists, as they examined them in the light of the setting sun. A *vicus* would usually grow up in a haphazard fashion around a fort, with huts, wineshops and brothels. But the size and orderliness of the Papcastle *vicus* were highly unusual, and discussions of what this might mean carried on late into the night.

Trench 1 was still producing surprises. Despite the fact that it was rapidly becoming waterlogged, Phil had uncovered a very complex array of buildings: a timber structure with a hearth, a deep feature filled with cobbles and three sides of a building on stone. The 'deep feature' on the external side of the line of building stones turned out to be an enormous ditch that went down at least 1 m (3.3 ft). With drains still on his mind, Mick proffered the suggestion that this might have been a drainage ditch next to the property.

But soon drains were the last thing he was thinking of as he and Tony, accompanied by a soundman and a cameraman, got a bird's-eye view of the site from a helicopter. They flew up the Roman road to Carlisle, where they could see quite clearly that the Solway Firth and the mountains beyond formed a very obvious border. Then they flew

Day Three

The TIME TEAM archaeologists got together early and decided that the ditch full of cobbles in Trench 1 was actually part of the foundations of a very large, probably administrative building. This discovery changed the team's whole attitude to the site. Now it was not a straggling *vicus* near the fort, but possibly a large settlement, perhaps like *Corstopitum* (Corbridge), a substantial base behind Hadrian's Wall.

The high status of this building was emphasised by a surprising discovery in Ray's garden. Tony Wilmott, an archaeologist with English Heritage who had joined us the evening before, noticed a piece of stone used as a step into the garden shed. On further examination this proved to be a cornice stone from the roof of a monumental building. We knew that it was Roman even though we could not establish its date or whether it had been part of the building in Trench 1. However, it did tell us two things: that the Romans had built as if intending to stay for a long time, and that they had felt secure enough in this settlement to want to display civic pride.

As the day progressed, Mike was able to make more sense of the jumble of building phases that had been found in Trench 1. There appeared to be four. The first dated from the late 1st and early 2nd centuries and included the hearth; bone finds and a flagon top came from this period. This layer seemed to be covered in 'made' ground – that is, soil that had been built up deliberately; in 1984, Adrian Olivier had found the same type of earth underneath the possible temple he excavated. The other three phases were impossible to date because no dateable finds had been found in context, but their sequence could still be discerned: first, a burned level, then the stones that Ray had originally uncovered, and finally the monumental building.

There was one dissenting voice as to the function of this last: because so many remnants of drinking vessels and mortaria for grinding food had been found, Lindsay Allason-Jones reckoned that it had been a very large taverna. Sue had made reconstructions of some of these finds. The earliest was a 2nd-century piece of black burnished ware – a flat-bottomed dish with straight sides, off of which the Roman soldiers would have eaten their dinners. There was also an 'indented beaker' made of colour-coated Nene Valley ware. This very large drinking vessel had an oddly narrow bottom, which would have made it very unstable. Perhaps, said Lindsay, Roman publicans used them because wine would be spilled and they would be able to sell more!

Ian had found a large piece of pottery wedged under one of the large stones in Trench 2 – the first truly stratified evidence for these being of Roman origin. According to Guy de la Bédoyère, the sherd was from a large storage jar, possibly used for wine, which could have been made locally or shipped up from the south.

After lunch, it was decided that this trench was finished and could now be backfilled. Guy was now less sure that

(Above left) Digger Jenni Butterworth recording the stones in Trench 2. *Mick Aston*
(Above centre) Phil next to the cobble-filled ditch in Trench 1. *Mick Aston*

the stones had been part of a monumental building foundation since the outer, smoother ones were really quite crude – 'Not good enough for a Roman wall,' he said, comparing them to those at Hadrian's Wall. Ian suggested that they could have been the base for walls made of wood or cob (compressed earth, clay or chalk reinforced with straw), with a sill beam running along the top of the stones, as he had seen in Dorset.

Back at the incident room, freelance conservator Karen Barker was finishing her work on the mirror found in Trench 1. Amazingly it retained enough of its silvering for Carenza to see her face in it – an eerie experience when you think that the last time it had reflected a woman's face had been almost 2,000 years ago.

Gilbert and Victor's mould had successfully emerged from the kiln, and now Gilbert lined it with clay which would then be fired in the kiln to make the final bowl. This would take longer than TIME TEAM had left, so we would have to wait until the post-production stage of making the programme before we would see the Buckinghams in Roman dress racing round the bowl, which by then would be coated in the shiny orange slip typical of Samian ware.

The geophysics team had found interesting E-shaped anomalies to the west of Trench 3 in Sibby Brows Field, and so our fourth and final trench was excavated here. Interest in this field was high, especially when the geophysics results were added to Bernard's site map and showed their relationship with surrounding features. Again the regularity of the walls and roads we were discovering was striking.

These findings could mean that this was simply an ordinary *vicus*, said Tony

Wilmott. However, it was much more likely that this was that rarity, a planned *vicus*, or even a complex of structures auxiliary to the fort, which was more military than civilian. For the *vicus* at Papcastle to have eventually evolved into a town would have been extremely unusual. In the south of England, this was not the case: first, there would be a fort and *vicus*, then the garrison would leave to go north and the *vicus* would become the basis for a proper town. However, in the north, garrisons were permanent and the stage at which a *vicus* could become a town simply didn't occur. In addition, there had to come a point when the *vicus* became less dependent on the fort in order to survive as a town. If the Roman garrison remained in place, the reason for this increasing independence was lost.

Therefore, what we had found at Papcastle was simply astonishing. A Roman fort that had been relatively overlooked by British archaeology had turned out to be a large, substantial settlement that had become increasingly permanent, eventually turning into a pioneer town, according to Tony Wilmott. Guy reminded us that, in nearby Carlisle in the 6th century AD, there had been a Roman arch and working Roman fountain, two centuries after the soldiers marched away. This could also have been the case at Papcastle.

At the end of the day, everyone went to Sibby Brows Field to view the excavations in Trenches 3 and 4. In the latter, the diggers had found the wall/street pattern continuing towards the east, as well as a Roman drain, which would please Mick! Gazing at the cobbled surface of one of the roads in Trench 3 as the sun set, Carenza said, 'Some people criticise what we do on TIME TEAM, but look – here we have added to knowledge. What we have found here will change the way we look at Roman forts.'

Final thoughts from Mick

I enjoyed Papcastle a great deal, for three reasons. First, we were actually able to help the Buckingham family after they had contacted TIME TEAM at least twice about doing a programme in their garden - it's always nice to work with families, members of the public, who are often fans. Second, even though we excavated such a small area, we were able to tell a good story that added greatly to the interest of Ray and Helen's finds of Roman pottery and other objects.

Finally, I had arrived without a warm sweatshirt, so I was overjoyed when, on the first evening, Helen presented me with a multi-coloured striped fleece that she had made. I was warm for the rest of that weekend, and I've worn it most of the time ever since!

Above left) Trench 4 in Sibby Brows Field showing cobbles and the Roman drain. *Mick Aston*
(Above centre) Decorated Samian ware found by the Buckinghams in their garden. *Mick Aston*

THETFORD

NORFOLK

WHAT MIGHT HAVE HAPPENED

The bishop was delighted with the new windows as the morning light filtered through them and cast a green glow on the stone floors. 'This is a more substantial reminder of God's might than the old cathedral with its rotting wooden sills and bat-ridden roof,' he thought. The position near the town was more attractive to him as well, since it brought in more souls and so provided a more secure basis for the Church. He also appreciated some of the town's suppliers of wine and food, who seemed prepared to curry his favour by bringing supplies to the cathedral. Then there were his plans for extra music more suited to the French mother church's new offspring.

The growing town could benefit from the endless stream of the Conqueror's soldiers as they continued their work to keep the newly won country in order. The cathedral would hopefully have many such visitors over the next few years.

Victor's reconstruction of the Dominican friary at Thetford.

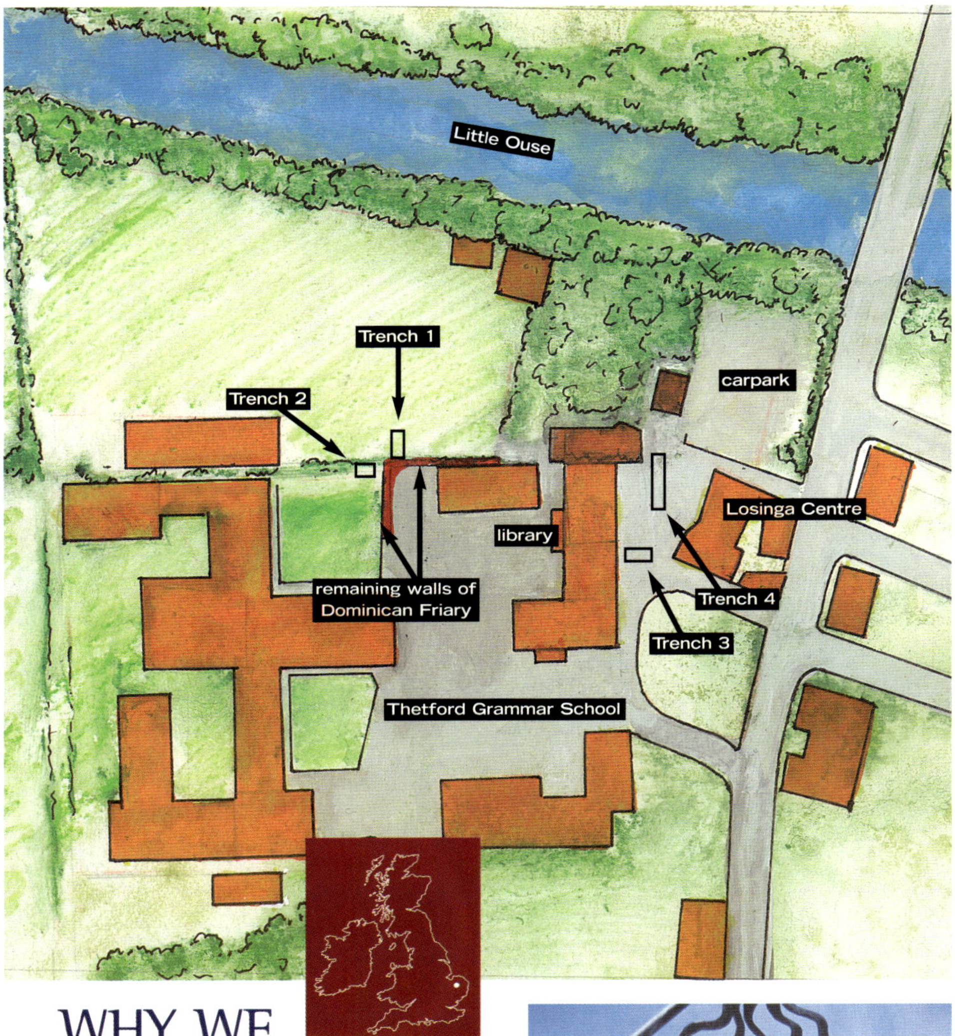

WHY WE WENT THERE

More than two years ago, three pupils at Thetford Grammar School – Tim Smith, Emily Crook and Holly Price – wrote to TIME TEAM asking us to unravel the history not only of the school but also of the two huge ruined flint walls that currently dominate the main school site on the south bank of the Little Ouse.

What intrigued us about this site were not only these walls, which were all that remained of a 14th-century Dominican friary, but the fact that this was once – briefly – the location of a Norman cathedral. But why would Thetford have been so honoured?

Thetford remained a relative agricultural backwater until the rapid expansion of the Saxon town in the second half of the 9th century. Although sacked twice by the Danes (in 1004 and 1010), by the time of the Norman Conquest, it was still the sixth most important conurbation in England (after London, York, Lincoln, Ipswich and Norwich) – a major trading, commercial, industrial and political centre with a mint and many religious houses and at least 14 churches.

The bishops of the conquering William I generally disliked the customs of the Anglo-Saxon church and, under the leadership of the archbishop of Canterbury, Lanfranc (1070–89), they remodelled it on the lines of the Norman church. One major change was to move the bishops' sees (headquarters) and their cathedrals from the countryside to more convenient centres.

In Norfolk this meant that, in 1071, the Norman bishop Herfast turned his back on the 'merely wooden' rural Saxon cathedral at Elmham in the north of the county and adopted urban Thetford as his see. There he took over Great St Mary's church and elevated it to cathedral status. This presumably meant that he rebuilt or embellished the existing structure or that he erected an entirely new structure, since he would have wanted his cathedral to reflect his great status. This was the high point of Thetford's existence: by 1086, the town's entry in the Domesday Book shows it in decline.

In 1091, Herbert de Losinga became Thetford's third bishop. In fact, he bought the post for £1,900 from Ranulf Flambard, the worldly cleric who was chief agent to William II Rufus. To Losinga's credit, he appears to have felt guilty about having committed this sin of simony (trading in sacred offices): in 1094 he resigned as bishop and went on pilgrimage to Rome, where he received absolution from Pope Urban II and was reinstated. The following year, Thetford received a body blow from which it did not recover until the mid-20th century: Losinga moved the see to Norwich and began to build the splendid cathedral that we can see today. The cathedral of Great St Mary at Thetford was redundant.

In 1104, the rights to what was now again the church of Great St Mary were bought by Roger Bigod, sheriff of Norfolk and Suffolk. Almost immediately the Cluniacs (*see box on p12*) moved in, turning the church and the rest of the site into their priory. However, it only took three years for them to outgrow this – in 1107, they established a new priory across the river, Roger Bigod laying the foundation stone just a week before he died. But it wasn't until 1114 that this establishment was completed and the monks finally left Great St Mary.

It lay fallow for more than two

Statue of William the Conqueror outside the castle at Falaise in Normandy where he was born. *Mick Aston*

centuries until, in 1335, it was given to the Dominican friars (*see box on p12*) who, in their turn, built a large friary. This was in operation until the dissolution of the monasteries in 1536; all that remains today are a substantial remnant of the north wall and a much shorter west wall, joined at a corner, next to the school playing field.

It was the succession of religious structures on this site that intrigued us. While excavating a Dominican friary would be fascinating on its own, it was the possibility of uncovering the lost Norman cathedral – or even the previous Anglo-Saxon church – that really captured our imagination. We may have had only three days to delve through a multiplicity of historical levels but we had the pupils of the school to help us.

Day One

TIME TEAM's architecture expert Beric Morley gave Victor his first briefing about what the 11th-century cathedral and the 14th-century flint-built Dominican friary might have looked like. Beric suggested that, for a model for the cathedral, we should use the abbey at Sherborne in Dorset, which was about 45 m (150 ft) long. It had parallel apses – two rounded ends – added to its east end, and we would be looking for similar ones at Thetford. In fact, Mick had already asked our geophysics team to

Monastic houses of England

BENEDICTINES
Founded by St Benedict, who realised that a religious community would have more impact than scattered hermits. Monks lived lives of prayer, hard work, self-discipline and good deeds, under a rule of poverty, chastity and obedience; wore black robes. St Augustine founded first Benedictine monastery in England at Canterbury in c. 601. More set up after Danish raids and settlement, especially by St Dunstan (later archbishop of Canterbury) from 940; at the Norman Conquest, there were 35 Benedictine monasteries and nine nunneries. By the late 11th century, many of these houses had become wealthy and less austere.

CLUNIACS
Founded in France with the aim of returning to St Benedict's original simplicity. Reached Lewes in Sussex in about 1078. Wore black like the Benedictines; spent most of their time at church services, leaving manual work to paid servants. By 1160, there were 36 Cluniac houses, most of them quite small; Thetford was one of the larger ones.

Mary Evans Picture Library

CISTERCIANS
Culmination of puritan reaction against the Benedictines. Founded by Robert of Molesme; first house in England established at Waverley, Surrey in 1128. Wore white. Built their monasteries in remote spots. Had severe rule based primarily on hard manual labour, which eventually made them prosperous. Divided their membership between *choir monks*, who attended all church services and ran the monasteries, and *conversi* or *lay brothers*, who did most of the heavy work. By the 13th century, there were 75 houses and 26 nunneries in England and Scotland.

CARTHUSIANS
Led by St Bruno; successfully combined monks living as hermits within a community. Lived solitary lives in separate cells, spending their days in prayer, meditation and gardening, only meeting in church and rarely speaking. In England, too severe to become popular; only established nine houses.

AUGUSTINIANS
The 'black canons', who followed the rule of St Augustine of Hippo; lived in communities like monks but went out preaching. Churches were large and they were known for their alms and hospitality. They eventually had 218 houses in England, the first being established at Colchester in c. 1100.

GILBERTINES
Only order founded by an Englishman – Gilbert of Sempringham in about 1131. Eventually had 26 'double house', with canons and nuns in the same community. Had separate cloisters and living quarters but a common church, split down the middle by a wall.

PREACHING FRIARS
New type of religious that arose in the 13th century. Professed poverty and owned no property – even their churches and priories were held in trust for them. Went among the people, preaching and doing charitable work, living on alms and collections. There were several orders in England: the *Dominicans* (Order of Preachers or Black Friars) from 1221; the *Franciscans* (Grey Friars) from 1224; and the *Carmelites* (White Friars) from about 1240.

(Top left) Sherborne Abbey: the Norman cathedral at Thetford may have resembled this. *Mick Aston*
(Top right) Aerial view of Thetford Grammar School, with the Little Ouse next to it.
Trenches 1 and 2 are adjacent to the bright yellow mechanical digger. *Mick Aston*

look for semi-circular traces in the school's Quad (between the library and the new Losinga Centre) where the east end of the cathedral should be.

The most obvious feature of the friary would have been the nave – a great airy hall in which sermons would have been preached. Crossing it would have been a walking space leading from the town to the friars' living quarters, and there would have been a chancel – a private chapel for the friars – at the east end. If it had been built 100 years earlier, the nave would have been dark and lit by candles, but its purpose as a place of preaching to the multitudes meant that it had to be large and open.

Excavation was quickly begun, watched over by Phil. The mechanical digger began Trench 1, at right angles to the outer side of the north wall of the Dominican remains. Then Trench 2 was started, extending out from the west wall, almost at right angles to Trench 1, with only a bit of a corner between the two left untouched. It was hoped that digging right down next to the wall would show if the Dominican structure was built on top of an older one – the cathedral? – or on 'natural' (the ground or bedrock). However, Trench 2 instead almost immediately revealed a modern 'midden' from the 1950s, full of broken crockery!

Back in the Quad, Beric, Carenza and some of the students were examining the east wall of the old grammar school, now the school library, for evidence of previous building. Inserted in the flint-built wall were a number of much older stones that Beric reckoned were Saxon. In fact, the wall showed traces of three buildings, including cross-sections of two walls that were now flush with the new one.

Geophysics had already surveyed the Quad and John now arrived with the results. A strong **resistivity** anomaly extended out from the east wall of the library and then made a definite turn to the north. However, the presence of two manhole covers suggested a pipe going east–west, and there was also supposed to be a gas pipe running from the library to the Losinga Centre. All this might have accounted for the anomaly, but, said John, a gas pipe should run straight through and not stop at a corner. The only way to solve this mystery was to hand-dig a trench, taking care not to damage the gas pipe.

In Trenches 1 and 2, Phil and his colleagues had dug down to the stone plinth on which the Dominican wall stood. Where they had uncovered the part of the wall previously hidden by soil, the flint was far less weathered than it was further up. Trench 1 had produced our first late medieval find: a green glazed floor tile and a fragment of window glass.

After lunch, Mick, Phil and Andrew Rogerson of Norfolk Landscape Archaeology examined a small pit that had been dug right next to the wall in Trench 2 to get a quick snapshot of what was down there. The flint mortar appeared to continue down, suggesting that the footings of the wall were built on top of something. They now wanted to join up the two trenches by digging right round the corner, but before they could do this, they would have to get the approval of the English Heritage architect responsible for this monument. After a persuasive phone call from Mick, they got it.

Phil and his team had also uncovered a hard mortared structure at the left-hand edge of Trench 1. It was decided to extend the trench to find out what this was.

The diggers had made good headway in Trench 3 in the Quad. First, three pieces of human bone were lifted out. It was hardly surprising to find these since hundreds of people had probably been buried in the church precincts during its long history; in fact, we were prepared for many more burials. Then, as well as the known gas pipe and just as the geophysics had predicted, they came upon the foundations of a wall. The Victorians had cut through this to lay a water pipe, in effect creating a perfect section of the wall, which was seen to be rubble faced with flint.

As the digging continued, a flat thick stone was found to run unexpectedly (at

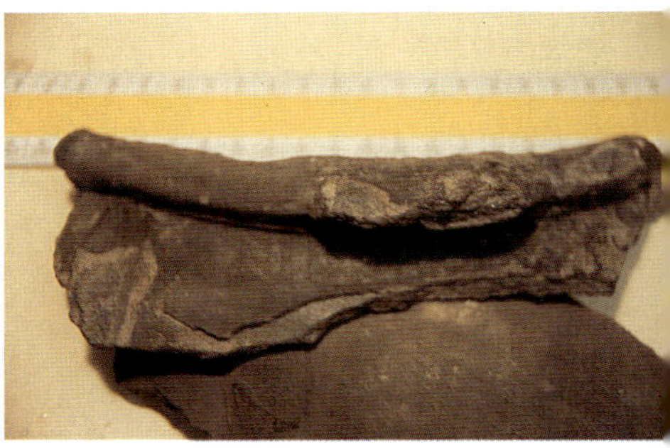

least unexpectedly to the geophysics team) at right angles to the south side of the wall, which appeared to have been hacked into to fit this stone. After the archaeologists conferred, it was decided that this was the foundation of a buttress. On the other side of the wall was a mortared floor on top of flint rubble, which would once have been covered in tiles.

The mechanical digger began the extension around the corner of the Dominican walls that would join up

(Above left) The remains of the Dominican friary walls, seen from the south. Mick Aston
(Top right) The fragment of 11th-century Thetford ware found in Trench 1. Mick Aston
(Above right) Sue Francis's reconstruction of the Thetford ware storage jar.

Trenches 1 and 2. Trench 1 had already been extended by 6.5 m (21 ft). At its bottom was a harder, possibly older surface that was cut through by the Dominican wall. There also appeared to be the foundations of another wall about 8 m (26 ft) from the friary.

It was in this trench that we finally found a piece of late Saxon pottery. Appropriately enough, it was a sherd of 11th-century Thetford ware, which might have been used at the Norman cathedral or even in the Saxon church that preceded it. It was part of a grey storage jar decorated with 'applied thumb strips' – strips of clay with roundels created by the potter's thumbs pressing the strips on to the body of the pot. This sherd went straight to Sue for a computer reconstruction.

At the end of the day, further geophysics results showed what appeared to be clear evidence of cloisters running north–south to the existing north wall. Mick decided that, since we almost 'knew' that the cloisters were there, there was no point in digging them up. Rather we should concentrate on excavations near the wall where various geophysical anomalies – for example, unaligned walls – could point to a series of buildings erected at different times.

Over dinner, discussion raged between Carenza, Mick, Phil and our medieval expert Dr Janet Burton, a lecturer in history at the University of Wales, Lampeter. One question kept coming up. While we knew about an Anglo-Saxon church, a cathedral and a Dominican friary on the site, we still didn't know if the Cluniacs built anything in stone during the 20-year hiatus before their quarters on the opposite bank of the river were ready. Was there, they asked, an interim structure between the cathedral and the Dominican friary? We hoped to know in two days' time.

Day Two

We arrived back at the grammar school under lowering skies; we were then faced with a cold wind and drizzle for the rest of the morning. Despite this, work in the trenches continued apace, with some of the students being taken under Phil's wing and given trowelling lessons.

In Trench 2, two walls had emerged on slightly different alignments and with one clearly built on top of the other. Mick now thought that the bottom one could well be part of the remains of the Norman cathedral. It was decided to extend this trench to follow the two walls.

Trench 1 was also being extended. Overnight, Mick's opinion had changed. He had decided that it would be a good idea to see if we could find where the cloisters began, believing that, at this friary, they were separated from the main church by an alleyway. And soon what might have been a cloister wall was being uncovered, and the student diggers had revealed the remains of a mortared floor.

Meanwhile, in the Quad, we could now see that the wall line in Trench 3 appeared to line up with one of the two wall cross-sections visible in the east wall of the library. This alignment would now have to be mapped, and then the library itself investigated to see if any traces of the wall seen in cross-section were visible inside.

To that end, Beric and a few of the students entered the library, accompanied by Alan Davison, who had been a pupil at Thetford Grammar in the 1940s. The library had been rebuilt in the 19th-

century but, as Beric now saw to his amazement, a 14th-century arch from the Dominican friary had been incorporated into the building. It would have been part of the north–south walkway leading from the town to the monks' living quarters. To the west would have been an arch of similar height but much greater width, leading to the large nave where the preaching had taken place. To the east, where Carenza was digging in Trench 3, would have been the chancel, the monks' private chapel. The library arch would also have been one of the four bases of the church tower.

When Alan was about 16, he and some friends had got the key to the library attic and there found the remains of a wall above the arch. Now Beric and one of the students peered up there themselves. Alan, like Beric, was surprised at how much of the medieval building was left. The land on which it was built had been taken over at the Dissolution by a Thetford man called Wilbertson and later left in his will for the foundation of a school. However, his relatives had contested the will and the matter hadn't been settled until about 1612. Thus for many years the site had been derelict, ripe for local residents to 'liberate' the fine stonework. Also, there was the question of why Wilbertson had bought the friary in the first place. Other than the ground on which the buildings stood, there was hardly any acreage attached, and some believe that he had purchased the property simply to sell off the building materials. Either way, it was lucky for us that so much still remained.

Out at the edge of the school playing field, Phil helped Simon Williams of

(Above left) Beric Morley shows how substantial the 14th-century friary arch inside the school library is. *Mick Aston*
(Above right) Trench 3, containing a portion of the friary church wall, as well as a water pipe and a gas pipe! *Mick Aston*

Anglian Flint to build a flint bench using medieval methods. Phil showed two of the students how to knap a large piece of flint so that there was one flat – external – surface and then a rock extension that would be mortared into the wall. Over the previous two weeks, Simon had prepared a traditional mortar made of sand and lime.

Trench 3 was beginning to produce the most exciting finds. A piece of tracery (the ornamental stone carving that appears in the upper part of a Gothic window) emerged, followed by masses of medieval stained-glass fragments, some quite large and showing patterns. An emergency call went out to expert David King in the hope that some of the glass could be identified.

Most of the action was now in the Quad. Because of the presence of gas and water pipes, it was impossible to extend Trench 3 towards the library or the Losinga Centre, so it was decided to dig another trench at right angles, extending towards the north – even if this meant removing some daffodils! We wanted to avoid digging *within* the friary because of the complications caused by uncovering floors and burials.

After lunch, the drizzle died away and we were even treated to a few moments of sun. In the new Trench 4 in the Quad, Mick the Dig and Carenza almost immediately came upon a wall that was later than the friary but had been built using medieval stonework, including a large dressed stone block and the base of a column. It was not substantial enough to be part of a building, and the best guess was that it had been a garden wall. This was recorded and then began the time-consuming process of removing it in the hope of finding an older structure beneath. Because this wall was outside the main friary structure, it might be based on one of the multiple apses that we hoped to find. Another archaeological conference in the Quad ended with the decision to extend the trench even further north.

Stained-glass expert David King arrived. A part-time school teacher and medieval arts consultant from Cromer, he ensconced himself in the photographic darkroom in the Losinga Centre to examine the many fragments of glass found on the site. When he finally emerged, he had some great news. He had discovered one piece bearing an oak leaf and another with an acorn, and stated that this naturalistic design dated from 1280 to 1350. He had also found other fragments that had been treated with a yellow staining technique that was used in the first half of the 14th century. Finally, another piece showed evidence of 'smear shading', in which a wash of paint was applied and then smeared with a hard brush; this was employed from 1330 to 1380. All these dates were spot on for the construction of the Dominican friary in c. 1335!

One of the students asked if the fragments could tell us anything about the main designs that the stained-glass windows would have once shown. This was hard to determine, said David, since the centres of the windows would probably have been smashed by 16th-century vandals to get at the lead. However, one fragment did show drapery, which indicated one or more figures. The glass that would have surrounded the main designs was much more in evidence, comprising bands of clear glass painted with naturalistic designs. Some of these designs were very similar to one still on view at Ely Cathdral and which was known to have been used by a medieval workshop in King's Lynn.

The glass found here also matched the date for the friary altarpiece, which still existed. The front part was now in France, but the back part resided in England, and when this had recently undergone conservation, a **dendrochronological** date of 1336 had been obtained.

At the end of the day, John Gater and Mick were in deep discussion, looking at

An example of English Decorated tracery within a stained-glass window.

Trenches 1 and 2 and the school playing field. They finally decided that the geophysics team would survey part of the playing field in 45-degree diagonal strips to obtain more precise results. If a site is surveyed in vertical or horizontal lines against known archaeology, it is possible to miss structures; diagonal lines would show up more of whatever lay under the ground.

Day Three

The TIME TEAM woke to a steady downpour and, on arriving at the school, were greeted with the quagmire that was now Trenches 1 and 2. But it wasn't only the rain and mud that dampened spirits: Phil and Mick both agreed that what they had hoped had been part of the cathedral in Trench 2 was actually the base of a buttress belonging to the Dominican friary.

More gloom came with the realisation that **ground-penetrating radar** (GPR) had failed here at Thetford. Nick Russill of the Cardiff-based geophysical consultants Terradat had been battling the wind and drizzle to survey the ground around Trench 3 in the Quad as well as a car park next to some school buildings south of the playing field. Radar reflects everything, even the most insignificant features, and there had simply been too many modern pipes in the Quad to make sense of the results. The car park read-out was equally confusing, and Nick and the geophysics team suggested that the car park may have been constructed over rubble or laid a number of times, scenarios that would lead to inconclusive results.

Suddenly Carenza's voice could be heard over the 'walkie-talkies' used by the team to keep in touch with each other. Addressing director Simon Raikes, she said: 'I think we've got a major breakthrough here.' Under the garden wall in Trench 4, she had found two substantial, finely carved pieces of stone, the edges of which were almost as sharp as when they had been first cut. Trench 4 was outside the friary and what had been found in it was distinctly different from that in Trench 3, which so far had been quite Dominican.

Then, disaster! Just as Carenza announced her find and it became imperative to dig Trench 3 deeper to see if, here too, possible Norman remains could be found at a lower level, a joint in a storm drain broke and the trench rapidly filled with water. However, swift action by production runner Jonty Sale, armed with a roll of Evo-Stick tape, meant that the break in the drain was plugged and the digging could recommence.

But things were still not going well. Just as the flooding was stopped in Trench 3, the digging in one end of Trench 4 seemed to have reached the water table and Carenza was soon standing in 25 cm (10 in) of muddy water!

She remained convinced that a Norman wall had been found. However, excavation had revealed a layer of tiles below the dressed stone that could be later – Beric simply wasn't sure. In addition, Mick the Dig, trowelling away on the other – dry – side of Carenza's Norman wall was finding only rubble, which could mean that this was a much less substantial feature than had at first been thought. As the archaeologists continued to argue among themselves about the status of the 'wall', it was decided to widen the trench by about 1 m (3.3 ft), to the limit of yet another drain, and a wooden fence was removed so that it could be made longer.

Back in Trench 2, the diggers had been instructed to go deeper to see if anything Norman remained under the friary wall. In Trench 1, the corner of what was thought to be the Dominican cloisters was clearly visible. While this trench would now be recorded and closed down, a geophysical survey would be carried out to see if it could verify the location of the rest of the cloister, which Bernard would then add to his database of the whole site.

Using the foundations of the buttress found in Trench 3, Bernard had been able to map out the rest of the Dominican chancel. This buttress appeared to have been the second one away from the known wall of the walking space between the chancel and the nave; this wall would have been at right angles to the eastern end of the arch in the library. Knowing this, Bernard was able to extend his plan to the probable east end of the friary church – now somewhere under the Losinga Centre, a building that in part, according to Mick, seemed to echo the church's chancel.

Stewart had been spending his time examining the historical documentation concerning the site. He concluded that all the religious groups who had settled here had probably found the site extremely constricted, with its boundaries limited by the river and by properties owned by others. The Cluniacs solved the problem of space by moving out, but why had the Anglo-Saxons and the Dominicans stayed? Bishop Herfast had established his cathedral here simply because it was an important location right next to the bridge crossing the Great Ouse.

Stewart also thought that the bishop would have added to the existing substantial Anglo-Saxon church only a new – and grander – east end, facing both the river and the road, to announce the change in status of the church. This building on top of or attached to the previous church would explain why the orientation was not truly east–west, which a Norman cathedral erected on a 'green field' site would have had. The slightly skewed orientation was continued when, in its turn, the Dominican friary was constructed on top.

In the continuing saga of Trench 4, opinion was shifting in Carenza's direction. When Mick the Dig's rubble was finally cleared away, the 'Norman-ness' of the wall became more persuasive. Stephen Heywood – of the historic buildings team from Norfolk County Council – identified a column base in it as early Norman, and another wall in the trench extension certainly looked to be from a time before the friary. The first wall was so smooth on

The remains of the Dominican church buttress in Trench 2. *Mick Aston* one side that it could have been a room interior, a particularly likely idea since a mortared floor was also revealed here. Now, in the remaining two hours of the dig, everyone was hoping to find evidence of a stone-built Anglo-Saxon church, which would be a relative rarity in this part of East Anglia.

A surprise visitor now arrived on site. Owen Thompson, a post-graduate student at the University of East Anglia, had been

examining the personal papers of Arthur Whittingham, surveyor of Norwich Cathedral, who had carried out excavations at Thetford Grammar in 1964. The plan that Whittingham had drawn up of the site had been thought lost, but Owen had just that morning found it in Norwich Record Office. It showed all the medieval friary buildings, some of which had been revealed by excavation and others that were probably more conjectural.

The new geophysics results from the playing field – which were much clearer having been done on the diagonal – tied in with the Whittingham plan. Comparing them to the plan and to the TIME TEAM excavations, Mick and Phil came to the conclusion that the structures in Trench 1 were not the cloisters but a building attached to their west side. In addition, the previous (less clear) geophysics survey was now thought to show garden features or buildings within the friary complex.

More walls were unearthed in Trench 4, which had been extended as far as it could be and excavated right down to the black soil of the former flood plain. Suddenly, when everyone had had a chance to take a fresh look at what had been revealed – and in the light of the conclusions reached for Trench 1 and the playing field – the joint opinion was finally reached that this and everything else found on the site was actually from the Dominican friary. The walls in Trench 4 were, in fact, probably part of the cloisters. We had not been able to uncover any sign of the Norman cathedral.

Despite this disappointment, the whole exercise had given us a snapshot of a period of power struggle, when bishoprics and their seats, the cathedrals, could change hands and locations within a relatively short time. It had also taught us that 'cathedrals' need not be the monumental structures we were familiar with, built over periods of 100–200 years and lasting for centuries. The cathedral at Thetford may have been just an enhanced Anglo-Saxon church, which was destroyed or changed out of all recognition when the Dominican friary was built.

Final thoughts from Mick

We live in a very secular age: not many people go to church and quite a few have no religion. So it is very difficult for many of us to appreciate how important Roman Catholicism – with all its rites and obligations – was to people in the Middle Ages. It is perhaps even more difficult for us to understand the calling followed at that time by the vast array of monks, nuns, friars, canons and so on. Thetford gave us a picture of this lost medieval religious world, and the finding of so much good quality evidence for the friary, while not our primary aim, was a major addition to knowledge about such sites.

I like medieval monasteries a lot, so I was very happy!

(Top right) Carenza and the wall in Trench 4. *Mick Aston*
(Above left) The early Norman column base found in Trench 4. *Mick Aston*
(Above) Victor and Steve's reconstruction of the friars' chancel in the Dominican friary church.

PLYMPTON

DEVON

WHAT MIGHT HAVE HAPPENED

The reeve sat warming his hands in front of the fire. His was one of the few houses in the town that had the benefit of such a blaze, the well-cut stonework retaining the heat all through the night. The recent troubles had coincided with a bitter winter, but it could have been worse. The poker that glowed in the grate would soon give his ale a warming touch, and the roasting meat from the plump sow had begun to give off a succulent aroma.

The civil strife had slowed, but not stopped, the usual supply of gifts from passing traders. However, he had his suspicions that some of the townfolk had taken advantage of the general lawlessness to hide away goods that ought to attract duty. Too many of the houses had deep cellars, and he had decided that the following day would see him paying some of his majesty's loyal subjects a surprise visit.

Victor's reconstruction of Chapel House in Fore Street.

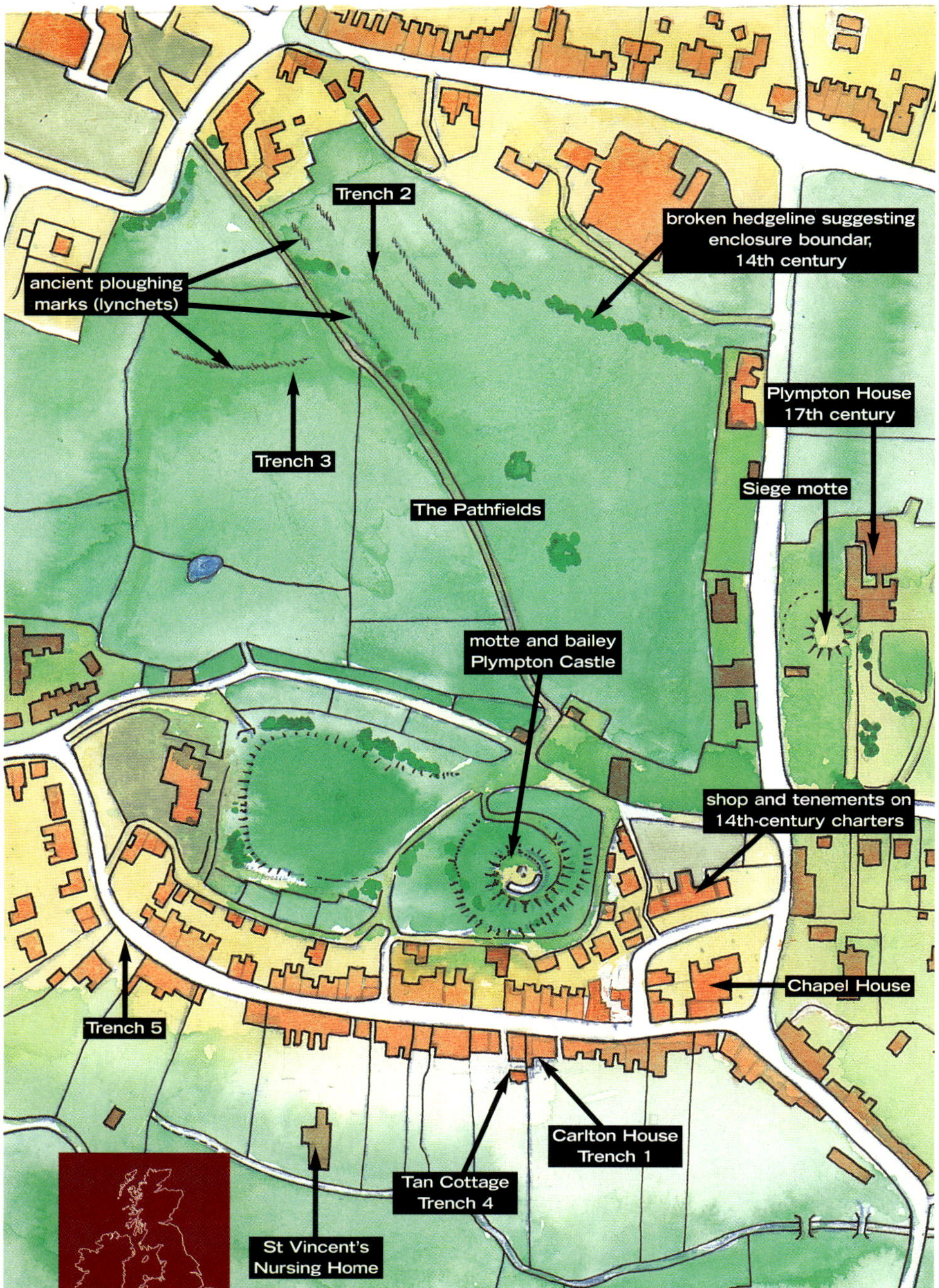

WHY WE WENT THERE

From the top of the Norman motte at Plympton Castle, near Plymouth, it is possible to survey the adjacent village of Plympton St Maurice. The great earthwork of the castle mound commands the surrounding landscape, just as it did when it was first erected in the 12th century. To the south, the main Fore Street follows its original medieval line, running parallel to and then curling around the western extent of the castle grounds or bailey. The characteristic long 'burgage plots' of a planned medieval settlement are still visible, stretching back from the street in regular lines behind the buildings. These would have been laid out when the *town* of Plympton was founded and then people invited to move in – a bit like planning a medieval Milton Keynes. The buildings themselves have been much altered over the years, typically now sheltering behind Georgian or early Victorian frontages, but careful examination can still uncover traces of their earlier origins.

The parish church of St Maurice, first mentioned in a deed dated 1300 and largely unchanged since the middle of the 15th century, rises on land to the castle's east. (The eponymous Maurice was a Roman legion commander who was martyred around AD 290 for refusing to take part in a ritual sacrifice.) To the north lies an enclosed area of undeveloped land known as the 'Pathfields' or 'Castlehayes'.

A long-standing application to develop a portion of private land at the Pathfields, adjacent to city council land used by residents, had prompted heightened local interest in the history of the area. Research coordinated by the Plympton Pathfields Preservation Group, set up in response to the development proposals, found that the fields could be traced back through documents and maps to at least 1529 (one former owner of the castle and its surrounding enclosure was the royal traitor Henry Courtenay, cousin of Henry VIII, who was beheaded in 1538). The group was convinced that there was a significant link between these enclosures - or 'hayes' as they were known - and the castle site, and that the Castlehayes had an important relationship to the castle going back even earlier.

The parish church of St Maurice. *Mick Aston*

At the same time that controversy had been brewing over the Pathfields development proposal, a local architect

had put in an application for planning permission to extend his cottage on a site just south of Fore Street. Early maps and illustrations showed that David Sheppard's Tan Cottage had formerly been part of a much bigger building, extending up to the main street and into a neighbouring garden. Internal renovation work had also uncovered a large granite jamb and part of a lintel of a medieval fireplace behind a 1960s' one, as well as finely cut granite and slate stonework in an internal wall and doorway. A massive chimney construction, making up an entire gable wall of the cottage, provided further evidence that here had once stood something much grander. Dr Keith Ray, then the Plymouth city archaeological officer, who had been called in to assess the planning application because it fell in a conservation area, felt that the proposed building work – and the associated demolition of an outhouse on the site of the planned extension – provided a unique opportunity to find out more about the history not just of David Sheppard's cottage but of the village as a whole.

The objective of our visit to Plympton, then, was to see how much of the medieval town that dates from the same period as its castle could be traced beneath the later additions, demolitions and developments. Many of the locals hoped that there was enough of it left for us to work out its original layout and boundaries, particularly in relation to the Pathfields site. As always, we had three days to see if they were right.

DAY ONE

A few metres down a side turning off Fore Street, Mick began Day One with a guided tour of Tan Cottage, in the company of Keith Ray and the cottage's current occupants, David and Sally Sheppard. Their home, which was to be one of the main focuses of our activities over the next three days, clearly contained remnants of what must have been quite an important building. As well as the fireplace, internal walls and chimney stack, there were also indications that at one time there had been a wall some distance to the rear of the existing property, perhaps marking the southernmost extent of a medieval building on the site. This may have continued beyond the boundary wall with Carlton House next door. A 1793 map of the site showed a building extending into what is now the adjacent garden, so to see if there were any traces of it left, Mick decided that he needed further evidence from beneath the surface of the gardens of both Tan Cottage and Carlton House.

There were two problems in obtaining this evidence. In the garden of Tan Cottage, a stone outhouse stood in the way of further investigation; while that of Carlton House was home to an elderly blind rabbit, who was unlikely to take well to teams of archaeologists disturbing his familiar habitat. The former difficulty was speedily resolved when David Sheppard announced that he was happy for the outhouse to be demolished since it would have to come down for his extension anyway. Better still, as his brother is a builder, he could commandeer the necessary equipment and personnel to speed the job along. The blind rabbit next door simply needed treating sensitively.

No sooner had the *ad hoc* demolition gang got to work removing the first slates from the roof of David Sheppard's outhouse than the geophysics team were beginning their search for signs of the possible medieval wall by surveying the lawn at the back of Carlton House. A faint line of **resistivity** suggested that there might be something there, so it was decided to place Trench 1 here, running north–south up the garden, parallel to the boundary wall with Tan Cottage and cutting across the line of the possible wall.

The geophysics team was also active over at Pathfields. The fields on this site would once have belonged to the old Saxon manor of Plympton. This was given to Richard de Redvers, a Norman knight, by Henry I around 1100, following which the castle was built and the medieval town laid out. The fields were claimed as pastures for the animals of the Norman lords.

There were a number of visible features of interest to us here, including a curving earthwork, a broken hedgeline that appeared to link up with others as part of an old pattern of field boundaries, and, on various areas of the Pathfields, additional banks and earthworks. **Magnetometry** readings revealed a curving anomaly matching the visible earthwork, which might indicate the existence of a man-made ditch. It was decided, if possible, to dig two trenches on Pathfields to investigate further. The first, Trench 2 – aiming to identify the nature of the banks and the old field boundary – was started immediately; the second, Trench 3, on the developer's land, would require his permission.

Local folklore has it that houses at the foot of Pathfields were once fishermen's cottages and that their boats used to be moored on the banks of the River Plym, which runs through the west of the village. This is now reduced to a shallow stream in the vicinity of Plympton and the tidal estuary is about two miles distant, but it

An aerial view of Plympton Castle. Fore Street can be seen running round the castle grounds. *Mick Aston* used to be navigable further upriver. A 1906 history of the area reported that, in the past, tidal waters almost reached the town, and 'at high tides, even in medieval times, it would seem that they washed the walls of the castle.'

The topographical evidence suggests that this is almost certainly untrue. But in the course of tracing the old borough boundaries, Robin found that they extended well beyond the burgage plots in the town and included a narrow access corridor to the River Plym more than two miles to the west. Robin and Stewart had never come across a boundary like this before. According to a document of 1599, it reflected the borough's struggle to maintain its links with the river and the sea, in order to remain a port after the watercourse became silted up with sediment – a consequence of the tin mining carried out further upstream. The town was eventually elevated to stannery status – that is, it became one of a small number of authorised tin-trading centres in the South-west. 'This town was sometimes a haven town,' said the document, 'but by means of the tinners the same by the sands in the course of years is clean quirted and choked and no haven there now at all.'

The Elizabethan oak tables in the Guildhall building on Fore Street, which we had taken over as our incident room during our time in Plympton, were by now groaning under the weight of the accumulating maps and other historical documents. There was also a steady flow of visitors bringing useful local knowledge and information to our experts. One resident had brought in a 1765 painting of Plympton, which appeared to confirm the existence of a larger building on the site of the present-day Tan Cottage. Robin was referring to this, the 1843 tithe map and the oldest map of the town – one from 1793 'survey'd and delineated by David Palmer' – as he worked his way through various early documents in an attempt to uncover the history of some of the burgage plots along Fore Street. Some of these documents were in medieval Latin, and they would have to be translated.

Local people were also helping Carenza and Beric as they carried out a survey of buildings in the main street. They were looking for other properties in the village that, like Tan Cottage, might have unusual architectural features or other items of interest. A lot of material had been reused at different times in the construction and reconstruction of buildings in what was then the town of Plympton, but the hope was that some original features might be found *in situ*. These could then be dated, either on stylistic grounds (by working out which architectural styles or materials were unique to particular periods in this area) or through the use of other techniques such as **dendrochronology**. This would then give us some clues as to how the town might have developed.

Meanwhile, the demolition of the outhouse at Tan Cottage had started to turn up some interesting finds even before the actual digging could commence. The walls contained some substantial carved medieval stones, including window sills, lintels and trefoil mouldings (David Sheppard announced his intention to incorporate these in the design for his new extension). Together with the discovery of some fine rope-edged carved beams at 53 Fore Street, next door but one to Tan Cottage, these were indicative of high-status buildings in the vicinity in the 15th and 16th centuries. There was not yet, however, any visible evidence of such a building from our excavations on the Tan Cottage site. Trench 1 next door in Carlton House had so far revealed only 19th-century garden rubbish and a narrow wall along the line of resistivity noted earlier, which was most likely a garden or outhouse wall from the same period. There was a lot more investigation still to be done.

The arch-braced timber roof of Chapel House. *Mick Aston*

DAY TWO

Carenza and Beric's buildings survey had progressed well. The people of Plympton, who turned out in their hundreds throughout the three days of our visit to observe and get involved in our activities, were eager to invite our specialists into their cellars, basements, attics and living spaces to seek out remnants of medieval structures. Among the most immediately interesting properties we looked into were Chapel House at 10 Fore Street and Pent House at 20 Fore Street.

Chapel House was perhaps the most exciting. Climbing up into the attic, we were faced with a complete five-bayed, arch-braced medieval timber roof. At the time it was built, these would have been fairly common in the West Country – a typical feature of medieval halls. Now, however, they are very rare in the area – there are no domestic examples surviving in Exeter and only one other in the Plymouth area, according to Keith Ray. Both the

standard of craftsmanship of the one at Chapel House and the fact of its survival intact were cause for much interest and enthusiasm. Since we had brought along medieval carpentry expert Damien Goodburn, we set him to work producing a copy of one of the cruck joints that are a feature of its construction, using the same methods and tools that would have been employed by craftsmen at the time. Wood samples were also taken in the hope of coming up with an accurate construction date from dendochronological analysis.

A little further up the street, Beric's initial assessment of Pent House, at No. 20, was that it had been through a number of rebuilding phases – he identified four – which might offer clues to the chronology of the development of the town if they could be dated accurately. The property had been built in a style common in the 15th century, he reckoned, with a passageway dividing two areas on the ground floor - a living area to the right as you faced it from the street and a service area to the left. There was a chimney and a kitchen at the rear of the service area (the presence of a chimney would have been seen as something of a status symbol in the 15th century), and the ground floor area would at some stage have served as a shop, probably fronting a market in the main street.

Beric estimated that, at some time between 1570 and 1630, the two rooms upstairs – which would originally have comprised a hall and an inner chamber – had been gutted, knocked into one and extended over the street. These would have been used for commercial purposes – possibly by a merchant - before being converted to residential use. Later still, the property had been subdivided again, becoming two separate cottages. To try to pin down these different building phases, samples were taken by dendrochronologist Robert Howard from the ground-floor fireplace, roof beams and uprights, as well as from the beam supporting the extension over the street at the front and a supporting beam bridging the passageway and running under the first-floor fireplace. Further core samples were taken for analysis from Nos. 22 and 24 Fore Street.

Back in the incident room, Robin had been joined by Angela Doughty, the Exeter Cathedral archivist and a medievalist, who would help him translate original 14th-century deeds, now in the possession of the cathedral, relating to various properties in Plympton. Remarkably, these beautiful fragile parchments have survived better than the buildings to which they relate, and by looking at them in detail, we were able not only to come up with useful information about the original medieval layout and boundaries of the town but also to eliminate one crucial red herring that could have seriously hindered our efforts.

This related to an earlier translation of one of the deeds, in which, on 7 February 1306, one Henry le Palmer granted

to Johanna his daughter his shop and solar in Plympton near the chapel of St Thomas the Martyr opposite the tenement which the grantor gave to Peter Grispin and on the east side of the tenement belonging to John son of Gilbert the tailor which shop and solar the grantor held of Thomas le Poltere to hold with a latrine adjoining the solar and the wall between the shop and the solar, which wall shall never be disunited.

The earlier translation had included reference to a 'ward wall', which had been taken to mean the outer castle

wall, a reference that would obviousy be crucial in helping to trace the location of the buildings referred to in these deeds. On retranslating the original deed, however, it was found that no such reference was actually there. It pays to return to original sources wherever possible and not to rely on other people's translations!

At Tan Cottage, the demolition site was now beginning to look more like an archaeological dig as the rubble was cleared away and a proper trench – Trench 4 – began to be excavated. Beneath an uninteresting, probably 19th-century wall, a much wider stone structure running east–west, with evidence of plasterwork on the southern side, was uncovered. There were also a number of pottery finds, including glazed earthenware, part of a pitcher and a cooking pot, and some sherds of very fine

(Top left) Medieval doorway at Chapel House. *Mick Aston*
(Top right) Phil and the wall in Trench 4 at Tan Cottage. *Mick Aston*
(Above right) A pot next to the wall in Trench 4. *Mick Aston*

pottery, probably imported. As more and more finds emerged from the ground, David and Sally Sheppard's enthusiasm grew – and David himself, much to his delight, unearthed a fine gold pin and tunic button. A piece of thin-walled, globular glass, possibly from a medieval vase, was also found in the early afternoon. It was decided to call in specialists from the Cornwall Archaeological Unit and Exeter Museum to help in identifying the various items.

On the Pathfields site, permission had been obtained from the would-be developer to investigate more closely the possible earthworks and boundary lines on his land. Trench 3 had been marked out ready for excavation, but although we were slowly piecing together an overall picture of the various features of the site, not a lot of finds of any great interest were uncovered from the dig. Along the line of nearby Trench 2, a clay bank had been identified, north of which were post-medieval plough soils and south of which had been found post-medieval bone, wood and sherds. It wasn't yet providing any conclusive information to assist in Stewart's efforts to establish the original boundaries of the site.

Carenza and Beric's survey, however, continued to turn up fresh evidence of original medieval structures and other features of interest. The cellar of 95 Fore Street was found to contain a now purposeless buttress and other i ndications of what were probably the bases of medieval structures. A carved granite window at 79 Fore Street (now St Vincent's Nursing Home) was identified as a reused piece of 16th-century carved parapet – a very expensive example of ostentatious display suggesting that the merchants of 16th-century Plympton were still relatively prosperous and unaffected by the rise of Plymouth, which had emerged as the major port and trading centre in the region by this time. And at the Rectory, at the top end of Fore Street near the church, there was great interest in the fact that the street level here appeared to be much higher than it would have been in medieval times. What secrets might be uncovered below street level in the Rectory cellar?

DAY THREE

The cellar in the Rectory is now about 2 m (6.5 ft) below the surface of the street. Inside, built into the street wall below ground level, the team was shown a bricked-in arch – local folklore suggested that it was the opening to an old tunnel from the castle. Again, legend proved unreliable. But when Charmian Evans, one of the organisers of the Plympton Pathfields Preservation Group who lives at the Rectory with her husband Paul, gave us permission to knock through the arch, we uncovered something just as interesting - a gap running between the front of the house and the street below ground level. The arch was in fact originally a medieval window that would have looked out on to the street before, at some later date, its level was raised.

All along Fore Street, there was evidence of the street level and original building line having altered over the years. The street had been wider in the past, as befitted a market street, before buildings had encroached upon it. In an attempt to get closer to establishing the original line, we decided to approach the owners of another property in Fore Street, a Georgian house set well back from the road, to see if we could put a trench in their front garden to look for evidence of medieval structures on the site. The property – at the opposite end of Fore Street to the Rectory, at No. 103 – probably incorporated several different burgage plots from the original planned settlement. Although we didn't have time to investigate the site fully, geophysics showed anomalies that suggested three earlier burgage boundaries.

Late in the day, this Trench 5 also began to add to our growing collection of finds from the dig at Tan Cottage. The arrival of Carl Thorpe, from the Cornwall Archaeological Unit, enabled us to start putting dates to all of these. A lot of the pottery was identified as St German's ware, which originated from just one known kiln but was common in the area from the late 1300s to 1590; some well-preserved pieces from a cooking vessel among our finds were dated to around 1490. The piece of glass discovered at Tan Cottage was reported to be similar to items found in the medieval waterfront of Plymouth when it was excavated in the 1960s; it was probably from a Venetian glass goblet, or an English copy, made around 1500. The large wall that had been uncovered at Tan Cottage, however, was definitely from a later date: a substantial piece of green glazed earthenware found securely in place in the foundation trench was definitively dated to around 1700, which meant that the wall could not be any earlier than that. If there had once been a larger medieval building on this site, we had not found any traces of its walls.

(Centre top) The Rectory on Fore Street. *Mick Aston*
(Centre above) The bricked-in medieval window in the Rectory cellar. *Mick Aston*
(Above right) The large wall in the Tan Cottage garden. *Mick Aston*

Likewise, next door in Carlton House, we had been unable to find any sign of a medieval structure coming through from Tan Cottage; the wall base that had been excavated running north–south up the garden was probably a boundary wall.

As well as the information from the pottery and other finds, more dating evidence also came in during the day from the dendrochronological analysis. A sample from the attic roof at Chapel House was found to have a felling date of around 1460–80. This was in keeping with the construction style and standards of craftsmanship that would have been expected at that time, but earlier in date than some estimations based on stylistic criteria alone. As Phil helped Damien, our medieval carpentry expert, put the finishing touches to his copy of a medieval roof beam based on those used in Chapel House, he could do so sure in the knowledge that he was employing the same techniques as those in use in Plympton at the end of the 15th century.

Some of the other 'dendro' results did not provide such clear-cut conclusions to our investigations, however. At Pent House, for example, Beric's rebuilding phases were largely confirmed by a felling date of the 1620s for the timber jetty extension over the street and a date of 1530–50 for a main beam across the house, probably relating to when the rooms on the upstairs floor were first knocked into one. But a beam bridging the passageway and running under the first-floor fireplace produced a much earlier felling date of 1270–1305.

Beric believed that this was a reused timber brought in to support the fireplace when the house was made much grander, possibly during the 16th-century refurbishment of the first floor. Keith Ray, however, suggested that a simpler explanation might be that the fireplace was the same date as the timber. Their disagreement was given added force by the fact that a timber from the fireplace at 24 Fore Street was dated to around 1275–1310. Again, Beric believed that this was a later insertion to the fireplace, while Keith argued that it was integral to the stonework around it. Beric insisted that the stylistic evidence strongly suggested that the fireplaces were of a later date, but Keith wondered whether the received stylistic opinion should be questioned in the light of the discovery of these pieces of timber from a much earlier period. In the end, both agreed to disagree, but if Keith is right, the architectural historians of the area might have to revise some of their chronologies by as much as 300 years.

The evidence from the Pathfields site as the dig came to an end was similarly inconclusive. Stewart described the earthworks as a 'quite remarkable' survival of a medieval field system made up of elongated open fields. These had, over the years, turned into large banks or lynchets (ancient ploughing terraces). The broken hedge-line represented a boundary possibly connected with parkland laid out on the site, most likely between the 16th and 18th centuries. This line cut across the earlier medieval field boundaries, of which there were other remnants elsewhere on Pathfields.

Finally, Stewart had also come up with an important addition to local history. Tucked away behind high stone walls in the grounds of a nunnery some 100 m (330 ft) from the castle was an earthwork that had long been thought of as a garden folly. Forty metres (130 ft) in diameter and 6 m (20 ft) high, the mound had, however, been overlain on one side by the current garden walls: this would not have happened if it had been erected as an intentional garden feature. The structure was also placed on the only piece of high ground that would

(Left) Sue Francis's computer reconstructions of *(top)* the green glazed earthenware jug dating from 1700 and *(above)* the 1500 glass goblet, both found at Tan Cottage.
(Right) Some of the tracery *(top)* and masonry that had been part of the outhouse at Tan Cottage. *Mick Aston*

command a view of the castle bailey and overlook the castle gate.

What Stewart had identified was a previously unknown siege motte, constructed for one of the two sieges of Plympton Castle, in either 1136 or 1224. Its size, structure and position were all that would have been expected of siege mottes (*see box*) during the turbulent early medieval period. Its distance from the castle – just out of range of archers but near enough to enable its occupants to rush out and attack the castle gate or rush back to safety in the event of a counter-attack – also fitted the description.

So what we had come up with was not perhaps the single boundary and clear history linking the Pathfields site to the castle that some of the local people had hoped for. But from our three-day look underneath the jumble of nine centuries of development since the Norman castle had been built and Plympton first laid out as a planned settlement, we had furnished some hitherto unknown pieces to the jigsaw of the town's history, and helped to kindle a reinvigorated local interest in its development.

Final thoughts from Mick

Although Plympton is now a village, it was once a medieval town, one of hundreds founded up and down the country in the 12th and 13th centuries - part of a Europe-wide urbanisation as trading and commerce took off in the early Middle Ages.

Subsequent development frequently removed all traces of such origins, but 'fossils' (not a derogatory term – such places are often the most attractive examples) such as Plympton preserve earlier buildings, street alignments and patterns of property boundaries. I like these places a lot because, although fashion and individuals' aspirations to grandeur often led to the alteration of frontages, much of the earlier fabric can still be found around the back and in the roof – not so much deliberately preserved as forgotten. There is still a great deal to be learned about these towns through careful examination and analysis.

SIEGE MOTTES

Many people will remember the classic 'motte and bailey' arrangement of Norman castles from their history lessons at school. The huge earthworks that made up the motte (and the stone structures that eventually replaced the original wooden towers and stockades) are still prominent features in many parts of England and Wales.

What is less well known is that, for many castle mottes, there are accompanying 'siege mottes', built during the recurrent periods of civil war and conflict in the centuries following the Norman invasion – in particular, during the anarchy of Stephen's reign in the early 12th century. Most of them are now little more than circular mounds in the landscape, often barely visible after many years of erosion or development, the wooden fortifications that would once have topped them having long since disappeared.

Their purpose was to provide a stronghold from which an attacking force could besiege an existing castle. To this end, they were generally built on high ground in positions commanding the approaches to the besieged fortification. They were usually no more than about 100 m (330 ft) away – within an archer's range of the castle and close enough to enable the besiegers to rush out and attack, and then, as necessary, rush back to safety. The siege motte discovered by the team at Plympton is 110 m (360 ft) distant from the castle on a ridge overlooking the castle gate and providing a view inside the castle bailey itself.

The construction of a siege motte often acted as a statement of intent as much as the base for an actual siege. It demonstrated that the attackers were serious and not about to go away. Faced with such determination from their enemies, the defenders would often surrender rather than face a prolonged siege.

(Top) Victor and Steve's reconstruction of what Fore Street would have looked like in the Middle Ages.

CHEDDAR GORGE

SOMERSET

WHAT MIGHT HAVE HAPPENED

The mouth of the cave was bathed in sunlight as the family huddled around the fire waiting for the hunters to return. From where they sat, they had witnessed the final stages of the hunt as the deer were driven past them into the narrow gorge that had no opening at the other end. They knew that the flint weapons prepared in the same cave earlier would make short work of the animals and there would be plenty of meat for the evening meal.

As the hunters returned, they all fell upon the pieces of meat – one child grabbed part of the deer's leg and thrust it into the fire, the skin still warm to the touch. As the fire singed the fur and began to cook the meat, the whole family sensed that, once again, this place had given them what they needed to survive the winter.

Victor's vision of hunters and their prey during the Palaeolithic.

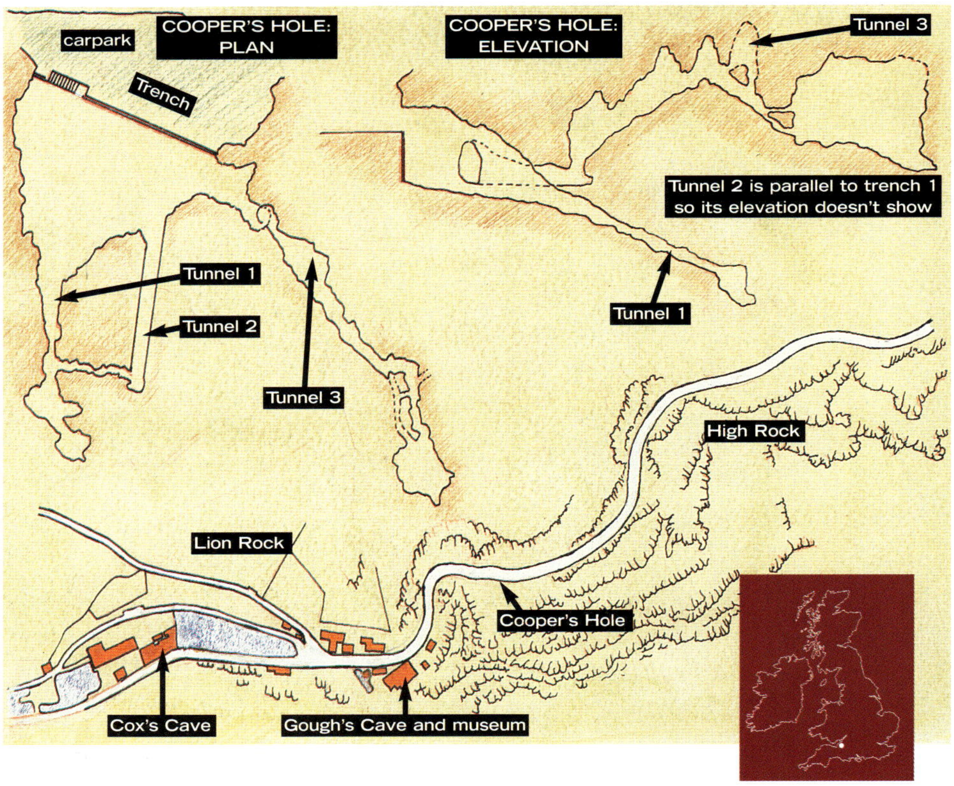

WHY WE WENT THERE

Cheddar Gorge in the Mendip Hills – 1¹/₄ miles long with cliffs rising as high as 150 m (500 ft) – cuts into carboniferous limestone formed about 300 million years ago. Limestone is water soluble, and over hundreds of thousands of years, the rock dissolved and formed cracks down which streams on the top of the hills would disappear. In turn, this flow of water created a cave system throughout the rock, which acted as drains, carrying the water to springs at the foot of the Mendips.

Cheddar Gorge itself is not (as was once commonly thought) the result of the collapse of a huge cave, but was carved out by water during the Ice Ages. This part of Britain was never covered by glaciers, but the climate became so cold that the water in the caves within the limestone froze. As a result, when the winter snows melted, there was nowhere for the water to escape; instead a lake formed that flooded over the edge of the Mendips at Cheddar, carving out the gorge. And as it was cut deeper, it opened up pre-existing caves in the limestone.

The Cheddar caves that are now above the water level were once below it, the floor of the gorge having risen over the centuries. Many of the caves are still subject to regular flooding, both by water running in from outside and from water rising from within. Some time during the Mesolithic period (*see box*), during the warmest part of an interglacial, the entrances to the caves became blocked. Water that had seeped through the limestone above – picking up dissolved calcite (crystalline calcium carbonate) on the way – dripped from their roofs. Over time, small stalactites (calcite 'icicles') formed from the top of the caves, and stalagmites (calcite mounds or tapering columns) built up from their bottoms. The stalagmite material also spread over the cave floors, creating a distinct white layer (known today as a 'stal' floor) that, in some of the caves, is about 0.3 m (1 ft) thick, dividing the Palaeolithic from the Neolithic.

Most of the caves have been thoroughly excavated, yielding some of the most important Stone Age archaeology in the country. The most famous is Gough's Cave, excavated by Richard Gough (and his sons and dozens of workmen) from 1898, on behalf of his employer, the Marquess of Bath, who owned the land. It was here, in 1906, that 'Cheddar Man' was discovered – the oldest intact human skeleton in Europe, dating from c. 7000 BC. However, when these early excavations were carried out, much of the potential information was lost or went unrecorded.

The present Lord Bath asked TIME TEAM to have a look at another cave further up the gorge. Cooper's Hole – named after a family who lived in it in the 19th century – was largely ignored by early archaeologists. In 1931–32, R F Parry, the manager of the then Marquess of Bath's property, found that the cave

(Top right) Aerial view of the Cheddar Gorge. *Mick Aston*
(Above right) The skull of 'Cheddar Man', found in Gough's Cave in 1906. *Mick Aston*

entrance was partially blocked with red clay and black charcoal that he believed had been washed down from the Roman and medieval lead mines at Charterhouse up on the Mendips.

The most extensive investigation of Cooper's Hole was carried out from 1959 by the intrepid men and women of the Mendip Caving Group, who wanted to find out whether it was the legendary 'Cheddar Hole'. In his book *Ex Historia Anglorum*, written in about 1135, Henry of Huntingdon told of the four wonders of England. One of these was 'Cheddar Hole' – 'a cavity under the earth which, though many have often entered and there traversed great spaces of land, and rivers, they could yet never come to the end'. This mysterious entrance to a lost underground world has become the Holy Grail to thousands of cavers (even though Henry of Huntingdon could very well have been referring to Wookey Hole, a massive cave some six miles from Cheddar).

The Mendip Caving Group drove a tunnel (Tunnel 1, *see plan*) 30 m (100 ft) through the silt, clay and rock deposits that now filled Cooper's Hole – only the very top of the opening arch is visible today. They later discovered a side passage (Tunnel 3) with ancient steps cut into the stal floor. (A rock fall has now blocked this tunnel.) However, the cavers' aim was to find the 'Cheddar Hole', not carry out any archaeology, although one of them, Chris Reynolds, did collect some of the artefacts that the cavers found – sherds of what appeared to be Iron Age pottery, an antler and quite a few bones including what was thought to be the jawbone of an Arctic fox – which are now kept at the Cheddar Gorge museum. There was also a particularly exciting find: a flint core that, it seems, showed distinct evidence of having been worked by a human, and which was discovered *beneath* the stal floor and so came from the Palaeolithic. Unfortunately, this was lost, having been left by one of the cavers on a bus after a few pints!

From 1983 to 1987, a group of Cheddar Venture Scouts dug a new tunnel (Tunnel 2), connecting the entrance of the cave to a spur of Tunnel 1. To do this, they built a mini-railway, using old fencing from the local primary school for the rails and a pushchair as a truck to carry up debris. Much of this debris had been deposited by severe floods in 1966 and 1968, which had finally defeated the Mendip cavers.

Lord Bath was keen for TIME TEAM to find out if the mud and rocks that now filled Cooper's Hole hid a 'showcave' similar to or even larger than Gough's Cave, which he could, after clearing, open to the public. But the Bristol University archaeologists Kate Robson-Brown and Larry Barham had a different agenda: they wanted this rare site to be scheduled to keep it safe from untrained excavators. But to do this, they first needed some evidence that humans had used or occupied the cave during the Palaeolithic – and TIME TEAM took up the challenge.

A CHRONOLOGY OF PREHISTORIC TIMES

PLEISTOCENE Climactic era characterised by fluctuating cold periods, beginning around 1.8 million years ago. Last Ice Age began to recede in Britain about 20,000 years ago and warmer climate encouraged human settlement. Rise in sea level that occurred then led to the North Sea severing Britain from rest of Europe in about 6500 BC.

PALAEOLITHIC Also known as Old Stone Age. The earliest phase of human development, characterised by the hunter-gatherer way of life. In Britain, it lasted for about 500,000 years until about 8300 BC. Divided into: Lower Palaeolithic (the emergence of early humans), Middle Palaeolithic (Neanderthal humans and flaked tools), Upper Palaeolithic (emergence of modern humans, blades and early art).

MESOLITHIC Transitional period between Palaeolithic and Neolithic, characterised by very small stone tools and sophisticated hunting practices. In Britain, it extended from 8300 to 4000 BC and coincided with the interglacial period.

NEOLITHIC Also known as New Stone Age. Characterised by development of settlements and cultivation of crops. Dates from about 4000 BC in Britain.

BRONZE AGE Characterised by bronze-working, which is linked with greater intensity of farming. In Britain, it lasted from about 2300 to 700 BC.

IRON AGE Period when iron became primary metal for weapons and tools, replacing bronze. Beginning in Britain in about 700 BC, it is generally regarded as having ended with Roman invasion of AD 43.

Box: *(left)* Victor and Steve's computer reconstruction of what Cooper's Hole might have looked like during the Palaeolithic

Day One

It was pouring with rain as we made our way to the incident room in a hotel overlooking the River Yeo. The sound of the water streaming over a weir just outside the window would later soothe many jangled nerves. The first task of the day was the briefing of our six diggers by Andy Sparrow of the Bristol Exploration Club, who would act as health and safety officer for the dig. As well as outlining the usual precautions to be taken when digging in caves, he said that the chance of 'bad air' was extremely remote as Cooper's Hole was too shallow. The only problem might be a build up of carbon dioxide, but the diggers would know quickly if this was a problem – they would become breathless and find working very hard. (They later experienced both things but not from any excess of carbon dioxide: the gruelling labour involved would stretch them to the limits.)

The diggers were then joined by our 'cave police' Kate and Larry, who explained the fragile nature of this sort of site. Then they confirmed what they had stated in earlier meetings with production staff: we would not be allowed to break through the stal floor; it must be kept intact for future archaeologists. But, cried the diggers, that means that we can't get at what we're looking for – evidence of humans from the Palaeolithic. Fortunately for us, however, the cavers who had previously dug in Cooper's Hole had broken through the stal in three places and we would be allowed to investigate the lower depths through these breaks.

The diggers trudged up the road to Cooper's Hole, a 12 m (40 ft) wide shallow opening in the bottom of one of the cliffs, with a carpark in front. Here, they donned their rubber suits, gloves, wellies, hard hats and lanterns and descended into the gloom beyond the mouth of the cave. Soon the heavy work began: sloppy mud was packed into a trug (a plastic barrel about 0.6 m/2 ft high with one side removed) attached to a rope; this was then laboriously dragged by hand to the surface ... again and again and again.

Outside, the geophysics team was

using **ground-penetrating radar** (GPR) to discover where the original cave entrance had been and what it might have looked like. A reference from the 19th century described it as 3.7 m (12 ft) high and only 1 m (3.3 ft) wide – much narrower than the present opening. Ascertaining this would help to refine the locating of the trench we planned to dig in the carpark.

Back in the incident room, Andy Currant, a palaeontologist from the Natural History Museum who had excavated part of Gough's Cave in 1988, examined some of the Mendip Caving Group finds. He discovered that what had been thought to be the jawbone of an Arctic fox actually belonged to a young (and relatively modern) dog. However, there was an antler that had been deliberately sawn, as well as some bone needles, a lead weight and a piece of beautiful Iron Age pottery – all signs that the cave had been used, if not inhabited, by humans in the distant past.

In Palaeolithic times, said Andy, long-term occupation was restricted to larger caves. Humans tended to live in large family groups, and the space needed to sit in comfort in a circle around a fire – and to have access past the fire to the back of the cave – seemed to have dictated the size of cave that was considered habitable.

Andy has a theory about Cooper's Hole and this part of the gorge. Ten thousand years ago, the floor of the gorge would have been about 7.5 m (25 ft) lower than it is now, and its sides would have been much closer together. This would have made the gorge virtually inaccessible to larger animals, and so it would have been an excellent animal trap for horse and red deer, which would have been chased up into it from the wooded slopes and lowlands below. Cooper's Hole would have been one of the nearest usable caves to the site of any killings, and thus it would have been an obvious candidate for seasonal living quarters or a hunting camp, with easy access to water, to wood from the surrounding slopes and to the open lands below.

Up at the cave site, John arrived with the GPR results, the multi-coloured printout bearing a striking resemblance to one of Mick's stripey jumpers! The GPR gave us an X-ray of a cross-section of the carpark. But instead of revealing rock formations that would have indicated a narrow opening, this showed a wide dip in the strata about 5 m (16.5 ft) down – that is, a wide entrance.

(Top centre) Kate Robson-Brown and Larry Barham – our 'cave police' from Bristol University. *Mick Aston*
(Above centre) Richard Trainer with his robotic laser theodolite, deep into surveying the cave entrance. *Mick Aston*
(Above right) A sherd of Iron Age pottery, found during the 1988 excavations of Gough's Cave at Cheddar. *Mick Aston*

To see the potential of Cooper's Hole, Carenza, Andy Currant and Bristol University geologist Dr Peter Hardy walked down to Gough's Cave, which extends about half a mile into the cliff. Peter explained how the cave had been formed by the limestone being dissolved by water from an underground river. The parts of the walls and ceiling where the water had been calm were now smooth, and where the water had eddied, they had been carved into fantastic swirls, holes and other shapes. Andy said that Cooper's Hole could be even bigger than Gough's Cave; the way you could tell was by looking at the calcite formations. He pointed out a stalactite with a truncated end, which now hung in the air about 1 m (3.3 ft) above his head but had once rested on the former cave floor. He also showed a distinct white line on the cave wall at the same level. This was the remains of the stal floor, just like the one in Cooper's Hole – but that one, now buried under deposits, was much further away from the cave roof, and who knew how far down the cave extended beneath the stal?

Back at Cooper's Hole, the mechanical digger had finally dug through the carpark tarmac to begin our trench. Although our real interest lay about 5 m below the surface (as shown by the GPR), even at its upper levels the trench revealed extremely distinct red and black **stratigraphy**, similar to what Perry had discovered in the cave deposits in the 1930s and perhaps from the same source. Phil also found some animal remains: teeth from a badger, sheep and, most importantly, red deer – the dominant species in the area from the Upper Palaeolithic until 200 or so years ago. However, without **radiocarbon dating**, it was impossible to tell how old any of these teeth were. Andy Currant guessed that the badger and sheep teeth were only a couple of centuries old.

As everyone else finished for the day, the diggers – led by Mick 'The Dig' Worthington – faced more long hours of labouring in Tunnel 1. So far they had only been bringing up modern material, complete with rusted soft drinks cans, small recompense for such hard, filthy toil.

Day Two

It was still raining, and this was bad news for us. Not only had Tony and Mick – up in the helicopter to try and get a bird's-eye view of the terrain – had to land when the clouds descended into the gorge, but the wet weather meant that even more water was dripping through the limestone into Cooper's Hole, making our diggers' task particularly onerous.

The geophysics team tried GPR inside the cave mouth, but were defeated by the clay, the least suitable type of soil for this technique. Then they attempted **seismic refraction**. Nick Russill (*see* Thetford) hit a metal plate with a sledge hammer. The sound waves generated by this bounced off the limestone (probably the stal floor) beneath the clay and were picked up by 24 'geophones' – probes wired up to a seismograph – with which the clay was seeded. Because sound waves take longer (600–1,600 metres per second) to go through clay than they do through limestone (1,000–4,600 m/second), John and Nick were able to calculate that the stal floor lay 3.6 m (11.8 ft) beneath the present entrance. Not only that, but it extended horizontally, indicating a generally level stratum quite different from the slanted appearance of the site.

It was also important to 'map' the inner dimensions of the existing cave. Expert surveyor Richard Trainer used a robotic laser theodolite to do this: the theodolite measured angles (and thus direction) and the laser measured distances; combined, these would give a

(Top) The diggers entering Cooper's Hole. *Mick Aston*
(Above) The beginning of the trench outside the cave. *Mick Aston*

position. This procedure was repeated at regular intervals around the cave mouth, and the data was added to Bernard's surveying software. It was then combined (with some difficulty) with Steve's computer graphics programme to produce a 3D reconstruction.

The trench in the carpark had been significantly widened. However, with expansion limited by, on one side, the road and, on the other, the retaining wall that the present Lord Bath's father had had built in the 1960s at the mouth of the cave, this was not enough to allow hand digging down to the depth where the interesting geophysics anomalies were located. Phil kept on excavating regardless, although wary of falls of soil from the sides of the trench. He uncovered very few finds – snail shells, a partial radius bone from a large mammal, a substantial vertebra from a red deer – but perhaps the environmentalist coming the next day would be able to glean more information from these.

Kate and Larry, our 'cave police', were concerned about the rapidity of the excavation in the trench. Palaeo-archaeologists usually proceed at a rate of centimetres per week because the finds are so few and often extremely tiny. Digging out great chunks with a mechanical digger does not figure in their world. However, although they kept their eagle eyes on what was going on, they realised that, if we were to have any chance of finding definite proof of ancient human involvement with the cave in the remaining one-and-a-half days and so get it scheduled, they were going to have to agree to a modification of working practices.

At about noon, the 8th Marquess of Bath – owner of the south side of the gorge (the north, uncommercialised side belongs to the National Trust) – visited the incident room where Andy Currant took him through what had been found in Cooper's Hole so far. One of the objects of most interest had actually been brought to light by one of the Mendip cavers: a large piece of antler, probably from a red deer. When this was placed under a microscope (attached to a computer for ease of viewing), Lord Bath could see marks indicating that it had been cut with a metal instrument and thus human activity had been involved. Because the metal used was tough enough to do the cutting, this probably happened no earlier than the Iron Age and perhaps much later. And because its location in the cave hadn't been recorded when it was found, we couldn't say for sure whether the antler had been placed there by humans or had been washed in during a flood.

The diggers in Tunnel 1 had finally reached the stal floor and the break made through it by the Mendip caver Malcolm Cotter. Unfortunately all this breach in the stal revealed was rubble.

Phil and his version of a *baton de commandement*, made of a reindeer antler. *Mick Aston*

However, when Malcolm revisited the spot where he had dug 39 years earlier, he remembered that he had encountered a collection of animal bones only about two hours' digging away. This goal would be tackled the next day.

Meanwhile digger Ian Powlesland was attempting to remove fertiliser bags full of spoil that had been dumped down Tunnel 2 some time in the past. His attempts to push the bags up the muddy, slippery slope simply resulted in the spoil falling back all over him. Calls of 'Mud Man!' greeted him as he emerged breathless from the depths.

Phil took a rest from the trench and joined Andy Currant in a shallow cave near the incident room for a demonstration of Stone Age technology. Phil, an expert flint knapper, took a triangular flint core and struck off a series of blades, each with one sharp end. From these, he created knives, including a 'Cheddar point' (a trapezoidal knife with a long blade, basically a cutting tool). He also showed Andy some flint tools he'd made with handles.

Then Phil took up a reindeer antler that had been soaking in water to make it softer and, using his Stone Age tools, bored a hole through the thicker end. Everyone had thought that this would take some time, but he achieved it in an amazingly quick 15 minutes. He was trying to replicate a 12,000-year-old *baton de commandement* that Andy had borrowed for us from the British Museum. No one knows exactly what these mysterious objects were used for. Phil thought that the present-day Inuit have similar tools that they employ to straighten arrows. Some ancient French ones have intricate engravings of horses on them so they may have been used with these animals, perhaps to hold ropes. Other suggestions have included a climbing/descending aid (again with ropes), a thong stropper (to de-flesh strips of animal skin), a willow wand de-barker, a counting tally (to keep prehistoric records) and – most far-fetched of all – a sex aid!

Back at the incident room, Sue took photos of some of the finds with a digital camera and then downloaded them into her computer. She also stored a view of the gorge, and then helped Victor transform it into a scene of how it must have looked during the time of the hunter-gatherers (*see p31*). They also turned a picture of Lord Bath into a fierce 'cave man'!

By the end of the day, the trench had been enlarged to about 5 m (16.5 ft) square and approximately 3 m (10 ft) deep, with stepped sides. However, the recent rain (which had finally stopped) had saturated the soil even under the carpark surface, and the sides of the trench at its deepest level were dangerously unstable. Shoring was needed, but all the boards that had

been brought to the site had been used to make a ramp for the cave diggers. A decision had to be made. After urgent discussions among the archaeologists, the mechanical digger revved up and, to the disappointment of everyone at the site, the trench was partially backfilled to make it safe. All the newly redeposited spoil would have to be dug out again in the morning.

Day Three

At last the weather seemed to have broken, and we welcomed the weak sunshine that filtered through the clouds. We also welcomed the arrival of the 'snail man' – palaeo-ecologist Paul Davies from Bath Spa University College – who examined the snail shells and other material that Phil had collected from various levels of the trench. Surprisingly, snails can tell experts a lot in terms of both environment and chronology. One specimen from the trench was known to have lived in closed woodland and could be dated to 6000 BC – the mid-Mesolithic – and it came from the same layer in which the red deer vertebra had been discovered, so dating this.

According to Paul Davies, the trench that TIME TEAM had excavated proved that this was a very important site as it showed a distinct ecological sequence from at least the late Palaeolithic or early Mesolithic (c. 10,000 BC), the end of the last Ice Age – a sequence that was unique in the Cheddar valley. It had also provided evidence of the oak woodlands that had covered the area once the ice retreated, and which gradually opened up as the region became populate d. There were microscopic flecks of charcoal in some of the layers, and one reason for this might have been humans burning down forests for agriculture and other domestic activities. However, there were a number of other ways that charcoal could have got into these soil layers, so this wasn't absolute proof of human activity here.

As the day proceeded, the weather improved immensely, becoming sunny and warm. This brought out the day trippers, but the dozens who turned out to watch the excavation at Cooper's Hole proved a friendly lot. However, it was a bit disconcerting to hear the guides in the open-top 'Gorge Tour' buses announce our presence every time they whizzed round the corner.

At the trench, the mechanical digger had delicately removed the backfill from the previous night and then continued digging further down. Because of the trench's instability, none of the archaeologists was allowed back in it. Finally, through a layer of scree, the digger bucket hit a slab of solid rock that was identified as part of the roof of the original cave entrance. Richard Trainer used a pair of Vector binoculars to see how deep it was. Designed for military targetting, these have a laser to measure distances and a digital compass to determine direction. According to the binoculars, the rock slab was at 3.7 m (12 ft), a measurement that almost exactly matched the geophysics seismic results. As we now knew the dimensions of the cave entrance, the trench was completely backfilled, but not before the stratigraphy on one wall had been recorded and photographed.

The diggers had to leave Tunnel 1 as it was becoming increasingly filled with water. So Malcolm's animal bones would have to wait to be rediscovered by future archaeologists.

Our attention now turned to Tunnel 2, where most of the dumped spoil and water had finally been removed. As an experiment, Bernard and Richard tried measuring the tunnel using a special pair of Vector binoculars designed to work at short distances. When they had finished, the diggers relatively quickly uncovered the stal floor. On one side of the tunnel, the stal had flowed into a V shape and below this was some distinctive orange clay, which had to date to the Palaeolithic. Some animal bones were found, and then ... nothing.

The sun was beginning to set as most of the TIME TEAM waited, holding their collective breath, outside the cave. There was so little time left, and we still didn't have what we had come to Cheddar for.

Then, when it was almost dark within the gorge, Carenza found it. In the orange clay under the stal in Tunnel 2, she gingerly extricated a small bone – a 6 cm (2.4 in) piece of a rib of a small mammal. It had been securely embedded in the clay and must have been there for a long time because it had taken on the orange colour of the soil. And not only that: on its side were fine scratches that could indicate that it had been scraped with a flint tool. We would have to wait for scientific investigation to be absolutely sure, but on the face of it, we had found real evidence of human activity in Cooper's Hole and perhaps from Palaeolithic times!

Final thoughts from Mick

I found Cheddar a difficult project. Palaeolithic deposits are so rare and, when found, need to be excavated so carefully that I doubted whether we could usefully do any research in the time available. However, given past disturbance to such early deposits in Cheddar and elsewhere, it was clearly important to get Cooper's Hole evaluated so that its future preservation could be assured. Because we managed to achieve this, theproject ended with a feeling of satisfaction.

I would have loved to have gone down into the cave (even if only briefly, as I hate small spaces underground). However, since I broke my leg two years ago, I still find it difficult to crawl, so I was relegated to above-ground activities.

Victor and Steve's computer reconstruction of a Stone Age Lord Bath.

SMALLHYTHE

KENT

WHAT MIGHT HAVE HAPPENED

The ship was now beginning to take shape. The workers swarmed over the vessel like ants, smoke billowed from the kilns and the constant hammering of the smiths echoed across the water. A visit from the king was rumoured, and the hectic work on the boats was matched by a similar hive of activity in the main street where the temporary houses and market area were being cleared of refuse.

They all knew that, once this ship was completed, they would have to move on. There was talk of a new grand dockyard at Chatham, and everyone looked forward to the prospect of living nearer the capital. However, despite the abundance of inns there and all the accompanying delights of a major port, life here had been healthier, even if the accommodation had been inadequate.

But they could not stay here even if they wanted to. Things were changing. The river had narrowed and this meant that an even longer wait for a suitable high tide would be required before the new vessel could be launched. It could very well be the last of its size to be built here.

Victor's reconstruction of Henry V's ship *Jesus*, made at Smallhythe.

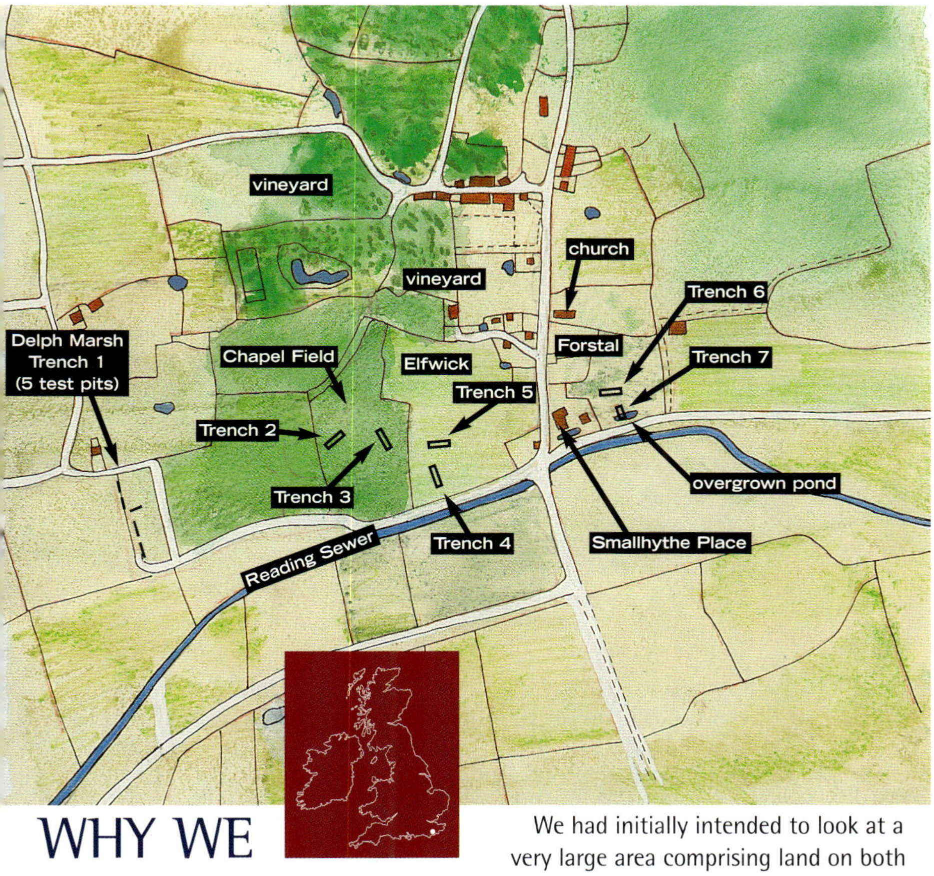

WHY WE WENT THERE

We had been told that we would be doing some maritime archaeology during these excavations, but as we arrived at Smallhythe, a straggle of houses and other buildings lining a road in leafy Kent, we looked in vain for any sign of the sea. In fact, the village is now about eight miles inland, and what had once been the mighty River Rother had shrunk to a drainage ditch - Reading Sewer. But 500 years ago, Smallhythe was the home port of a ferry that crossed the Rother and we knew from historical documents that many ships and other sailing vessels had been built here, underneath where sheep now grazed.

We had come to Smallhythe at the invitation of local resident Peter Luckett. He was organising the construction of a Millennium diorama of the borough – 'the town and hundreds of Tenterden' – to celebrate the quincentenary of its incorporation as a 'limb' of the Cinque Ports (*see box*). It was intended that the diorama would show the ancient shipyard at Smallhythe, but except for a handful of references in old manuscripts, there was almost nothing for Peter and his colleagues to go on. They were hoping that TIME TEAM could help.

We had initially intended to look at a very large area comprising land on both sides of Reading Sewer. However, the fields were owned by multiple landowners, many of whom had decided not to cooperate with us. This is a problem frequently encountered by archaeologists – they just can't dig where they want to, regardless of the desires of those who own the land. We were forced to work with what we had permission for – and, in the end, we were grateful that our search for the lost dockyards of Smallhythe had become, by default, so focused.

Day One

The first morning was devoted to sorting out the lie of the land before any serious archaeology could be considered. While most of the geophysics team surveyed Chapel Field, where clumps of nettles indicated some kind of disturbance below ground, Sue Ovenden began her **seismic refraction** study along the public footpath to the west of Delph Marsh. Further down the same path, Jane Siddell of the Museum of London Archaeological Service (MoLAS) and Keith Wilkinson of King Alfred's College, Winchester set up their powered augur. They would be attempting to get core samples all along the path to establish which parts of the fields had once been under water and

THE CINQUE PORTS

This was a group of towns on the south-east coast of England that, until the 15th century, had to provide ships and men to the Crown to defend the coast against invasion and to provide transport across the Channel. The confederation probably had its origins in Roman times and, by the 12th century, comprised five ports (hence the name) – Dover, Hastings, Hythe, Romney and Sandwich. Later, Rye and Winchelsea also became a part, and other towns – including Tenterden – had a looser association. The loss of Normandy to the Crown in 1204 meant that the towns formed the front line against the French, and during the rest of that century, the Cinque Ports played a major naval role. Thereafter they became increasingly absorbed into the general coastal defences of the navy. However, the office of Lord Warden of the Cinque Ports still exists as an honorary distinction; the Queen Mother has held this post since 1979.

thus part of the old River Rother. However, Jane was a bit worried since, over the centuries, the river could have meandered all over the flood plain.

In the barn across from the incident room – which was situated in Tenterden Vineyards' Rural Museum, filled with such estoteric machines as a beet chipper and a chaff cutter – Damien Goodburn, from the Museum of London and an expert in medieval ship building, was beginning to make a small section of a mid-15th-century warship using replicas of medieval tools (*see box*). He first had to shape the oak boards to make them slightly wedge-shaped so that they would overlap each other – the prime characteristic of a clinker-built ship.

To establish a chronology of shipbuilding at Smallhythe, Robin and Tony talked to Dr Ian Friel, the curator of the Littlehampton Museum who had worked at the National Maritime Museum for many years. According to Ian, the first reference to Smallyhythe dates from 1252, and earliest date for anything to do with the sea was 1321 when two men were charged with piracy. However, Smallhythe is particularly exceptional because it is one of the very few places in England where a medieval shipbuilding industry is known to have existed, being active between 1400 and 1545. Of course, ships were built all around the coast, but it has been difficult to pin down the locations of ship-building quarters, even in large ports. It was a very impermanent sort of industry – it was only in the 16th century that fixed dockyards began to be constructed – and the concrete knowledge that it happened here was one of the things that made Smallhythe so interesting.

Another reason for coming to this out-of-the-way spot, Ian continued, was that the second largest ship ever built in medieval England – the *Jesus* – was constructed there in 1416 for Henry V, who came to Smallhythe personally to view its progress. It is quite possible that he sailed in the *Jesus* to Trouville in France to begin his campaign to conquer Normandy, two years after his victory at Agincourt.

The *Jesus* was very large indeed – 46 m (150 ft) in length with a 32 m (105 ft) keel, and 14 m (45 ft) in breadth. It was a '1,000 ton' ship, a 'unit of measurement of a ship's weight or volume in terms of its displacement of water with the loadline just immersed' (*Oxford English Dictionary*). Today a 'ton' is specified as 1 kg (2.24 lb) or 1 cubic metre (35 cu. ft), but when the *Jesus* was launched, 'ton' referred to a 'tun' – a standard wine barrel that was approximately the same size as Robin Bush with his hands on his hips! The *Jesus* was capable of holding 1,000 of these.

In the incident room, Carenza was putting together a jigsaw puzzle of about 30 **aerial photographs** from the RCHME (*see p113*) showing the Smallhythe area after flooding in 1960, before flood control measures had been taken. The areas where there was standing water should give us some indication of the probable extent of the original river, which had disappeared through silting and drainage. These areas might also give us clues as to where the slipways and other features of shipbuilding in Smallhythe might have been.

One of the most western fields available to us was the long and thin - and thus distinctly oddly shaped – Delph Marsh. 'Delph' means 'diggings' and there was a local legend that this field had once been a dry dock. Because of this and its anomalous shape, Carenza, Mick and Gus Milne – a lecturer at the Institute of Archaeology and director of the Thames Archaeological Survey, which had been responsible for the discovery of a number of shipbuilding sites on the

Thames foreshore – decided to excavate here without first doing a geophysical survey. This Trench 1 would be a 'machine trench' – that is, a very deep trench dug with a mechanical digger. The spoil from it would be checked with a metal detector for any evidence of human activity.

John and Chris arrived with geophysics results from Chapel Field, midway between Delph Marsh and the main road. These showed a large area where some type of metallic component was present, but Chris was almost positive that this was modern. However, there were two other, more modest anomalies, also associated with nettles, and it was decided to dig Trenches 2 and 3 here.

After lunch, Tony and Carenza walked down the road from the incident room to Smallhythe Place (*see box on p40*), to speak to Margaret Weir, custodian of the Ellen Terry Museum there. She showed

(Top left) Aerial view of the main site at Smallhythe. *Mick Aston*
(Above left) Aerial view of Delph Marsh, churned up with trenches and tracks from the mechanical digger. *Mick Aston*
(Right) A mosaic of the aerial photographs showing the flooding in 1960. *Mick Aston*

them some nails that had been dredged out of the pond next to the house and which the National Maritime Museum had identified as medieval ship nails. She also said that the pond – complete with paddling ducklings – was believed to have been a dry dock, like Delph Marsh. Because it was on National Trust property, we weren't allowed to excavate here, but Margaret pointed to the field next door, known as the Forestal, where there was another overgrown pond. The field and the pond bank would be another geophysics target.

Things were not going well on the excavation front. The three-part Trench 1 in the north of Delph Marsh had yielded nothing to indicate human activity. Gus did say that the peaty black soil at the bottom, which contained pieces of wood, could be the remains of a prehistoric forest, but Jane Siddell wasn't so sure - she thought that the woody remains were too structurally intact to be that old. In Chapel Field, Trench 2 had been virtually abandoned as only modern bits of metal and a drain cover had been found. According to Phil, Trench 3 looked to be turning out the same, but digging would continue there until this was confirmed.

Jane and Keith's auguring had come to a halt. Already delayed by the late arrival of some two-stroke engine fuel, now two of the augur's sections had welded together at a depth of 12 m (40 ft) and they were wrestling to release them. Before this happened, they had managed to complete only two cores, out of the 10 they had been hoping to achieve that day. Because the cores are so long, they could only check their contents on site through the viewing space in the augur, and then they were discarded. They were unable to preserve them for future research, as can be done with smaller cores. However, palaeo-archaeologist Nigel Cameron was able to take samples from them to carry out diatom analysis (*see box on p40*).

Sue Ovenden's seismic study had also run into trouble. First, she had had difficulties with the computer designed to pick up the signals, then she encountered interference from TIME TEAM's television crane. Sorting out what results she

AN EXPERIMENT IN MEDIEVAL SHIPBUILDING

For the last half century, *writes Damien Goodburn*, archaeologists have been studying the rare remains of medieval and Tudor ships and boats, but it is only in the last 25 years that much attention has been paid to how they were actually built. In fact, many details of how shipwrights worked during this time are still not understood, and the 'cameo' at Smallhythe provided an opportunity to experiment with theories about how some of this work was done.

In the late Middle Ages in England, the 'clinker' style of shipbuilding was predominant. Shipwrights formed the hulls of vessels by first assembling the slightly overlapping oak boards and then fitting the curved oak frame timbers. Most of the boards were split out of large straight logs and trimmed with axes. Then they would be fitted together and fastened with distinctive iron rivets – known as 'rove nails' or 'clench nails' – and washers called 'roves', which were forged in strips and snapped off as they were used. The areas where the boards overlapped were waterproofed, or 'luted', with tarred hair, rolls of wool or moss. But just how the fastening and waterproofing were carried out remained more or less a mystery.

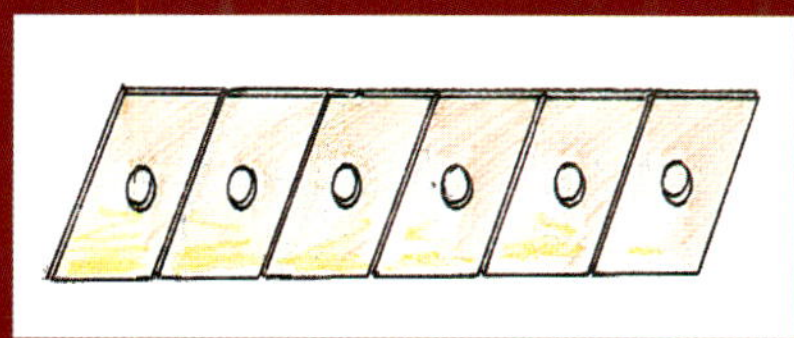

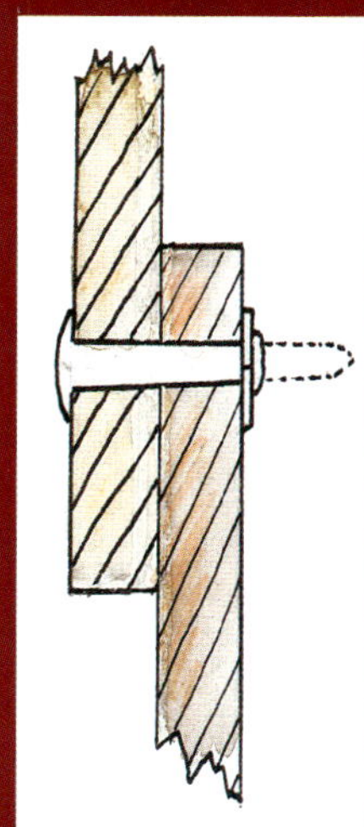

At Smallhythe, a small section of a medieval-style clinker ship hull was created to test two shipbuilding details. First, marks on the rove nails in medieval ship boards found in London had seemed to suggest that a hammer with a chisel-shaped end might have been used to cut off the nail tips and expand them over the rove, but other researchers had said that pincers or files may have been used to cut off the nail tips. Second, we wanted to learn whether it was practical to tar the rolls of wool luting first or simply stick them to the tarred overlaps before the final riveting or 'clenching' up.

Replica wrought-iron nails were forged on site, and we found that, with practice, these could be relatively easily 'clenched' just using a chisel-ended hammer on the nail tip while a heavy hammer was held on the head. This would have been a two-person job in a medieval shipyard, performed by 'clenchers' and 'holders'. In addition, when some of the nails found at Smallhythe were later X-rayed, they were seen to have distinctively flattened tips.

The messy experiment in tarring the luting suggested that soaking wool rolls separately was impractical as they absorbed far too much pine tar. This went everywhere and on everybody during the clenching up! The medieval evidence was replicated far better when the wool rolls were laid in the tar on the overlap of the boards (already pre-bored for the nails), which were then fastened together.

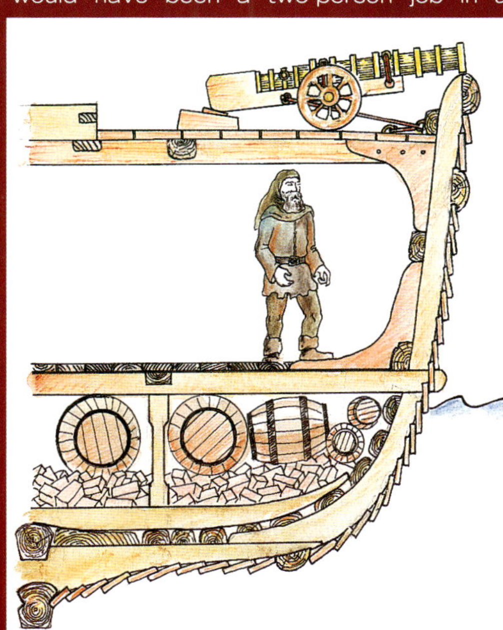

Thanks to this small exercise in experimental archaeology, we have gained new insights into the work of shipwrights at Smallhythe and elsewhere in medieval England.

SMALLHYTHE PLACE

This Kentish yeoman's house with close-set wall timbers and undulating floors was built in the early 16th century, not for a farmer but – it is said – for the 'port reeve', the harbour master of Smallhythe. In 1899, it was bought by the renowned actress Ellen Terry, who lived there until her death in 1928. It is now a museum in her honour, filled with her furniture, china and mementoes from decades in the theatre. The house and grounds, which also contain the Barn Theatre created by Terry's daughter, are now owned by the National Trust and are open to the public.

had got was taking time and not a little patience.

Meanwhile Stewart had completed his survey of the fields to which TIME TEAM had access. The most promising of his findings were in Elfwick Field, to the east of Chapel Field, where he had identified rectilinear earthworks that could be slipways. When a geophysics survey was done of this area, a strong anomaly was found that might be the former edge of the River Rother, as well as some strong signals that could well mean burning or smelting. Given the other disappointments we had had, this gave us something to be getting on with the next day.

Day Two

While outside the strong wind and spitting rain was making everyone else uncomfortable, in the calm of the incident room Sue Francis, having put Carenza's aerial photographs on to a computerised map of the area, was highlighting the flooded parts in blue. This exercise produced some surprises. For instance, Delph Marsh, instead of being flooded as one might have expected had it been a dock, was the only place in that section that was not under water. However, the two 'suspect' areas – the two ponds – at Smallhythe Place where the geophysics team was now surveying both looked promising.

Sue then superimposed contour lines, which showed where the height of the land changed. The shape of the lowest of these closely matched the edge of the flooded area but fell about 4 m (13 ft) above it, giving us what looked like the Smallhythe 'beach'.

The flood line also showed fine detail, including areas that, according to Gus, could well be prime candidates for slipways in Elfwick Field. We were looking for the detritus of shipbuilding, he said, not substantial structures. Much medieval shipbuilding had not been carried out at what we would recognise as docks, but rather in more informal slipways just above high water.

Elfwick Field – now almost universally referred to as 'Stewart's field' – had become our prime focus. Two trenches had been dug here. Trench 4 was another machine trench, created to discover the whereabouts of the foreshore and to give us a definite reference to locate whatever else might be found in this field. Stewart

DIATOM ANALYSIS AT SMALLHYTHE

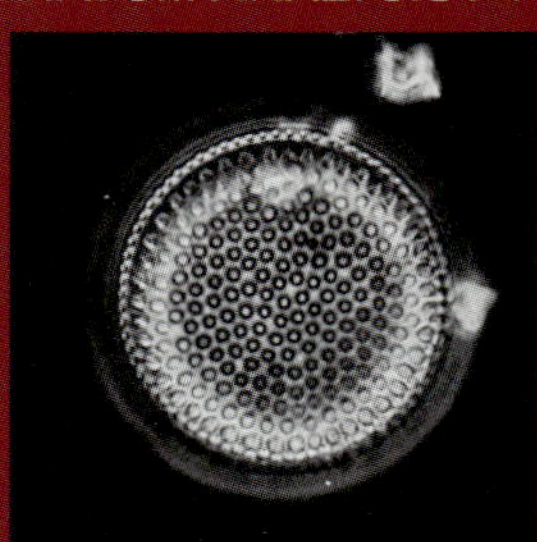

Diatoms are microscopic algae that live in water and are characterised by their ornamented silica shells, *writes Nigel Cameron of University College London's Environmental Change Centre.* Growing as single cells or in colonies, they may be free-living in the water (when they are known as 'plankton') or attached to or moving in and on submerged surfaces.

After diatoms die, their shells are often preserved in the sediments of ditches, ponds, lakes and rivers and in coastal and ocean sediments. There are many thousands of diatom species, and which species grow where is dependent on such water quality factors as the level of acidity, phosphates (from sewage inputs, for example) and saltiness. By looking at the range of species present in a sediment sample of a known age, the water quality and other aspects of the former environment can be reconstructed.

At Smallhythe, samples were prepared from a sediment core 3 m (9.8 ft) long, which contained material that was likely to have accumulated over several thousands of years. (An independent dating method such as **radiocarbon** would be required to confirm this.) A sequence of mud and peat layers was visible in the core. By analysing the diatoms in these sediments, we could find out whether the water that once covered the site was fresh, brackish or salt.

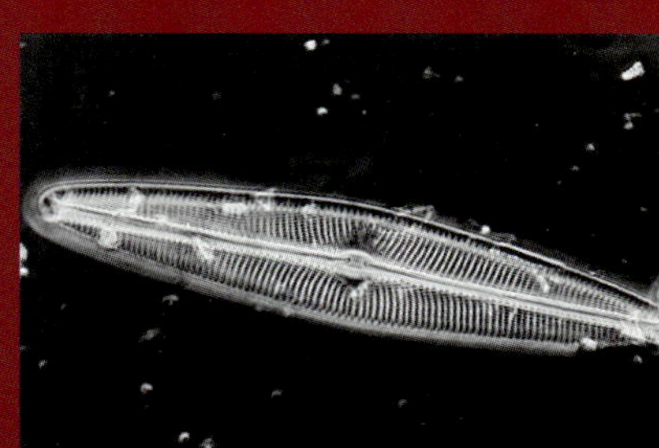

Today, the surface of the coring site is on dry land eight miles from the sea. However, marine species found in the middle part of the core indicated that a water channel that had once been there had been tidal in the geologically and perhaps historically recent past, and that, in the earliest part of its history, it had been freshwater.

(Top box) Aerial view of Smallhythe Place with its pond. *Mick Aston*
(Centre left) Jane and Keith recording a soil sample in the augur. *Mick Aston*
Box: Two of the diatoms found in the sample at Smallhythe. *Nigel Cameron*

and digger Jenni were both pleased so far: in the trench, top soil gave way to 'beachy' sand, which probably indicated the shallows just below the shore. Trench 5 was being excavated at right angles to Trench 4 and about 15 m (50 ft) further up the field, where Stewart's possible slipways might be. Already we had made our first find dating from the period under investigation: a medieval ship's nail.

This had been identified by Damien Goodburn, who was also excited by another 'find' brought to him by researcher David Coward. This was a medieval axe head that, from the way it was offset to one side, had been made for a right-handed worker and, said Damien, was very likely to have been used in shipbuilding. David had found it in a Smallhythe antiques shop where it had been brought by a local gamekeeper who had discovered it in someone's garden. Thus the axe head had virtually no 'context', but it did give us some idea of what we might find 'in context' ourselves.

After lunch, Trench 5 increasingly became the star of the moment. Dozens of nails and roves had been unearthed, which Damien agreed were definitely medieval and evidence of at least ship breaking and repair, as both nails and roves had been used. (Only an unbroken strip of roves would be absolute proof of shipbuilding - the shipwright would have snapped off each piece like squares of chocolate.) There was also a great deal of brick rubble, and from the relative thinness of the bricks, they appeared to be pre-17th century. Mick suggested that they could have been part of a ship's ballast or the remains of its oven – both had been found with Henry VII's ship, the *Mary Rose*.

Conservator Dana Goodburn-Brown had removed some of the spoil from Trench 5 and had taken it up to the incident room. Here she dried it using a hair dryer and ran a magnet – actually a speaker from one of TIME TEAM's Land Rovers! – over it. She was looking for tiny beads of iron that would once have been the sparks that had flown off red-hot metal shaped by a medieval smith, as well as microscopic flakes – hammer scale – that would been scraped off the forged iron work. These finds would show that forging – and thus ship repairing, if not actual shipbuilding – had been carried out somewhere on the site. When Dana examined the results of her magnet work under a microscope, she found both beads and hammer scale.

During the afternoon, Sue Ovenden had sorted out the problems with her seismic study and had finally come up with some results. She had found definite evidence of the old river. There had been two channels: the one nearest the shore was about 10 m (33 ft) deep and 50 m (164 ft) across, and the other, much larger one was 30 m (98 ft) deep and 130 m (427 ft) across. The shallower channel was of more interest to the archaeologists because the size of the ships that could have been built at Smallhythe would have been limited by its dimensions.

In the Forestal field by Smallhythe Place, the overgrown pond had been dredged but this had produced nothing of interest. However, Trench 6 dug next to it – where geophysics had identified a large anomaly – had already, in its first few hours, given up nails and what looked like iron slag.

(Top left) Trench 4 with its 'beachy' sand layers. *Mick Aston*
(Above left) Medieval ship nails found at Smallhythe. *Mick Aston*
(Top right) The brick structure in Trench 5. Mick Aston
(Above) The medieval axe head found in an antiques shop in Smallhythe. *Mick Aston*

In the hotel bar that night, there was a discussion about the geophysics, seismic and auguring results. Gus now agreed with Jane that the pieces of wood found in Trench 1 in Delph Marsh were not from a prehistoric forest. Instead he thought that we had not dug deep enough as the 'peat' found there was too new. So it was decided that, first thing the next morning, Jane would carry out a number of auguring transects of that field, to see if or when the area had silted up – if this had happened in prehistoric times, the place would not have been suitable for medieval shipbuilding. They also wanted to discover how steep the foreshore had been at this point; if it had been fairly steep, it would have been ideal for slipways.

Day Three

As Jane set to work in Delph Marsh, Trench 5 in Elfwick Field was providing continuing excitement. What had been thought to be brick rubble was becoming much more substantial. What appeared to be a corbelled roof with a hole in it (for a flue?) might be the top of a furnace or kiln. To find out, Phil was digging out the interior. Meanwhile, even more nails and other bits of debris from ship building/repair/breaking had been found.

In Trench 6 in the Forestal, the great geophysics anomaly proved to be a metal bucket, tea kettle and jelly mould – laughter and red faces all round! However, just a metre or so away, Mick the Dig and Carenza had uncovered what might prove to be the find of the shoot: nails and very dark soil shaped in a distinctive curve. Could the dark soil be the decayed planks of a medieval ship or smaller boat?

Dana had also been raiding the spoil heap here. She had found a substantial amount of hammer scale and balls from sparks, enough to suggest the close proximity of a smith.

A section had been cut through the pond bank and designated Trench 7. Although nothing had been found in the spoil from the pond bottom, nails were found in the bank. This and other evidence – including the fact that the

two ponds at Smallhythe Place were parallel to the shoreline, not (as one would expect) at right angles to it – led to the conclusion that the ponds had never been docks. The ponds had probably been formed when the levee along Reading Sewer was created some time after the area's medieval heyday.

At lunchtime, John Gater, laptop at the ready, rushed on to the dining bus to show producer Tim Taylor the latest geophysics results from Elfwick Field. Previously he and his team had surveyed only a small portion of this, which led to the discoveries in Trench 5. Now, having expanded the search to about a hectare (2.5 acres), they had found what appeared to be quite strong evidence for settlement along the main Smallhythe road. But would there be time to put in another trench to test this out?

At Smallhythe Place, Carenza and Mick the Dig were disagreeing about what they had uncovered in Trench 6. But regardless of whether it was or wasn't the remains of a ship left here to rot and become buried back in the late Middle Ages, we had ample evidence of some kind of ship construction, repair or breaking at this spot.

Over to the west, in the field between Delph Marsh and Chapel Field, Jane had finished four transects of bore holes into what appeared to have once been a large inlet or bay, according to the 1960 flood photographs and the contours of

the surrounding land. But would it have been deep enough for ships to have sailed in it? The results – achieved through Jane's back-breaking labour with the motorised augur – showed that it would have been much too shallow, and therefore the centre of shipbuilding at Smallhythe would have been further to the east.

And to the east was where Trench 5 was producing the biggest mystery of

(Top centre) The metal bucket and the tea kettle (containing the jelly mould) that created a large geophysic anomaly in Trench 6. *Mick Aston*
(Top right) Working on the brick 'kiln' in Trench 5. *Mick Aston*
(Above right) Carenza clearing the 'boat' remains in Trench 6. *Mick Aston*

the dig. What had initially seemed to be a corbelled roof over a possible furnace had proved to be more of a horseshoe-shaped brick slot. Further uncovering of the surrounding area had revealed an oval edge of clay that had been heated so fiercely from the inside that it had been baked to form bright red brick. There was also a significant amount of chalk or limestone inside, but if it had been a lime kiln, used to make lime mortar, where was the large residue that one would expect to find? No ship's nails had been found directly inside this enigmatic feature, but plenty had come out of the ditch or channel that excavation had revealed right next to it.

As the end of our third day was quickly approaching, it was decided that we didn't have time to put in a trench within the strong geophysics evidence of settlement on the hill above what had once been the shore, along the main thoroughfare of the present village. But we were virtually certain that this was where Smallhythe's working population had once lived.

In the barn opposite the incident room, Damien and his crew had managed to construct, from hand-picked oak timbers, three boards and the supports ('futtocks') to which they would have been attached with nails identical to those found in trenches 5, 6 and 7. The ones he used had been specially forged on site, a process that had produced spark balls and hammer scale virtually identical to that found by Dana in trenches 5 and 6.

Now the caulking of the boards – technically called 'luting' – was carried out. In the Middle Ages, this appears from documents to have been provided by women, and since their names coincided, it is probable that many of them were the wives of the shipwrights. In the first step of Damien's experiment, wool was teased out and rubbed along the thigh until it formed a long, loose rope, similar to what would have been needed for spinning. Then this was soaked in pine tar, warmed up to make it less viscous. Meanwhile the two boards were each tarred on one side where they would meet when attached. The luting was laid on to this and the boards nailed together. (For the technical results of this experiment, see box on p39.)

To prove that the now complete clinker-built section was waterproof, Tony persuaded Phil to crouch behind it and be sprayed with water from a hose. As we had all hoped, only mist reached Phil over the top of the boards. Then Tony aimed the spray directly at Phil and then sprinted away! With a roar, Phil chased after him with the hose, and both ended up soaked to the skin while the crew fell about laughing.

At the end of Day Three, we could say that we had found, not a massive complex of quays and docks, but an informal working area of slipways, with a settlement of shipwrights and other workers – as well as their wives and families – close by. The slipways could have been established virtually anywhere suitable along the shore of what had then been the wide River Rother. In his mind's eye, Tony could imagine the *Jesus* being launched here, carrying Henry V's troops east down the river and across the Channel to fight in France.

Stop press:

When Mick the Dig returned the next day to 'make good' the trenches behind Smallhythe Place, he found in Trench 6 a piece of elm planking, with perhaps the remains of animal hair caulking, and a futtock complete with holes for clench nails. The entire structure bore an uncanny resemblance to the ship section built for us by Damien. Mick the Dig now calls this discovery 'the one that got away'!

Final thoughts from Mick

Smallhythe was a really interesting project. The evidence for medieval ship building has turned out to be very important – almost unique in the country and far beyond what we had expected.

For me, one of the most intriguing aspects was the change in the landscape since the Middle Ages. It was very difficult to imagine that the green fields had once been a wide estuary. We went to the coast in the helicopter and then followed the former outline of the estuary and river inland. We could clearly see the flat land with drainage ditches, as well as the medieval town of Rye and Henry VII's Camber Castle - formerly on the coast but now marooned inland. It is often a surprise to realise that the landscape is not static but constantly changing, even if this is not appreciated in a lifetime!

Victor and Steve's reconstruction of what Smallhythe would have looked like in its shipbuilding heyday.

BURSLEM

STOKE ON TRENT

WHAT MIGHT HAVE HAPPENED

This was the last load of the new pottery to be tested, and the workers were still full of expectations. Each time they had looked for the lustrous cream finish to emerge from the still baking-hot kiln, only to be disappointed. Now, as they peered in and a shaft of sunlight entered the gloom and caught the edge of the stacked plates, they knew that the master potter had got it right.

Josiah Wedgwood had already decided where the first consignment of this new china would be sent. If the royal family could be persuaded to eat off it, the rest of the country would follow. Cream-glazed dishes would be found in every family's cupboard, and not only in Britain. His dream of becoming china maker to the world was about to become closer to reality.

Victor's reconstruction of the Ivy House works in Burslem during Josiah Wedgwood's tenure on the site.

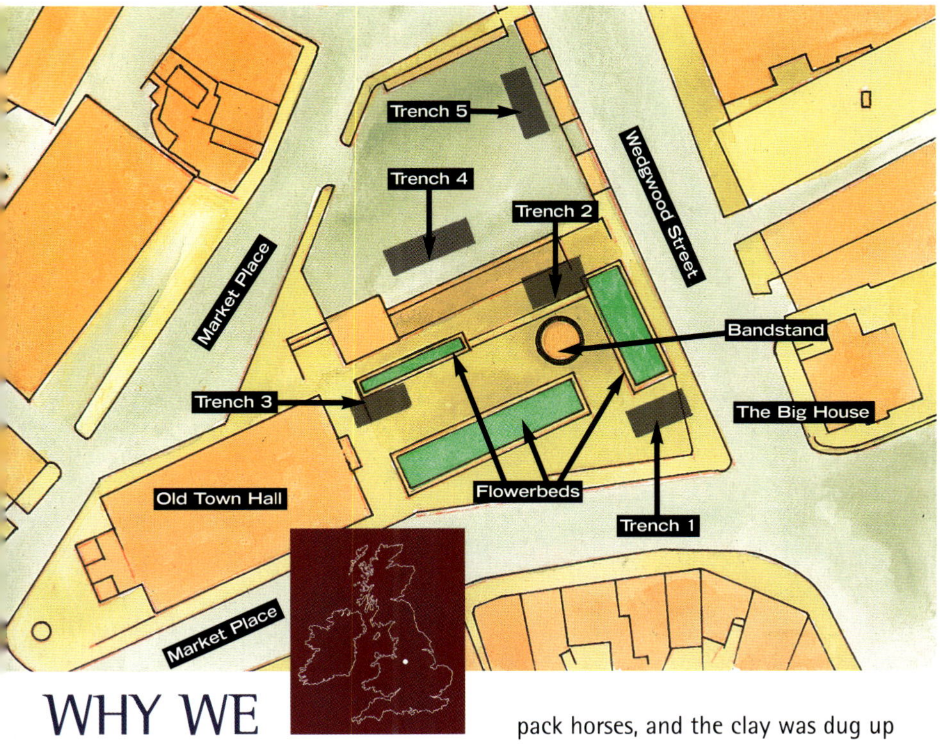

WHY WE WENT THERE

Today, Burslem – one of the 'six towns' that make up Stoke on Trent in north Staffordshire – is in obvious need of redevelopment and investment. It was with this in mind that the Burslem Community Development Trust approached TIME TEAM. Not that we would contribute financially to the renovation of the town, but we could help in two other ways. First, featuring Burslem on the programme would give it welcome publicity, and second, we could carry out some of the archaeological evaluation needed before the Trust's big project could go forward. This was an exhibition centre to be called 'Ceramica' and it would eventually celebrate the industry that, in the past, had made Burslem world famous.

In the early 18th century, Burslem was isolated and impoverished. There were no roads, only muddy tracks, and the area was sparsely populated because the land was too poor for farming. However, it did have two things that made a huge impact on its future: coal and clay. Virtually all the cottagers had pottery kilns in their back gardens, and they moulded the clay to make relatively crude dishes and other containers that would be fired in the kilns – heated red-hot with the coal – and then sold to local hawkers. Because there were no roads, the coal had to be carried in on pack horses, and the clay was dug up wherever it was found, with the result that the area was littered with 'potholes'.

Josiah Wedgwood (1730-95) was the youngest of the 12 children of Thomas and Mary Wedgwood of the Churchyard pottery works at Burslem. Josiah had two much older cousins who were more successful than his father. Thomas and 'Long John' Wedgwood amassed so much money through manufacturing salt-glazed ware that, in 1843, they were able to build the first house in Burslem to be roofed with slates, which they called the 'Big House'.

Following the death of his father in 1739, with only two years of schooling under his belt, Josiah began working for his eldest brother at the Churchyard works. Completing his apprenticeship, he went into partnership with Thomas Whieldon and spent his evenings carrying out experiments to perfect various pottery techniques; he wrote up the results – in a secret code – in his 'Experiment Books'. At the same time, he courted his cousin Sally (Sarah) Wedgwood, whose father refused to let him marry her unless he could match the £4,000 he was giving her as a dowry.

In 1758, the 28-year-old Josiah ended his partnership with Whieldon and, using his savings, set himself up as a master potter. In May the following year, his cousins Thomas and Long John leased him a small pottery works called the Ivy House for £10 a year. This consisted of a house, workshops and bottle ovens. He employed 15 workers, some of them children, and trained them well, while insisting on strict discipline. He continued his experiments, perfecting a cream-coloured earthenware that soon superseded the salt-glazed stoneware that had been the staple product of the district. He also arranged for his brother John, a merchant, to represent him in London, so extending his sales beyond Staffordshire.

At the end of 1762 or early in 1763, just three years after setting up at the Ivy House, Josiah had outgrown the premises and moved to the Brick House works, leased to him by another potter. From then on, he never looked back – he matched Sally's dowry and married her in January 1764 – and eventually his marvellous ceramics gained an international reputation.

But it was Wedgwood's first venture as sole proprietor at the Ivy House works that became the focus of TIME TEAM's investigation at Burslem. For the Trust's projected Ceramica exhibition centre

(Top right) Crane view of the Big House, built by Josiah Wedgwood's cousins and still standing opposite the TIME TEAM excavation site. *Mick Aston*
(Above right) Engraving of Wedgwood's Ivy House works, based on a picture drawn from memory by one of Wedgwood's descendants. *Trustees of the Wedgwood Museum, Barlaston, Staffordshire, England*

was to be constructed right on top of the park and carpark next to Burslem's Old Town Hall – and thus right on top of where the Ivy House had once stood. Would we be able to find any trace of Josiah's first factory?

Day One

Despite the fact that it was the second week of June, it was freezing cold and pouring with rain as we made our way to our most city-centred site of the series. The park where we would be excavating was covered in raised flower beds, benches, slab paving and a 1960s bandstand. In addition, so that we could get on with our work in relative peace and safety, the entire area had been surrounded by wire fences. As a result, as the three days passed, we felt increasingly as if we were animals in a zoo, there for the entertainment of the local residents. The latter, though, proved to be some of the friendliest we had encountered, ever welcoming and bemused as to why we had come to such a place!

While the geophysics team began traversing the tarmacked carpark with **ground-penetrating radar** (GPR), Stewart carried out a survey of the area, using old and new maps and his own experienced eyes. The history of the site, which was located on rising ground, contained one major potential headache for us: in 1835, a large meat market was built over most of the area we were to concentrate on. If it had been built *into* the hill, with the soil (and anything it contained) having been removed to create level ground, it was unlikely that we would find anything of note. However, if it had been 'stepped' into the hill, so that there would have been various levels within the market itself, we might be lucky. However, Stewart was working on the basis that much of the market area had been scraped clean, and by placing transparent overlays of plans of the Ivy Hall works, the market and the present park on top of each other, he was trying to find any odd corners that might have survived with older material.

In the incident room, Robin had uncovered documents showing the conveyancing of two plots of land in, respectively, 1832 and 1848 – one, for the Blue Bell tavern, between the town hall and the market and the other on the edge of what was now the carpark (the buildings on the latter had been demolished in the 1950s). It appeared that these plots might have survived right through from Wedgwood's time. If this were true, they would have been unaffected by the construction of the market and so were prime candidates for trenches.

Meanwhile, Trench 1 had been started in the south-east corner of the park, on the corner of Wedgwood Street and Market Place, an area identified by Stewart as possibly untouched by the meat market. However, after only inches of material had been removed, black-and-white and red Victorian floor tiles were found that were undoubtedly part of the market.

Stoke on Trent is near Rocester, the home of JCB, the manufacturers of mechanical diggers, and the company had lent us the services of some of its most experienced drivers. The latter created virtual ballets with their machines as they manoeuvred around the park with its flower beds, steps, pavements and benches, and we were soon applauding their expertise.

After lunch, John reported potentially very good results from the GPR in the carpark. Unfortunately, however, the rain had got into the works and John and his colleague Sue Ovenden had had to suspend the last part of their survey until the machine dried out. They had tried to continue with a smaller machine at a different frequency, but this hadn't 'looked' as deep as the wet one.

Trench 2 was begun in another 'niche' identified by Stewart, to the north of Trench 1, underneath one end of a shelter that ran the length of the park. The JCB first had to demolish some wide steps, then prise loose the paving slabs and remove them. Then it squeezed into the limited space and began digging. Shortly after, traces of a structure were seen and we had our first pieces of pottery: some inferior 19th-century cream ware, probably discarded after firing, and some mottled ware from 1650-1720. The latter was invariably used for pub drinking vessels, and so these pieces could have been discarded by pottery workers.

The Wedgwood Museum had arranged for Josiah Wedgwood's 'Experiment Book' and his 'Commonplace Book' to be lent to us, but only under the watchful eye of a uniformed security officer. The 'Commonplace Book' – which contained details of Wedgwood's finances, minutes of meetings, descriptions of other potteries, accounts of journeys he took, letters to his children, among many other things – gave us, according to

(Above) A selection of 'finds' from Stoke Museum, consisting of pieces of medieval and early post-medieval pottery (some reconstructed) excavated at sites in and around the city. *Mick Aston*

(Top left) A Wedgwood teapot and hot water jug in creamware. *(Trustees of the Wedgwood Museum, Barlaston, Staffordshire,England)*

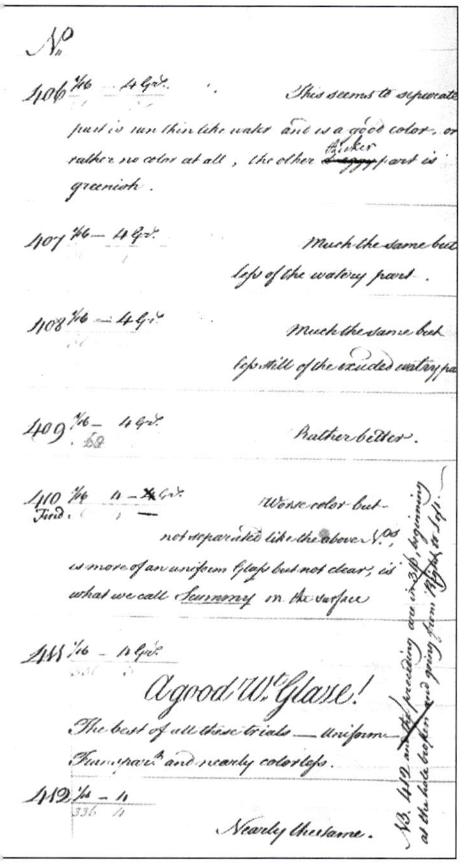

No

406 76 — 4 Grs. This seems to separate

part is run thin like water and is a good color, or

rather no color at all, the other thicker part is

greenish.

407 76 — 4 Grs. Much the same but

less of the watery part.

408 76 — 4 Grs. Much the same but

less still of the exuded watery pa

409 76 — 4 Grs. Rather better.

410 76 — 4 Grs. Worse color but

not separated like the above Nos

is more of an uniform glass but not clear; is

what we call Scummy on the surface

411 76 — 4 Grs.

A good Wt. Glaze!

The best of all these trials — Uniform

Transparent and nearly colorless.

412 76 — 4

Nearly the same.

(Top left) A page from Wedgwood's 'Experiment Book'.
Trustees of the Wedgwood Museum, Barlaston, Staffordshire, England.

Robin, 'a portrait of a true man of the Enlightenment'. The 'Experiment Book', on the other hand, showed Wedgwood's fanatical persistence: he perfected his white glaze only after 111 trials.

As more earth was removed from Trench 2, multiple suggestions of what we might have found were proffered. Some were sure that the brick structure that was gradually being revealed was a drain. Then someone said that it might be one of Wedgwood's prototype kilns – the brick structure could actually be a flue. Still others quickly damped down this enthusiasm. However, as a sherd of medieval pottery was recovered and more and more laid brick came to light, it was hard not to hope for the ultimate goal: the base of a kiln contained within a bottle oven (*see box*). But, so far, there were none of the distinctive concentric circles of bricks that would mean a kiln bottom.

So as a winter-like night drew in, TIME TEAM repaired to The Leopard pub across the street. According to his diary, Josiah Wedgwood had come here for a drink and a discussion about the building of the Trent Mersey Canal that would eventually enable him to transport his wares throughout England and the world.

BOTTLE OVENS

Until the 1950s, Stoke on Trent – including Burslem – was an extremely unhealthy place to live, not least because of the smoke that emerged from the thousands of bottle ovens scattered throughout the town. Today there are only about 40 still standing, with seven preserved at the Gladstone Working Pottery Museum at Longton.

'Bottle oven' very accurately describes the appearance of these structures. The ovens consisted of two distinct parts. The outer, bottle-shaped shell – the hovel – acted as a chimney, protected the actual oven from the elements and gave the workers some control of the ventilation. It could be as tall as 21 m (70 ft).

The round oven or kiln was inside, with a passageway between it and the hovel so that the workers could get at the firemouths around the bottom, below the oven floor, which would be stoked with coal to heat the structure – it could take up to 14 tons of fuel to fire a load of pottery. The oven had a domed roof (crown), walls 0.3 m (1 ft) thick and iron bands (bonts) running right round to strengthen it as it expanded and contracted during firing.

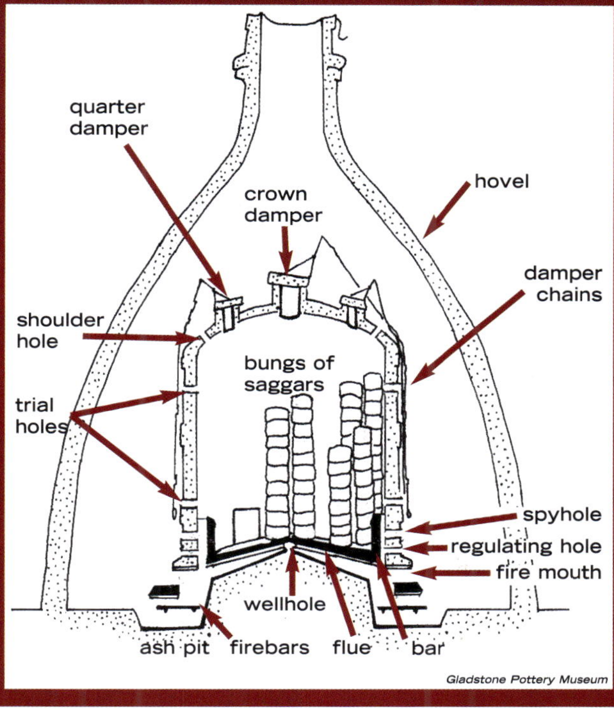

The unfired pieces of pottery would be placed in round clay containers called saggars to protect them from the smoke. The saggars would be taken into the oven and piled up on top of each other in stacks known as bungs. When the oven was full, the doorway (clammins) would be bricked up and the firing begun. It would take about 48 hours for the oven to reach its maximum temperature – between 1,000 and 1,250°C (1,830-2,280°F) – which would be maintained for two or three hours. The fires were then allowed to go out.

Day Two

While Carenza went to the Gladstone Working Pottery Museum at Longton, a few miles away, to see how pottery was made in the 19th century (*see box*), work continued in Trenches 1 and 2 and Trench 3 was opened at the other end of the shelter area, near the entrance to the Old Town Hall.

In Trench 1, one of the JCBs hammered apart the substantial concrete level – made with pottery sherds instead of gravel! – that underlaid the tiling floor. At first, it was thought that this operation would destroy everything underneath (of which there was little hope anyway), and closing down the trench was contemplated. However, as someone commented at the time, 'Just mention closing down and watch how they work!' – and, sure enough, the diggers soon came up with bits of 18th-century pottery and what they suspected might be a kiln.

That was also what was found in Trench 2 after debris had been removed – a 19th-century kiln. According to Mick, this would have to be recorded and then part of it removed, to see if there is something older underneath.

But it was the new Trench 3 that now took centre stage. At first, the sweeps of the JCB revealed nothing in the soil and then only the odd sherd. Then, suddenly, it uncovered a huge deposit of broken pottery of all types, including what one of the experts said were pharmaceutical items, including heavy earthenware inhalers. All this was excavated by the rubbish binful. David Barker, keeper of archaeology at Stoke Museum, reckoned that the pieces were all made in the 1830s – still outside the small three-year window we were aiming for. But with all the pottery we were finding, we were travelling backwards through Burslem's industrial history.

After a cloudburst that drenched everyone queuing for lunch – and created a stream that poured into Trench 3 until diverted – the sun apperared intermittently and the temperature rose.

In Trench 1, digger Jenni Butterworth – whose passion is early slipware – was ecstatic: 'This is the best time I've had this series!' Miraculously, tucked away underneath the meat market, a small deposit ditch had lain undisturbed, as had the edge of what had once been a kiln. Numerous pieces of slipware were found dating from about 1700. These included pieces that, when stuck together, formed a virtually complete official ale measure, with a badge on the outside as proof of this. Perhaps this had come from the Blue Bell pub? In addition, quite a few animal bones and teeth were discovered, but from a time before the meat market. It was suggested that these might have been added, baked and ground up, to the clay for a kind of bone china. This trench would now be recorded and closed down.

Our pottery experts told us that the huge number of broken pieces of pottery in Trench 3 had all come from the firm Enoch Wood & Sons, which was still in operation nearby. Enoch Wood had been notorious for 'flytipping', getting rid of his waste pottery in any available hole, where or not he owned the land. He had also been an antiquarian and many of the earliest examples of Burslem pottery in Stoke Museum had come from his collection. It was said of him:

EW was a thorough antiquary naturally, and whenever in the neighbourhood of Burslem excavations were being cut or foundations laid EW would be ... watching and looking out for fragments of old pottery for his museum.

He had probably also been on the lookout for places to dump his waste!

The team from Stoke Museum were busy cleaning up the sherds from the Wood flytip we had found, all of which would be assessed and packed away for future reference. It was quite possible that the discovery of this dump could lead to the matching of pottery patterns with their previously unknown manufacturer.

Once the sherds had been cleared away from Trench 3, a structure was found in the bottom that, at first, was thought to be a mine shaft. Local historian Fred Hughes sincerely hoped it wasn't. Because these shafts were invariably left in a dangerous condition, the presence of one here would mean shutting down not only the TIME TEAM dig but also the whole Ceramica project! Luckily Phil finally deemed it to be the rather badly preserved remains of a kiln floor, which would mean that we had located a previously unknown bottle oven on this site. Mick the Dig instructed the JCB operator to move the existing spoil heap to one side and widen the trench. Getting underway, the JCB driver happily began to rip up the park benches.

In the carpark, John and Sue Ovenden had finally completed their radar survey. In the area closest to the park, there was some activity next to a strong signal that John thought was probably where the wall of the meat market had been. Another JCB drilled a series of holes through the tarmac and then scraped it off to begin Trench 4.

A cobbled floor appeared at one end, then a cut containing a modern electricity cable and finally a concrete structure. The floor was likely to have been from a cottage known to have been here from about 1835. Could the concrete structure be the roof of the tunnel that was known to have led from the now-demolished police station to the cells in the cellar of the Old Town Hall? After much discussion, however, it was decided that this was a World War II air raid shelter!

Elsewhere in the carpark, the radar survey results conformed to structures known to have once been on the site, except for the space where the old police station should have been – this was a complete blank on the printout. However, this could have been the result if, when the police station was demolished, the hole had been filled in with clay, which cannot be 'read' by ground-penetrating radar.

The final decision of the day was to begin another trench - Trench 5 - in the car park, opposite the blank police station area.

(Top left) The ale measure found in Trench 1. The yellow disc is the official badge. *Mick Aston*
(Above left) Jenni Butterworth shows off the c. 1700 slipware found in Trench 1. *Mick Aston*
(Above centre) A fraction of the pottery dumped by Enoch Wood in the 1830s and found in Trench 3. *Mick Aston*

Day Three

Carenza was again absent from the site as she and Victor had gone to the modern Wedgwood factory to recreate one of Josiah's vases. Meanwhile, as the marvellous archaeology in Burslem kept everyone there on the hop, so did the weather. Brilliant sunshine was followed by cloudbursts, complete with hail. 'Next come the frogs!' said someone, only half joking.

In Trench 5, Mick the Dig had uncovered a row of bricks that, at least on first view, seemed to be slightly curving. He fully expected to come up with yet another bottle oven, but only more excavation would show if he was right.

Trench 3 had been widened and more of the 'floor' uncovered. Contrary to earlier expectations, this was now reckoned not to be a kiln, undiscovered or not, but simply a jumble of deposited bricks. However, here it was extremely easy to see the yellow-ochre layer of Etruria marl clay from which much of the pottery we had encountered had been made and which had originally been the source of Burslem's wealth.

The remains of the 19th-century bottle oven in Trench 2 were now very clear; the outer, stepped sides – three courses high – would eventually be

cleaned up to show how crisp the brickwork still was. But it was the excavation under part of this that was generating excitement that could be felt by everyone nearby. It revealed all that TIME TEAM had been hoping for: the first pieces of pottery from the 1759-62/3 window when Josiah Wedgwood had been working here. And, as an added bonus, there were some large fragments of cream ware, which Wedgwood had been the first to produce at Burslem. As word of these finds was whispered throughout the cast and crew, great grins appeared everywhere. But that wasn't all. The

diggers had also found a layer of older (pre-19th century) brick floor. There was too little to definitely tell its function, but its upper surface did show evidence of great heat, so perhaps this, too, had been a kiln - and perhaps one of Wedgwood's!

Also found in this part of the trench was a moulded corner of white pottery. Our experts took one look and said that it was the corner of a teapot that had been made in the shape of the Big House, which still stood opposite the park, and had been manufactured by Josiah Wedgwood's cousins Thomas and Long John in about 1730. When an intact example was brought from the museum, it was easy to see just where our corner would fit.

Mick the Dig had promised that Trench 5 would produce the discovery of the dig, but even he had to admit that, up till now, his trench had not been nearly as interesting as Trenches 1-3 – even his row of bricks had turned out to be quite straight and so not a bottle oven. However, when he consulted Stewart, the latter verified that, according to a plan of 1835 that

TRADITIONAL METHODS OF CERAMICS MANUFACTURE

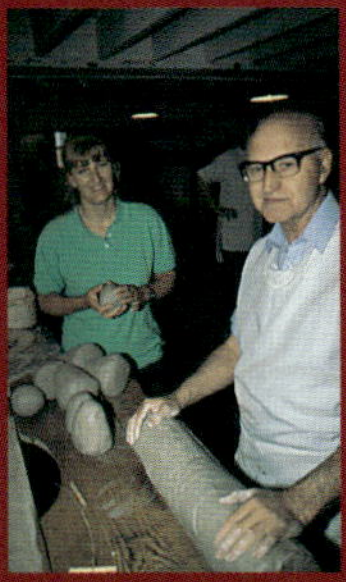

Although great technical advancements have been made in the manufacture of ceramics over the last three centuries, traditional methods continue to be used, *writes Gaye Blake Roberts of the Wedgwood Museum*. The potter still sits at the fast-moving throwing wheel – now powered by electricity rather than manually operated – and skilfully forms the clay into the required shape. Some items are more satisfactorily created by casting. The caster pours slip (clay in a liquid state) into plaster moulds that absorb the water, leaving a thin coating of clay on the inside. When dry, the clay contracts and so is easily removed from the mould.

Cups are made on a machine called a 'jolly', which employs a mould to shape them. The handles are created in one of three ways: by pressing the clay into a mould, by casting or by cutting a long strip of clay into appropriately sized pieces. They are then fixed to the cups with a tiny amount of clay mixed with water. Plates are manufactured by a combination of mechanical and hand processes –

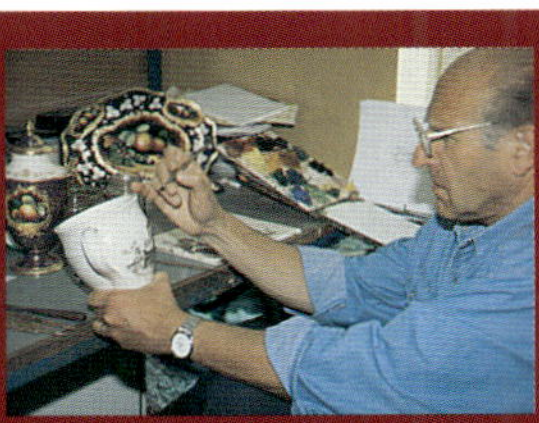

techniques that have not changed over the years.

Decoration plays a major part in the production of most ceramic wares. Free-hand painting in enamel colours directly on to a piece's glaze takes great skill and dates back to the earliest days of the Potteries. Transferring printing designs by means of a copper plate and tissue paper pull was the first method of mass-producing identical patterns, and subsequent methods of decoration include lithography, where the pattern is encased in thin sheets of plastic. Gilding is the last step in the decorating process, and is applied by hand using 22-carat gold.

The most important part of manufacturing ceramics – and the riskiest – is the firing of the pieces. This was originally carried out in the coal-fired bottle ovens that once dominated the Staffordshire skyline. Today it is done in electrical or oil- or gas-fired ovens, which has both increased the standards achieved and speeded up the process.

(Top centre) The base of the kiln in Trench 3. *Mick Aston* *(Top right)* The corner of the Big House teapot. *Mick Aston*
Box: *(left)* Carenza and a Wedgwood potter preparing clay; *(centre)* Victor painting the enamel on the glazed vase; *(right)* the completed vase, showing the Ivy House works. *Mick Aston*

he and Bernard had examined, this was the back wall of the Ivy Hall works! Even though we couldn't say if the works had extended this far in Wedgwood's time, this was quite a significant find.

After lunch, it was decided to carry out just a little more excavation in Trench 3, the team not being satisfied with the jumble of bricks at the bottom. A bit of digging and a drain was uncovered, then what appeared to be the floors of two workshops on either side of it, one containing a hearth. These, too, were believed to date from the Ivy House period.

Meanwhile, curator Debbie Ford had had another look at the 'pharmaceutical items' found in Trench 3, especially the 'earthenware inhalers'. Debbie gently turned one of these over and it suddenly became an early lavatory pan! However, even these were significant because, being dated to about 1835, they are earlier than those produced by Doulton, which would become the dominant manufacturer of sanitary ware.

However, it was Mick the Dig's Trench 5 that proved to be the crowning glory of TIME TEAM's excavations at Burslem. Mick the Dig had decided to insert a test pit next to the wall he had found and soon he had come up with a great number of shards of medieval pottery dating from the 14th to the 16th century. According to city archaeologist Bill Klemperer, while they had found the odd fragment of medieval ceramics and around Burslem, they had never uncovered anything as wonderful as this collection. It would, he said, change the way archaeologists viewed the history of pottery production in the entire area.

The architects of the Ceramica exhibition centre visited our excavations and confirmed that their present designs would cover up all the archaeology we had revealed. But they were surprisingly enthusiastic about what we'd found and said that not only would they alter their plans to protect the archaeology but they would also try to incorporate the bottle oven bottom - and Wedgwood's floor - in Trench 2 into the permanent exhibition!

Final thoughts from Mick

The excavation at Burslem was a really good experience. Not only were the local team - Bill Klemperer, David Barker and others - incredibly helpful and enthusiastic, but everyone in the town seems to have paid a visit to the 'fences' to see how we were getting on!

The archaeology, though 'recent' as far as many people were concerned, was very exciting. Most of us had never seen so much crockery - just the sorts of stuff that you would find in your garden. But this time, with David Barker around, we were able to learn the precise dates of the designs and shapes as the technology improved. I just wonder what the museum will do with all the many dustbins of pottery we left them!

(Top left) One of the Big House teapots and the sherd found by TIME TEAM. *Mick Aston*
(Top right) Steve and Victor's vision of the Ivy House works next to the still existing Big House in Burslem.
(Above) Kiln waste found at the end of excavation. *Mick Aston*

BEAUPORT PARK

EAST SUSSEX

WHAT MIGHT HAVE HAPPENED

They all felt proud of the new bath house as they sat in the streaming interior. Not many administrators in places in the empire dedicated to their industry had had the foresight to construct facilities like this, so near the workplace. It might not have the fine mosaics of the governor's bath house, but it still contained all the necessary elements and the lockers had been a splendid touch.

As they scraped away the grime of another day's production, they felt satisfied with their labours. The metal they created through excavation and fire was good, and the seam of iron ore seemed capable of meeting the increasing demands of the fleet and the empire's farmers. It was their iron that held the ships and buildings of the Romans together and formed their ploughshares and weapons. No men more deserved a reviving bath at the end of the day.

They indulged themselves with another bowl of wine before the cold plunge that would bring them back to the realities of living in this farflung outpost.

Victor's reconstruction of the Roman bath house at Beauport Park.

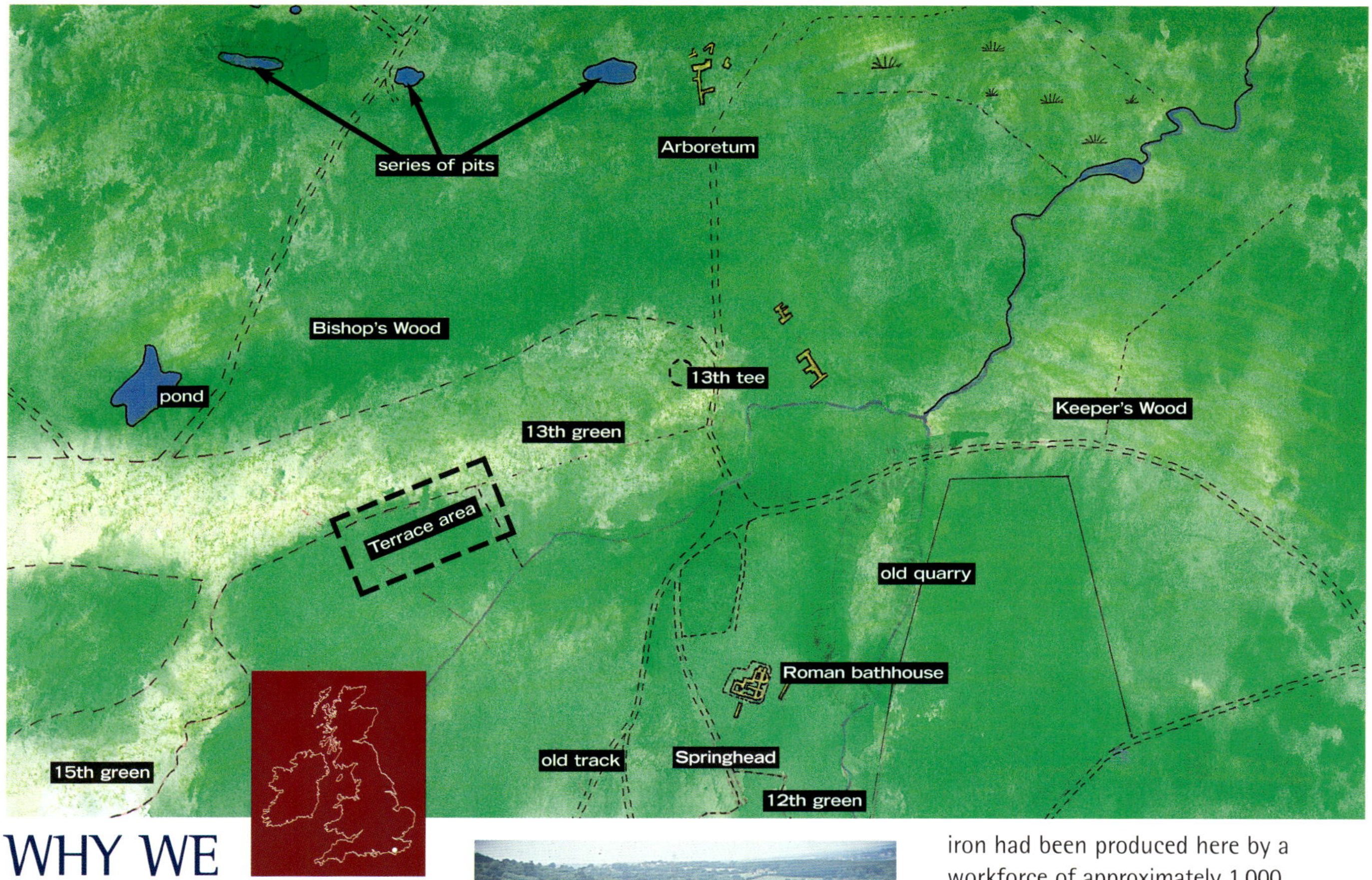

WHY WE WENT THERE

In 1869, a church rector discovered a huge bank of iron slag – the waste product after the ore has been smelted – in the grounds of a 1,000-acre estate in East Sussex known as Beauport Park. The bank, which had been created by Roman iron-working, covered over 1 hectare (2.5 acres) and contained an estimated 100,000 tonnes of slag. However, shortly after its discovery, most of it was carted away to make metalled roads in the area. However, it still merited an annotation on Ordnance Survey maps: 'Site of Roman bloomery [iron-working].'

In the late1960s, it was this citation that attracted classics master Dr Gerald Brodribb to Beauport Park. After obtaining permission from the owner, he excavated wherever he wanted, using divining rods to locate Roman roads and tracks. One day in 1970, while employing his rods, he 'got a reaction and began to dig immediately revealing good quality masonry and tile. This turned out to be the bath house.'

Gerald and some volunteers spent the next two years excavating this extra-ordinary survival – a Roman bath house with about 60% of its original masonry still standing. However, although the bath house and a large area to the north of it were scheduled as an Ancient Monument and taken under the wing of English Heritage, no funds have been forthcoming to exhibit the site to the public and conduct further research. It was with this in mind that Gerald approached TIME TEAM.

Aerial view of the bath house (covered by the corrugated iron shelter), the forest and the 13th fairway of the golf course. *Mick Aston*

We, too, were intrigued by the bath house, but only as a focal point of an area of Roman industrial activity. Gerald and his volunteers had found coins that dated the ironworks to AD 80–250, and Dr Henry Clare, co-director with Gerald of the Beauport Park excavations, had estimated that about 30,000 tonnes of iron had been produced here by a workforce of approximately 1,000.

We were convinced that, as well as the bath house, there must be other, high-status structures on this site, such as the commandant's house and administrative buildings. But where were they? The thick forest, some of the least disturbed in the south-east, hid most of the features that would give us clues. In addition, a large proportion of the land on which we could expect to find previous Roman activity had been turned into a golf course in the early 1970s.

As we approached the site on our first morning, we knew that we were going to be tackling one of the most difficult sites in the history of the series.

Day One

First thing, on a beautiful sunny, warm morning, Gerald, now a venerable 82 years old, gave Mick and Tony a tour of his pride and joy - the Roman bath house that has been described as the best- preserved small Roman building in northern Europe. Entering the ramshackle corrugated iron shelter that kept it away from the elements, Mick and Tony were immediately impressed. The front, south-facing wall was 2.4 m (8 ft) tall at the west end and 13.5 m (45 ft) long. One of the three windows in this wall has the second highest Roman window ledge in Britain.

THE CLASSIS BRITANNICA

Fleets (*classis*) of ships provided the Roman Empire with both sea power and logistical support. Instead of sailors, the men who sailed in them were soldiers who simply used sailing vessels to get themselves and their equipment from A to B.

In Britain until the late 3rd century, the *Classis Britannica* appears to have operated almost entirely in the logistics role: transporting the invasion army; helping provision the army in northern Britain; and managing the iron industry in the Weald of what is now Kent and Sussex. The onset of raiding by Germanic tribes from what is now northern Germany and southern Scandinavia changed the role of the navy until, by the end of the occupation, the fleet was divided into several smaller units integrated with cavalry forces and based within fortifications in southern and eastern Britain: the forts of the Saxon Shore.

Inside, it was hard to judge the height of the walls because 0.6 m (2 ft) of sand had been laid to preserve the clay-tiled floor. In the changing room (*apodyterium*) were the remains of lockers – niches in one of the internal walls with large clay tiles on the bottom, which would have once had wooden frames and doors. Beauport Park is one of only six places in the world where Roman lockers survive; the others are Chesters on Hadrian's Wall, Pompeii, Herculaneum, at Herod's palace at Masada and two places in Spain.

All but one of the rooms were heated, and extremely well-preserved box flues (*tubuli*) could still be seen. Heated air from the furnace outside the bath house would have escaped through these after circulating under the floors. On some of the walls were the remains of plaster and traces of paint. Gerald pointed out that, in some places, there were two or three layers of paint of different colours – as if the commandant had ordered the bath house to be redecorated. However, because of a lack of funds to conserve the paint, it has deteriorated badly since the bath house was excavated.

Many of the roof tiles and bricks used to build the bath house were stamped with the letters 'CL BR'. These showed that the bath house and the rest of the iron-working site was operated under the aegis of the *Classis Britannica*, the Romano-British fleet (*see box*). It might

(Top left) The south-facing wall of the bath house. *Mick Aston* *(Centre left)* One of the well-preserved box flues in the bath house. *Mick Aston* *(Above left)* One of the rare bath house lockers. *Mick Aston* *Box:* Victor's reconstruction of a Roman ship.
(Above centre) One of the terracotta tiles from the Roman bath house bearing the stamp 'CL BR' for 'Classis Britannica'. *Mick Aston*

seem strange for a navy to run such an operation, but, in fact, the *Classis Britannica* was more like the Royal Engineers than the Royal Navy.

The bath house owed its preservation to the collapse of part of the iron slag bank, which had completely covered it at some unknown time in history. Before this happened, and after the Romans abandoned the site in about AD 250, squatters had moved in. We know this because, among other things, they removed floor tiles to make a hearth.

North-west of the bath house, down a track to an area of dense forest between the 12th and 13th greens of the golf course, was a 'platform' of relatively flat land where Gerald – and his divining rods – had decided was the most likely location of the house of whomever had been in overall charge of the iron works. This could have been a commandant; alternatively, if he had lived at Dover, a much bigger centre, as Guy de la Bédoyère, one of our experts, thought, the head man could have been a procurator.

The use of dowsing to locate archaeological features is controversial, and the few times it has made an appearance on TIME TEAM, it has been unsuccessful. Mick is particularly dubious about dowsing, but Gerald was able to point to quite a number of finds that had been unearthed here at Beauport Park because of signals from his divining rods, not least the bath house. We would just have to wait and see what happened this time.

After the undergrowth had been strimmed away from the platform, the geophysics team got down to work. However, Stewart was already expressing the opinion that, because of the small size of the platform, finding a substantial building was highly unlikely; the geophysics results were also relatively negative. Despite this, a trench was begun.

Guy explained how the iron works at Beauport Park would have once been similar to a Gold Rush town in the American Wild West – highly polluted from the works and very rough and ready. Most of the trees would have been chopped down to make the estimated *50 tonnes* of charcoal burned every day to keep the works going, although there must have been some sort of woodland management scheme to ensure a constant supply of young saplings and branches. The smoke from the charcoal making and burning would have saturated the air, and those residing here would not have lived very long. This fact made some of the archaeologists begin to question whether we were correct in assuming that anyone in a high-status position would have ever actually lived here.

In the garden outside the incident room, Jerry McDonnell of Bradford University and Jake Keen, an ancient technology expert, were beginning to build the furnace for our iron-smelting experiment (*see box*). Phil, meanwhile, had gone to a local quarry to dig out iron ore from the surrounding clay, which was also being used to make the furnace.

After lunch, the trench in the platform was greatly enlarged with a mini-digger. In addition, two smaller trenches were dug, based on the evidence of signals from Gerald's divining rods.

Further down the path, Jenni Butterworth and some local volunteers were excavating the depression that had been left when a very large tree had fallen over. The dirt within the upturned root system of the tree showed a definite line, with, on one side, the natural orange-coloured soil and, on the other, 'made', almost black earth containing a great deal of slag and pieces of charcoal. It was thought that, if the tree was turned back upright, this line could form part of a Roman road or path. In the end, however, we came to the realisation that the tree had simply grown over a Roman midden (rubbish dump), from which a pot rim – one of our few Roman finds during this dig – was unearthed. Then the trench was recorded and closed.

Geophysics had escaped the forest and, guided by Stewart, had investigated the 13th fairway of the golf course, coming away with some startling results. However, we could do everything except dig there, so the next day we would have to be satisfied with excavating on the margins within the woods.

Day Two

At breakfast, everyone compared the mosquito bites, nettle rash and bracken scratches they had received the day before. What made them itch and sting more was the fact that these hardships were being faced with no relief in the form of archaeological success.

The trenches on the platform had proved to be almost totally sterile. All that had been found were a few sherds of abraded Samian ware and a handful of golfballs, and so the trenches were recorded and shut down. This was a great disappointment to everyone but especially to Gerald who for years had pinned his hopes on this area being significant to the site – his divining rods had certainly thought it was. He had to accept that, in this instance at least, dowsing had failed miserably, but he appeared to take this setback well.

Heads were now put together to try to come up with another part of the park where there might be remains of this Roman industrial community and (1) was away from the golf course and (2) was outside the scheduled area. These restrictions severely limited our choices.

Deep in another part of the forest, under two huge, magnificent oak trees, Stewart had located a promising mound-and-ditch feature that could possibly have been made by human hands. Carenza and Phil trudged out to find it, accompanied by Ian and the mini-digger – and a crowd of eager Beauport Park Trust volunteers – but after a mechanical section was dug through it, which showed it was artificial, all that was found was a fluorescent orange golfball!

The anomaly located by geophysics on the 13th fairway was, according to John, 'the size of a cathedral', but most of it was under the greensward. Luckily, the company that owned the golf course had relented and was now allowing us to extend our excavations further into the fairway, as long as we kept to the 'rough' on either side. As a result, a trench was quickly inserted under Phil's guidance.

Mick and Stewart took to the skies in the helicopter in a near-desperate search for new sites, made especially difficult

ROMAN IRON SMELTING

The Weald of East Sussex, where Beauport Park is situated, contains extensive deposits of iron-bearing clays, with nodules of ironstone. The Romans – or, rather, the slaves and other workers under them – collected this iron ore and then roasted it to get rid of any moisture that might have accumulated within it and to break it into smaller pieces.

Then a mixture of roasted ore and charcoal was heated in a clay furnace. This comprised a small clay-lined pit about the size of a bucket – the crucible – with a clay chimney structure on top. We can only guess at the height of the latter since none has survived. At the bottom of the chimney were a number of openings into which the mouths of the bellows

made of animal skins would be placed. It took a great deal of muscle power to maintain the operation of these bellows so that the correct temperature would be reached. To smelt iron, it was necessary to achieve 1,000°(C) (1,832°(F), although the Romano-Britons would have had to judge this by eye, from the colour of the burning material within the furnace.

This extreme heat would eventually result in a spongy mass of iron known as a 'bloom', as well as slag, the waste material that would flow out of the furnace like treacle and then set hard. Since this method of smelting only extracted about half the iron available, pieces of Roman slag contain quite a bit and so are relatively heavy.

The blooms were further refined and shaped by being hammered by a blacksmith while they were still red hot, giving purer 'wrought' iron. This could be done on the spot or after the blooms had been transported to where the iron was being turned into such products as knives, hammers, ploughs, weapons, nails, horseshoes and other necessities.

because of the dense tree cover. However, they returned with two possibilities: a flat area on the highest ridge, just behind the incident room; and an unusual **cropmark** in a field belonging to a nearby farm, which just might be a villa.

All this activity resulting in so little led to a great deal of discussion about the nature of the site. So far, the method of investigation had been what someone had called 'poke and hope'. However, to do it properly, said others, would take three or four years of landscape survey, gradually refined to identify appropriate places for geophysical survey and, ultimately, excavation. Knowing that there must be much here to discover but being unable to find it was extremely frustrating. But then, said still others, it might be that the very fact of the bath house's existence had resulted in a skewing of the archaeology so far – without it, it might have been easier to see the whole area in context.

And who was the bath house for? We

knew that it would have been quite near an extremely unpleasant, polluted area, so would a commandant or procurator have actually wanted to live near that? When we looked at the bath house more closely, we found that – although it had been redecorated – it was a fairly basic structure, with none of the high-status decoration (for example, mosaics) that one would expect if it had been used by equally high-status personnel. The arguments continued ...

The afternoon brought a stream of bad news. The trench on the 13th fairway had come up with absolutely nothing, despite the extremely good geophysics results. When Phil banged his trowel against the bottom, a sharp *clang* could be heard – an indication, he said, that the ground underneath was packed solid and not tumbled up as it would have been if people had built there or used the area for some other purpose. And the extremely promising cropmarks? They turned out to be a series of modern land drains!

We lifted our eyes unto the hills from whence cometh our help – and found Stewart emerging from the wood with news of a collapsed wall up on the ridge. Other than the bath house, this was the first archaeology that we had found above ground.

Meanwhile, an urgent telephone call had been made to English Heritage, with the suggestion that it might be useful if we were allowed to tidy up and record some of the test pits and trenches created by the Beauport Park Trust volunteers within the scheduled area, which would also give us the opportunity to examine a part of the site known to contain plenty of finds. The answer: go ahead as long as the English Heritage man on the spot agreed (he did).

So the day ended with at least two promising leads to follow. This was a relief to everyone – rarely had TIME TEAM come up with so little by the end of Day 2!

Box: *(top left)* the iron-smelting furnace with *(from left)* Jake Keen, Phil, blacksmith Reg Miles and Jerry McDonnell *(Mick Aston)*; *(top right)* operating the bellows to increase the temperature *(Mick Aston)*; *(above left)* hammering the slag from the bloom *(Mick Aston)*; *(above right)* the final product: a piece of iron *(Chris Bennett)*.

(Top right) The cropmarks that were modern land drains, not a villa! Mick Aston

Day Three

By mid-morning, it was all change: the trench on the 13th fairway, which the day before had been deemed sterile, was suddenly found to contain extremely important information. At dinner the previous night, John had been adamant that either we hadn't dug deep enough or we hadn't looked at what we had dug up closely enough. The **magnetometry** readings, he said, had shown that there was definitely something there that had been at a high temperature at some time. All we had to do was really look!

In the morning, he continued his campaign by taking Jerry up to the fairway. The University of Bradford archaeometallurgist immediately pointed out flecks of burned soil, charcoal and slag. Then, with a large, red, cartoonish magnet, he picked up bits of mineral that had been heated (otherwise it wouldn't have been attracted to the magnet).

Most likely, said Jerry, this had been where the iron ore had been roasted prior to smelting. Not far away was the quarry where the ore would have been mined; further down the hill, in one of the trenches dug by the volunteers in the scheduled area, the bases of two smelting furnaces had been found; and even further along were the slag heaps. All this gave us a great deal of the context for this industrial landscape.

When a slot was dug into the middle of the trench, small pieces of burnished ware cooking pots were found, and later, Phil trowelled out three contiguous sherds of what Guy said was the bottom of a crude pottery flagon – just the types of things that one would expect to have been used by workers in such a rough environment. A sort of continuation trench – separated from the first trench by the width of the fairway – was started, to investigate the limits of the 'noise' (further strong magnetic anomalies) picked up by the geophysics team. However, nothing of interest was found here.

Up on the ridge above the incident room, a start was made to make sense of the tumbled-down wall that Stewart had found. But all that came to light was confusing rubble, and as our last day began to pass quickly, the diggers began to despair at ever arriving at a hypothesis

of what this might have been.

Deep in the wood in the scheduled area, Jenni was tidying up the trench in which the furnaces had been found, straightening the sides and bottom so that accurate recording could be carried out. Helping her, Guy unearthed the bottom of a Roman glass flagon – a square base of green-blue glass moulded with an X.

Back in the incident room, John was running more geophysics results through his computer. This time, he found an extremely interesting anomaly further down the 13th fairway – but would we be able to dig there? He contacted one of his team, Louis Harvey, by radio to find out. Luckily, Louis replied that the anomaly was in the 'short rough' to one side, where we were allowed to excavate.

Because we didn't have enough diggers to work here and up on the ridge, the decision was reluctantly taken

to abandon the ridge trench and move all the diggers down to the new one on the fairway. However, this was almost in the direct line of fire from the 13th tee. So, when the diggers began to excavate, one of the production runners was assigned to watch the golfers; whenever one began to tee off, the runner would signal to the diggers who had to leap out of the trench to get out of the way!

In a part of the forest known as the Arboretum, which contains hundreds of listed trees including a gigantic Monterey pine, Carenza, some of the Beauport Park Trust volunteers and a digger from South East Archaeology were trying to make sense of a trench that had been dug by the volunteers over the years. Under the top soil was a metalled Roman road, and beneath this were a variety of pits, some containing burned material and pieces of pottery.

However, it had proved impossible to place any of these things in context or to date them because the parts of the trench had been excavated with little or no recording of what had been above the levels now evident; in addition, various 'steps' had been dug into the trench that bore no relationship to the actual archaeology. One of the volunteers had made a stab at some recording of the trench, but it was not in a form that would make it usable by archaeologists, and it also omitted various important pieces of information.

After Carenza showed Phil what had been going on here, he very gently explained the consequences to the volunteers, while applauding all the hard work they had done for almost three decades. Then he offered to help them develop a more recognisable form of recording, the results of which could then be passed on to South East Archaeology and the Sites and

(Centre) Sue's reconstructions of *(top)* the pottery flagon found in the trench on the golf course and *(above)* the glass flagon discovered in the scheduled area.
(Above right) The confusing trench dug by volunteers in the Arboretum. *Mick Aston*

Monuments Record (kept by the local council) for future generations.

Back at the new trench on the 13th fairway, the diggers – in between dodging golfballs – had uncovered a small charcoal-filled depression that Jerry thought would turn out to be a hearth or even a furnace. In the end, however, they found it to be much more than this. In fact, it appeared to be a charcoal pit at least two arms' breadth in diameter and at least 1 m (3.3 ft) deep with a baked clay lining – concrete evidence of human industry on this now pristine hillside.

Stewart had returned from his wanderings over hill and dale and through bracken and nettles to deliver his view of the Beauport Park landscape in Roman times. A large vein of iron ore exposed in the valley of one of the two streams had provided the Romans with the reason for developing the site in the first place. An industrial community had built up in proximity to this, complete with buildings and a network of paths. The confluence of the two streams had been the perfect location for the bath house – one stream had brought clean water to it and the other had taken dirty water away. In addition, water would have been used in the industrial process, and there had been a great deal of wood for charcoal.

Following his field survey on the high ground, Stewart had found no evidence for a high-status commandant's house or other buildings. It looked as if we had found evidence for ore crushing and burning on the high ridge that was now the 13th fairway, and slag had been dumped on the other side of the stream, which eventually encroached on the bath house (and, much later, buried it).

The Beauport Park industrial community was, said Stewart, one of a web of others in the Weald. It was certainly not a high-status location. When the few *Classis Britannica* administrators came to visit for, say, two or three weeks, they would have stayed in a reasonably substantial building (also still to be found) and used the bath house, which was a relatively crude example. In between these visits, the bath house might have been used by the work force and it could have been quite a status symbol for them.

So while we had spent the best part of three days looking for high-status buildings to go with the bath house, we had found instead that it was the bath house that was probably one of the few substantial buildings on the site. The bulk of the evidence had revealed a place where, nine centuries ago, a community of people had toiled in a terrible environment for their Roman masters, leaving little behind to mark their passing.

Final thoughts from Mick

Despite the lack of 'spectacular' finds - either buildings or objects - Beauport Park was an enjoyable excavation. The weather was good and the wooded Wealden countryside magnificent.

In many ways, the project demonstrated the problems of working in woodland. It is difficult to do field-work, geophysics gets obstructed by trees and it is often impossible to know where you are!

In the end, I think many of us felt that we needed a lot longer to survey in the woods - recording any surviving earthworks and digging test pits and evaluation trenches to identify and isolate the positions of the archaeology. But we really didn't have the time to do that!

(Top) Our iron smelters as, according to Victor and Steve, they might have been in the 2nd century AD.
(Above) The 13th fairway of the golf course as it could have appeared 1,800 years ago – courtesy of Victor and Steve.

REEDHAM

NORFOLK

WHAT MIGHT HAVE HAPPENED

For the farm workers at the marshy field's edge, the drone had become familiar. For the last two years, the bombers had frequently passed overhead on their outward and return flights. On a clear day, the paintings on the fuselages could be seen, as well as the damage from German fighters and flak. It often seemed a miracle that the planes were still flying at all.

Now with the end of the war possibly in sight, there had been fewer flights, but today the sky seemed filled with planes. The change in one aircraft engine's note caught their attention and they looked up. Two planes suddenly emerged out of a cloud bank, and were quickly followed by a third, which appeared to cut through the tail of one of the others. The farm labourers were already running for help as the two bombers fell to earth.

Poster for the 1944 William Wyler documentary *The Memphis Belle*. *Kinema Collection*

WHY WE WENT THERE

In February 1944, the British and American air forces joined together for the 'Big Week' – a series of combined, round-the-clock bombing operations against the German aircraft industry intended to reduce the Luftwaffe's strength in anticipation of the forth-coming D-Day landings. On 21 February, 34 aircraft of the 549th and 550th squadrons of the 385th bombardment group of the US Army Air Force based at Great Ashfield, Suffolk took off on a raid on the Diepholz aircraft depot in north-west Germany. The operation was successful and all but one of the planes turned back towards England.

On reaching the Norfolk coast, they were ordered to descend through dense cloud in groups of three to reduce the risk of collision. One of these groups – comprising three B-17 'Flying Fortresses' – was lead by Captain John N 'Hutch' Hutchison Jr and his crew of nine, plus a photographer who was aboard to record the mission. On their port side was the aircraft captained by Lieutenant John A Terrace, and on the starboard were Lieutenant Warren J Pease and his crew of nine. All the airmen in the Hutchison plane were anticipating their entry into the 'Lucky Bastard Club' as this was their 25th and last mission ... and Great Ashfield was only minutes away.

When the formation emerged from the clouds, only two of the planes were there: the Pease aircraft had disappeared. Suddenly the missing plane broke through the cloud, descending just behind the Hutchison B-17. Pease abruptly pulled up as if to level off, only to have his tail caught by the Hutchison plane and break off. The tail tumbled to earth, carrying with it the rear gunner, Staff Sergeant Junior M Falls. It was later discovered by would-be rescuers: Falls was dead, although his body appeared untouched; he was later found to have a broken neck.

Meanwhile Pease's tail-less plane continued upwards. Then it seemed to hang for a few breathless seconds before falling back on top of Hutchison's aircraft, breaking it in two. The shattered remains of the lead B-17 immediately plummeted to the ground at the edge of Mill Dyke, killing all 11 men on board. To witnesses, the rapidly descending Pease plane appeared to even out and some even thought that it could have made a possibly survivable belly landing, but then it hit a dyke close to a wood called Decoy Carr at Reedham Marshes. When local residents rushed to the site, all they found was a water-filled crater surrounded by smouldering debris.

The crew of the USAAF *Sly Fox*, including 'Hutch' Hutchison *(fourth from left)* and five others who later died at Reedham. *Ian McLachlan*

An American salvage team spent four weeks in the area, 'recovering' the bodies from the two planes. (This meant removing at least 65% of the notional body weight of all the men, whose bodies would have been shattered out of all recognition.) The salvagers would have had scant regard for the structure of the planes, simply ripping them apart to get at the airmen's remains, then (as frequently happened) piling the wreckage back into the crater and covering it over. (It is less likely that the aeroplanes themselves would have been salvaged: at that time, there were many crashes and minimal facilities for metal salvage.)

And there the Flying Fortresses (and any unsalvaged body remains) were left, and the sites gradually reverted to nature. Then, in 1964–65, a group of young cadets from the local Air Training Corps, led by the 16-year-old Ian McLachlan, unearthed part of the Hutchison plane in Mill Dyke and carried out research to find out who had been involved and what had happened. This, for Ian, was the beginning of a life-long interest in aircraft excavation. After many years of investigating other sites, in 1976 he returned with a group of like-minded enthusiasts to Reedham Marshes, where they recovered two propellers, a machine gun and various bits of the navigator's kit from the Pease plane before their mechanical digger slid into the quagmire and was only winched free with difficulty.

When TIME TEAM came to consider following up Ian's work at Reedham, we were struck by the very difficult challenges that this dig would present us. First, it could be dangerous. Although it was highly unlikely that any bombs would be discovered (most or all would have been let loose over Germany), there would undoubtedly be many, many bullets plus machine guns and pistols, all of which would have to be dealt with by an RAF bomb disposal team. Pockets of aviation fuel might also still exist, which as well as being highly flammable can cause severe skin reactions if touched.

Second, digging through peat was a very different matter from the type of site usually encountered by TIME TEAM. The **stratigraphy** of Reedham Marshes consisted of a surface cover of 0.6–1 m (2–3 ft) of waterlogged top soil and peat, under which was about 1m (3.3 ft) of thick grey clay. But most important of all was the third layer: at least 4 m (13 ft) of unstable peat, a deep brown, semi-dry soup. And it was highly likely that what was to be found would be very deep, necessitating much bigger mechanical diggers than we had ever used.

Finally, the site itself was environmentally highly sensitive. To reach what we wanted to find, we would have to pump water out of a dyke and probably from the bottom of trenches. However, this water could easily be contaminated by aviation fuel, so it could not be returned to the ground. Instead, we would have to construct a 'lagoon' 150 m (500 ft) away from the excavation to which the water would be pumped. Here, in a series of stepped reservoirs, the quality of the water could be assessed. It would then be filtered and treated appropriately before being sprayed back on the ground.

The night before the dig began, a meeting was held of all those involved, to impress upon them the dangers they might be encountering over the next three days. The RAF bomb disposal team even handed round bullets, having first made them safe – contrary to popular opinion, untreated bullets such as these, often misguidedly kept as souvenirs, can kill. We were also introduced to our experts. As well as Ian McLachlan, accompanied by a dozen or so fellow aviation excavators, we were joined by Bob Spangler, an American 'crew chief' responsible for the maintenance of Flying Fortresses during the war who would be our 'namer of parts', and aircrash investigator Bernie Ford, who would try to piece together what happened during the last moments of the two planes that were to be the focus of our investigation.

Day One

As an overcast day dawned, TIME TEAM appropriately began operations on an almost military scale. From the incident room at Hall Farm, a convoy of four-wheel-drive vehicles drove more than a mile down a dirt track to a marshy field bounded by dykes and the wooded Decoy Carr. Already in place was a camouflage tent housing the RAF bomb disposal team who would look after any ordnance recovered during the excavations. Geophysics were hard at work traversing the probable site where the Flying Fortress had crashed, and standing by was a large mechanical digger and a huge 360 tracker digger, both with an unusually long reach, the better to dig deep holes.

(Top left) One of the Air Training Corps cadets pulling out part of the Hutchison Flying Fortress in Mill Dyke in 1964. *Eastern Counties Newspapers Ltd*
(Above left) Lieutenant Warren J Pease in flight gear. *Lawrence Pease/Guy de la Bédoyère*

A small trench was dug on the site of one of the 'hotspots' that geophysics had discovered. However, water began to pour through a fissure in the side and the trench soon filled up with water. (Later, when this was drained, no sign of metal was apparent to a detector.) Another trench about 4 m (13 ft) away was begun and this soon produced finds. At first, these were primarily random pieces of steel and aluminium, which could have come from almost anywhere on the plane. But eventually Phil found a relatively large structure that Bob Spangler said was a retracting screw of the forward undercarriage.

Most of the very small finds – including an increasing number of bullets - were discovered by the many metal detectorists on site. A remarkable number of different kinds of detectors had made an appearance, not only those operated by our geophysics team and the RAF bomb disposal unit but also many owned personally by the aviation excavators helping us on this dig. As a result, discreet comparisons were being carried out and not so discreet derogatory comments were being made – very much a case of 'toys for boys'.

Stewart was convinced that the same investigation processes that were normally applied to discovering archaeological sites could be applied to air crash sites. He walked around the surrounding area, looking to see if there were any marks to show where the plane might have skidded before crashing, as some witnesses had insisted, and whether any trees showed signs of having been damaged by the crash and then regrown. In the end, he found a small crater-like depression along the edge of the dyke to the east of Decoy Carr, which corresponded with a fresh impact crater visible on air photography taken in 1946. In addition, he was able to pinpoint the spot where a photograph of the crash site had been taken only a few weeks after the event. Comparing this evidence with the present-day scene, it was easy to identify exactly where the plane had ended up – and all the signs identicated that that had been an extremely violent end.

Already the differences in working methods between the aviation excavators and the TIME TEAM archaeologists were beginning to clash. Although the strangest things can happen to aircraft after a crash, the fact that we had found what was apparently part of the bottom of the plane at the top of our trench seemed to prove to some of those on site – and particularly the aviation excavators – that these pieces of the plane had been pulled apart by the American team who had recovered the bodies and then simply piled the wreckage back into the hole and covered it up. (There were also mutterings among the TIME TEAM diggers that they may have been part of the backfill from the excavators' 1976 dig.)

In any event, these finds did not represent significant stratigraphy in any archaeological sense, and so to the excavators, it made no sense to dig carefully around the remains with small trowels or to record each layer carefully as the archaeologists, led by Phil, were doing. At this rate, they said, we would find nothing significant in the three days available – a sad waste of an opportunity and, more to the point, of the availability of the large machines on site, which could move mountains and were being required to move spadefuls.

The archaeologists disputed this, saying that there was no way of knowing what had been found so far. The fact that the enthusiasts had done so many other excavations of aircraft did not really prove anything because they had always tackled their sites so roughly. If they had used archaeological methods, they might have drawn different conclusions. It was important to discover the context of what we had found so far and only then decide what to do next.

Despite the archaeologists' best intentions, some shortcuts were being made by those working on the site. Lots of finds – again, mainly unidentifiable bits of metal – were being ferreted out of the spoil heaps through metal detectoring. Although Jenni and Pete Bellamy tried to ensure that everything that came out of the trench was given a number and put in a specific finds tray, they were soon overwhelmed by unlabelled bits and pieces. Bernard had been asked to give three-dimensional locations for finds using his theodolite, but this soon became unmanageable and the idea was abandoned.

Meanwhile Phil painstakingly cleared away clay from the relatively large pieces of metal in his trench, and Pete

(Above left) The 1944 American salvage team with wreckage from the Hutchison plane. *R Zorn*
(Above right) View over the site with the two mechanical diggers. *Mick Aston*

THE PEASE FLIGHT CREW

1st Lieutenant Warren J Pease (*pictured left*): pilot
2nd Lieutenant Edward B Brown: co-pilot
2nd Lieutenant Bernard Kaplan: navigator
2nd Lieutenant Robert E Jenkins: bombardier
Technical Sergeant William R Clift: top turret
Technical Sergeant William Gill Jr: radio operator
Staff Sergeant Franklin C Owsley: ball turret
Staff Sergeant Junior M Falls: tail gunner
Staff Sergeant Harold E Dickason: left waist gunner
Staff Sergeant Gail F Bruner: right waist gunner

produced a grid made of wooden slats and string so that Jenni could begin to draw up the layer that Phil had uncovered. Pete later denied that methodology had gone out of the window. 'We've never done this sort of site before,' he explained, 'and so we've been following behind the volunteers. However, I think we've now devised a way of working that will be acceptable to everyone.'

Finally it was agreed that the trench would be extended to one side. Phil was agreeable to this as he had realised that there was a distinct difference in the clay outside the area where the parts of the plane were coming from and the clay within it and he wanted to see where this colour difference ended – did it delineate the hole that the Americans had dug and then covered? Ian McLachlan and his colleagues were quite relieved that more progress was promised, although it wasn't really enough to satisfy them completely. A particularly sensitive metal detector operated by the men from RAF bomb disposal had indicated that there was something 'very large' tantalisingly below the surface.

While all the polite arguing was going on, geophysics had surveyed the land on the opposite bank of the dyke. More hotspots had been revealed and there was talk that this may be where the bulk of the bomber had come to rest. At the end of the day, as the wind picked up and carried rain with it, it was decided to open a trench here. But the big question was: how were we going to get one of the monstrous diggers to the other side of the dyke without sinking it?

Day Two

In the incident room, Stewart was questioning air crash investigator Bernie Ford. Both found it odd that, according to the official report of the collision of Pease's and Hutchison's planes, dating from 29 February 1944, a mere eight days after the accident, a 'lack of details' precluded 'the issuance of any statement of responsibility' – although, it continued, 'it is the opinion of the

accident committee that the combat crews become too lax when approaching the home base.'

The question of how the Pease plane could have flown having lost its tail was also puzzling them. All the experts said that this would have sent the aircraft into an immediate crash dive. But one of the official witnesses, a marsh labourer working to the east of Reedham church, had testified:

> *The left-hand [Pease's] plane appeared to go up on losing its tail, then levelled out after losing height, appeared to turn and then suddenly dived into the marsh.*

In addition, three railway workers about half a mile from the crash site had reported:

> *This plane lost height, but kept level and going towards Decoy Carr. When a short distance from the Carr, this plane tipped down nose first, began to turn and crashed into the marsh ... When the planes crashed, the petrol tanks exploded and the wreckage instantaneously caught fire.*

However, Bernie pointed out that, once the tail had gone, it would have been very difficult for anyone witnessing what happened next to have distinguished between the wings and the fuselage.

The larger of our two tracker diggers had made it to the other side of the dyke, across a newly made clay dam topped with 'mats' – huge wooden sleepers bolted together. There it waited for further instructions.

The small sterile trench had been closed, and the remaining one had been squared off, substantially enlarging it. The digger driver, guided by TIME TEAM diggers, delicately lifted out bucketsful

(Above centre) The first debris from the B-17 appears in a trench. *Mick Aston*
(Above right) Phil and the armoured back of the pilot's seat. *Mick Aston*

of top soil and clay. An increasing number of larger finds were uncovered, including a part from one of the four engines (which would have been attached to the spark plugs) and pieces of fusilage. But there were some more intimate discoveries. One was the base of the seat on which would have sat the navigator Bernard Kaplan or the bombardier Robert Jenkins. Other – and even more telling – objects included the armour plating that would have formed the back of the pilot's seat and a piece of thick Perspex from the front cockpit window. As it gradually dawned on everyone that Warren Pease would have looked out of this window and that this was the seat in which he had died, the tragedy that had occurred more than five decades before suddenly seemed much closer. This feeling became even stronger when the remains of a military boot were brought out of the clay.

Excavation stopped as the diggers cleared everything just above the beginning of the peat level – below this, the soil would be like chocolate mousse. Only the mechanical diggers could excavate this, and because there was always a danger that the trench sides could collapse irreparably, it was agreed to delay this procedure. In the interim, it was decided to extend the trench sideways down to the same level, to see if there were more small finds to be had.

In the incident room, a tape of William Wyler's *Memphis Belle* was shown to Phil, Mick, Tony, Stewart, Carenza and Guy de la Bédoyère who, although a Roman expert who had helped us at Papcastle and Beauport Park, is also a keen World War II aviation enthusiast. This full-length documentary of a B-17's mission over Germany had been made in 1944, the same year in which our plane had crashed. It was the closest we could get to finding out what combat must have been like for the crews of these Flying Fortresses, although it couldn't duplicate the shuddering, enormous noise and bitter cold. Mick and Tony, who had made a visit to the RAF museum at Duxford to see one of the few remaining B-17s,

were able to describe how huge these aircraft were and how terribly small was the space into which the ten crewmen would have been crammed.

One of this dig's missions was to try to increase our information about the circumstances of the collision. We had discovered that some of the most important eyewitnesses had never had the opportunity to testify to the accident committee. The members of crew of the third plane on the scene, captained by Terrace, had been shot down and captured four days after the tragedy and had so been unavailable to tell their stories. Stewart, Bernie and Tony rang two of them: Bob Goldsmith in Ohio, the ball turret gunner who had been in the fuselage, ready for landing, and had seen everything plainly from the waist gunner's opening; and co-pilot Eugene St John in Florida, who had actually been flying the plane. As co-pilot, he had been sitting in the right-hand seat and so would have been able to watch the formation leader Hutchison closely.

Goldsmith and St John, both in their 70s, remembered essentially the same things about the collision and the crash. The aircraft piloted by Hutchison (as leader), Terrace and Pease all went into a cloud in a correct, tight V formation, with about 50 m (165 ft) between the cockpits. But only two planes – Hutchison's and Terrace's – emerged from the cloud. Suddenly, as both Goldsmith and St John watched in horror, Pease's bomber emerged from the cloud in a relatively steep dive. It quickly pulled up, but by this time, it was on a collision course with the underside of Hutchison's plane. It hit that plane between the fuselage and the third engine, which caused the right wing to begin to detach itself. Then, as Pease's plane continued upward, its tail was severed, possibly by the propellors of the other aircraft. This caused Pease's bomber to fall back on top of Hutchison's aircraft; this sealed the latter's fate and it began to spin and tumbled straight to the ground. Meanwhile, Pease's tail-less plane, which no longer had any stability, began to plummet. As it did so, the back of its fuselage moved forward so that, when it too crashed seconds later, it had virtually turned over.

All this took place in a flash. The two aircraft fell from a height of only about

(Top) One of the few remaining B-17s – the *Mary Alice*, now at the RAF museum at Duxford, Cambridgeshire. *Mick Aston*
A military flying boot *(centre)* and glove *(above)* found during the excavation at Reedham. *Mick Aston*

245 m (800 ft) at a rate of approximately 220 knots per hour (191 mph) in the space of only five seconds. Goldsmith noticed that two men jumped or were sucked out from one or the other of the planes (he didn't know which), but both were still doomed – neither parachute had time to open before they hit the ground. Meanwhile St John in the third plane had banked his aircraft steeply away from the collision, so avoiding, by a very small margin, becoming involved in the disaster.

This version of events was of particular interest to Bernie Ford. Earlier that day, he had examined the two propellers that Ian McLachlan's group had excavated from the Pease crash site in 1976, and had seen that one of the pair was 'feathered' – that is, the pilot had activated the switch that turned the blades so that they were edge-on to the wind. This is done in prop planes when an engine malfunctions and the pilot wants to avoid the flat blades of the propeller acting as a drag.

This told Bernie that, while in the cloud, Pease had experienced engine trouble, possibly from flak encountered during the raid on Dieplotz. He would have been busy feathering the propeller and looking at the related controls, rather than watching the horizon level elsewhere on the control panel. He could have inadvertently allowed the nose of the plane to dip and go into a shallow dive, and once he was out of the cloud, his eyes might still have been on the controls rather than looking forward to see how far out of formation he had strayed. Once he did realise that something had gone wrong, he would have been below Hutchison's bomber. When he pulled up his plane's nose to level off, he would have been unaware of the plane above him.

Bob Goldsmith added a personal detail that brought the tragedy of these events into sharp focus. As he had watched Hutchison's plane come out of the cloud, he 'could see Hutchison clearly in the cockpit and he had his feet up and was sucking a big cigar – celebrating the 25th and last of some rough ones.' But instead of going home to the United States, all 11 of that crew – and the 10 in Pease's aircraft - ended up in a cemetery near Cambridge.

Back in the marsh, we were still looking for the physical evidence of that tragedy. The extension of the trench to one side had been discontinued. After the spoil that had previously been placed in this area had been cleared, the geophysics team had gone in, but after a small trench had been dug, the only anomaly that had come to light turned out to be a piece of reinforced concrete!

While the archaeologists on site were understandably frustrated by the few orthodox techniques that they had been able to carry out, their philosophy was having an effect on the aviation excavators. One of them admitted that they were somewhat embarrassed about the way in which they had carried out their digs in the past – more or less simply wrenching large pieces of aircraft out of the ground and tossing back the less interesting (to them) smaller bits. It was true, he said, that they had never tried to figure out why and how these military planes had met their fates. However, in their favour he told how they had had to pay to rent mechanical diggers from their own pockets, and because of this lack of funds, saving time was of the utmost importance. Painstaking trowelling was simply something they could not afford, even if they had been aware of its importance in terms of adding knowledge to the record.

After a discussion, it was decided to extend the trench in the opposite direction and across the dyke. It was now believed that the plane had ploughed into the dyke at an angle, and it was hoped that we would find more substantial parts of the 30-ton aircraft in this adjacent area.

As the largest mechanical digger began to scrape away the clay, the immense weight of the machine made the unstable ground shake as if there had been an earth tremor. Meanwhile the other tracker digger began to remove foul-smelling mud and vegetation from further down the dyke, to eliminate a blockage. Once this was gone, as much water as possible was pumped out of this portion of the dyke, which had been dammed at both ends. The water travelled through a series of pipes across the field to the 'lagoon' that had been erected on the far side.

Once the water level had fallen, we were left with mud about 1.5 m (5 ft) deep and an unknown depth of peat. For the first time, we penetrated below the clay, with the arm of the largest mechanical digger descending up to 1.8 m (6 ft) into the muck and pulling up peat ready for the garden centre. But we waited in vain for the much desired sound of metal clunking against metal – that is, finally locating a large part of the aircraft. Instead, as the digger carefully removed clay from a previously

(Top) Live machine gun ammunition recovered from one of the trenches. *Mick Aston*
(Above) One set of the propellors of the Pease B-17 excavated by the aviation enthusiasts in 1976. *Mick Aston*

untouched area, Carenza, Phil and Ian recovered some small, yet touching finds, including a cap visor and strap.

The day's digging ended as drizzle descended and the previously sun-drenched countryside became damp and forbidding. Tomorrow we were going to dig much deeper.

Day Three

Following a depressing evening watching England lose at the World Cup, cast and crew had an uphill battle trying to raise their spirits at the dig. As a cold wind whipped the clouds above our heads, our mechanical diggers went into action.

Stewart had devised a new plan. He had looked closely at one of the photographs of the crash site taken in 1944 and had spotted what appeared to be significant aircraft parts sticking up from the ground. He talked to Bob Spangler and discovered that these came from the rear of the wings. He then conferred with the geophysics team, and by correlating anomalies, a picture of how Pease's plane had come down emerged. We now knew where the wings had entered the ground and could adjust our digging to try to find them, especially as we had recovered one of the red lights from the end of a wing.

The big trench was enlarged at an angle to the dyke. Now was not the time for trowels – it was the moment for the big plant to shine. Like two dinosaurs bending down to nibble at the marsh grass, the long arms pulled out an increasing amount of clay and peat and piled it in growing spoil heaps, which were immediately covered by men with metal detectors.

Suddenly, while a group of children from the local primary school gaped, an intact machine gun emerged from the mire, closely followed by another. These were immediately commandeered by the RAF bomb disposal team, who carefully cleared them of bullets to make them safe.

Stewart thought that it was probable that both machine guns came from turrets somewhere behind the cockpit, where they would have been facing backwards – if they had been in the front turret, they would have been the first part of the plane to take the impact and would have been severely damaged. This was disputed by Bob Spangler, who pointed out that this type of machine gun was always mounted in one of the front turrets. Someone else pointed out that the slim cylinders would have entered the soft ground of the marsh fairly smoothly; it was the large, flat fuselage that would have felt the full force of the impact. In the event, Stewart was proved right: when Pete later examined the surviving B-17 at Duxford, he confirmed that the gun mountings we had found were the same as those in the ball turret.

Once the digger had excavated almost to the bottom of the clay level, one of the RAF men jumped into the trench and surveyed the area with the military metal detector, which was more powerful than anything else on site (the software that geophysics was using to interpret their signals had proven disappointing in determining depth). Unfortunately the military detector did not find a sign of any metal objects in the trench, so it was reluctantly backfilled.

We now had only one other place to look - right under the digger, which was on a line with the areas where we have found pieces of the aircraft. The digger moved off its platform of wooden mats, picked these up and shifted them over to one side, remounted the mats and recommenced digging. Again the bottom of the resulting hole was surveyed by the RAF man – and again no sign of metal resulted.

We were left with a mystery. Either the remains of what had been a 30-ton aircraft were much further down in the peat than any of us had imagined, or someone had removed the larger parts of the plane. Could the American team that had stayed in Reedham for four weeks in 1944 have taken the engines, wings and other large parts for scrap? This seemed unlikely, but not impossible. A local man who had been in the village at the time of the crash admitted that the villagers had taken some souvenirs, but 'only as much as they could carry' – which ruled out the enormous engines. We simply had no idea what had become of the majority of the plane.

But what we did know now was how these 21 young men had come to die in a foreign land, and the thoughts of many of us were haunted by the image of the plummetting aircraft crashing into that peaceful field.

The grave of Warren J Pease, in a cemetery outside Cambridge. *Guy de la Bédoyère.*

Final thoughts from Mick

I found the making of this programme a very moving experience. As a small boy, after the end of the war, I was very excited by aeroplanes and I knew a lot about them, and being asthmatic, I had plenty of time to make models. But as an adult with my own teenage children, and after seeing the newsreels and the 1944 Memphis Belle *film, the whole bombing campaign of World War II became much more poignant.*

Archaeologists often say that their aim is to dig up the 'people' of the period at which they are looking. Usually we have very little to go on, and the details of individuals and events are not very clear. Reedham was different: some of the people involved in the event were still alive and we had personal possessions of young men whose names were known. In the end, I found it all a bit too much to take.

BAWSEY ST JAMES

NORFOLK

WHAT MIGHT HAVE HAPPENED

The attacks had increased, the warnings had become more frequent and the ships from the north had become a sight that the inhabitants of the peninsula had learned to dread. The invaders cared little for their sacred traditions, and the buildings offered no protection.

As the sound of horses' hooves could be heard approaching the hill, the brothers gathered together for refuge and the villagers joined them.

One man who had fatally left his departure too late stood at the water's edge, clutching his basket of fish. He knew that it was impossible for him to make it across to the others. The blow that felled him came from a skilled swordsman and he felt little in his final moments. The downward slash of the sword sent him tumbling into the grass, the silver fish scattering around him as the horsemen headed for the hill.

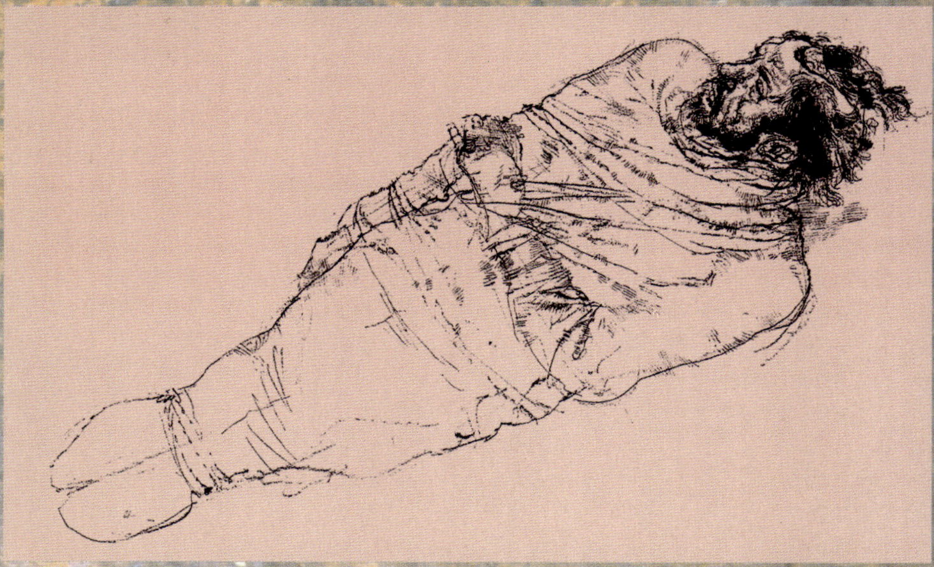

Victor's reconstruction of the burial of the man with the sliced skull that was excavated at Bawsey St James.

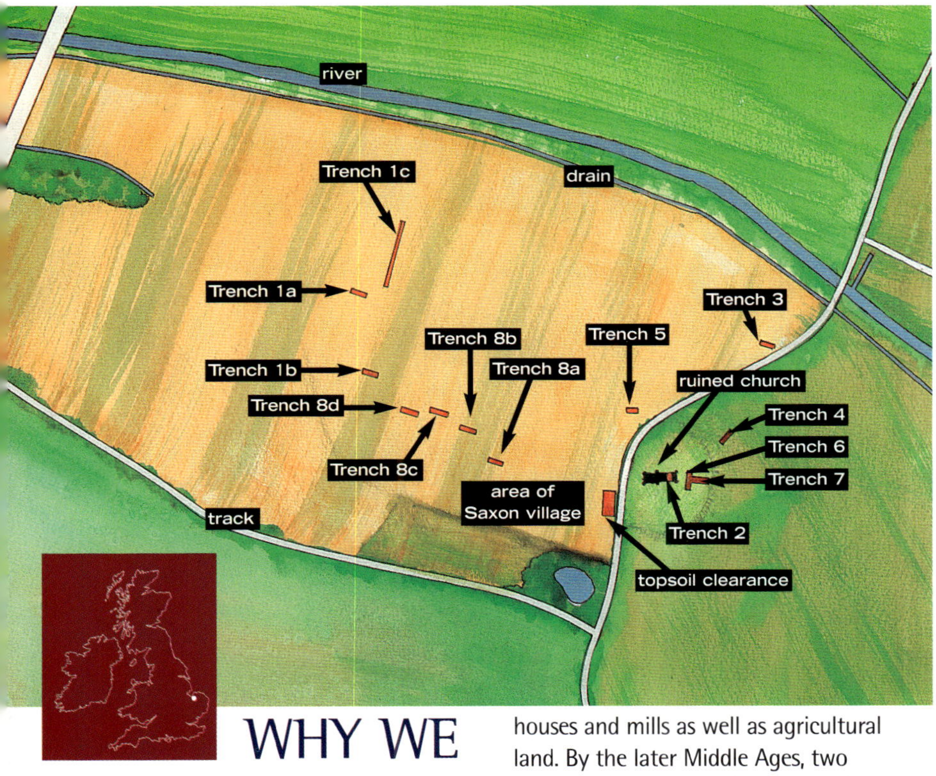

WHY WE WENT THERE

Choosing the site for a TIME TEAM 'Live' is a tricky business. Somehow we have to be sure that there will be enough archaeology for us to show viewers over the four or five hours of transmitted programmes over the August Bank Holiday weekend, and the archaeology has to be interesting enough to bring people back to their televisions throughout the three days. So we made a list of 'interesting' sites and began hunting.

Bawsey St James in Norfolk soon crept to the top of the list, and we investigated its historical record. As a parish and manor, it had existed since pre-Domesday times as part of the Freebridge hundred and a half (a 'hundred' was an administrative unit), comprising the city of Lynn (later King's Lynn) and a group of West Norfolk manors. All this was owned by Archbishop Stigand of Canterbury until the Norman Conquest, when it was seized and awarded to Odo, Bishop of Bayeux and half-brother of William the Conqueror. So from an early date, the economy of Bawsey and its surrounding manors was linked to that of Lynn.

Bawsey itself has two entries in the Domesday Book. According to these, William Malet, friend of William I and supervisor of the burial of King Harold after the battle of Hastings, owned property there, as did the count of Brittany. At that time (c. 1086), Bawsey appears to have been relatively populous, with salt houses and mills as well as agricultural land. By the later Middle Ages, two monastic houses owned property there and two others owned portions of two mills. However, the medieval settlement was soon to be destroyed due to enclosure, when common land (used by common people) was taken into private hands. A visitation by Bishop Redman to the parish church in 1597 recorded the somewhat lapsed state of church administration and the fact that the graveyard was unfenced and had been for some time.

There was no written record of what happened at Bawsey during the Saxon period or earlier. There was, however, physical evidence. We discovered that the Sites and Monuments Record (SMR) for Bawsey was huge, listing all the metal detecting and agricultural finds from the site – everything from Bronze Age pins, Iron Age torc wire, Romano-British pottery, Saxon metalwork of all descriptions (particularly coins) to medieval odds and ends – but none of this had ever been plotted on a map to make sense of it. Finally, an **aerial photograph** showed clearly visible **cropmarks** delineating what appeared to be a huge enclosure beneath the present-day surface – a boundary ditch some distance away from and encircling the church – together with other indications of past human occupation and activity.

So here we had a site that seemed, on past experience, to be rich in finds and to have been almost continuously occupied from the Bronze Age to the Middle Ages. It also had an extremely visual focal point in the ruins of the Norman church. But it was the possibility of finding the Saxon settlement here that finally decided us, for this era of British history is the most mysterious of all.

(Top right) The ruined Norman church at Bawsey St James, with the temporary Anglo-Saxon village beyond. *Mick Aston*
(Above) Victor's reconstruction of the settlement that may have occupied the site at Bawsey St James in late Anglo-Saxon times.

Day One

Fifteen minutes to one on Saturday, 29 August, the beginning of the Bank Holiday weekend, and the first transmission of *Time Team Live 98* was about to get underway. By the time the titles rolled on television screens across the country, the largest contingent ever assembled for a TIME TEAM programme had already been digging for several hours in the fields around the ruined church at the centre of our site. Built more than 800 years ago by the Normans, the church would once have risen majestically from the flat East Anglian landscape, a high-status, continental-style structure that would have impressed and inspired the local inhabitants of the period. Now it was at the heart of an operation involving, said Tony, 'legions' of archaeologists, historians, diggers, conservators, geophysicists, **field walkers**, metal detectorists and other assorted experts and volunteers as well as crew– some 140 people in all, compared with the usual TIME TEAM complement of around 40.

They were gathered here for a three-day investigation into the history of this site. The outside broadcast caravans, catering buses and other paraphernalia of a large-scale live television under-taking were parked up by the farm buildings a quarter of a mile from the church across the fields. A telecommuni-cations mast erected for the occasion towered over the site; the incident room was already established and busy in a large barn (free from the nesting pigeons with which the team had had to share facilities at last year's live event); and four-wheel-drive vehicles transported people hither and thither across the site while a helicopter buzzed overhead.

By the side of the dirt track leading to the church, meanwhile, the Saxon re-enactment society, Angelcynn, had set up a mini Saxon village. Here, under the enthusiastic eye of guest presenter Hugh Fearnley-Whittingstall, its members would be smelting metal, striking coins, weaving and dying cloth, making clothes, constructing a Saxon oven and preparing a traditional Saxon feast for the Sunday evening – with everything being done as closely as possible to the methods of more than 1,000 years ago.

The reason for the Saxon emphasis was that one of the objectives of the weekend was to try to ascertain what existed on the site before the Norman church was built. Previous finds in the area dated from prehistoric through to medieval times, but according to Andrew Rogerson, of Norfolk Landscape Archaeology, who was ultimately responsible for the site, the 'really exciting period' was likely to be the middle Saxon, around AD 650-850. This was when local finds of high-status Saxon jewellery have been dated, and was also the most likely time when a Saxon settlement might have been constructed. Andrew had briefed the team about a previous excavation on the site in the 1930s, which had apparently uncovered evidence of an earlier rounded wall at the east end of the church, probably the foundations of an apse predating the existing church. Unfortunately, virtually no records existed of that dig, and another of the tasks of the weekend would be to try and identify afresh precisely what was uncovered then.

As the team assessed their initial priorities for the weekend, the helicopter, one of the most costly items on any TIME TEAM operation, quickly proved its worth, giving Stewart and Mick an early overview of the site to help them form an idea of how it may have appeared in the past. And the aerial photograph – described as 'superb' by Mick – also offered a stunning insight to the previous layout and possible uses of the area.

The evidence from the air suggested an obvious immediate strategy of dig-ging several trenches across the line of the ditch to track and date it. Carenza took charge of the first of these, Trench 1 (later to become Trench 1a), at the ditch's western extremity, several hundred metres from the church. Phil – our usual digger-in-chief who, having a slipped disc, wouldn't be doing any

digging himself this weekend – was particularly interested in what Mick described as a 'confused area' on the aerial photograph, to the north of the church. 'There is obviously something exciting going on,' said Phil. It was decided to organise the field walkers and metal detectorists to see what, if any, patterns emerged from surface finds. The geo-physics team was also busy surveying the site to see what evidence of pre-existing structures or human activities could be discerned from **magnetometry** readings.

Inside the church itself, Neil Holbrook of the Cotswold Archaeological Trust, familiar to the team from his work with us on the 1997 live event, was supervising the digging of Trench 2. This was in the same location as the 1930s' excavation, and by the time of the first live broadcast, it had already revealed a well-preserved 15th-century glazed-tile floor. This consisted of good-quality tiles laid out in two alternating colours to form a chequer-board pattern; our experts identified them as having been imported from Holland.

The church was a hive of activity by this stage. Archaeological surveyor Richard Trainer was deploying state-of-the-art laser and computer technology to take measurements and produce a three-dimensional computer model of the ruins; this would eventually be imported into Steve Breeze's computer software for the final reconstruction. And a father-and-son team of stone masons had been engaged to reconstruct a 12th-century arch leading

(Above left) One of the five television crews prepares to film while Chris and Carenza are engrossed in the geophysics results. *Mick Aston*
(Above right) Aerial view of the site. *Mick Aston*

into the church tower, which had collapsed at some time between 1975 and 1985. They were using a lime mortar mix, made up of lime, sand and stone dust, based on an analysis of the original material used in the arch's construction.

An examination of the voussoirs – the large curved stones that formed the arch – has shown that two of them had typical Anglo-Saxon interlace carvings on the back. They had probably once been Saxon grave markers, reused by the Norman church builders. Together with the fact that two complete Saxon gravestones have been found on the site in the past, this provided strong evidence for the existence of a Saxon burial site here. We were

expecting to uncover human remains during the weekend, and forensic archaeologist Margaret Cox was at the ready to see what these might tell us about the previous occupants of this place.

As the day progressed, the team developed a clearer picture of how the site might have appeared in the past. Stewart was busy mapping the old coastline by reference to geological survey maps and sedimentation data, enabling him to assess which areas, once under water, had been drained or had silted up and raised above present-day sea level. Although the site is now about five miles from the sea, Stewart's research showed how, 1,000 years ago, it would have formed a small peninsula on the coast. The hill on which the church stood would only have been connected to the mainland by a narrow landbridge to the east.

The site, unique on this stretch of the Norfolk coast, would have been very distinct topographically and hence strategically or symbolically important. This was reflected in the architecture of the church, which would have been of considerable status. Stephen Heywood, architectural historian with Norfolk County Council, explained how the normal arrangement for a parish church of this period would have been to have a small tower at the west end, adjacent to the nave. Here, by putting the tower in a central position, between the nave and the chancel, the builders had imitated some of the great churches built soon after the Norman Conquest, such as at Norwich.

It was likely that any earlier Saxon building here would have been of similarly high status. Historian Dr Dawn Hadley pointed out that the site layout as it was beginning to emerge was typical of the topography of Anglo-Saxon monasteries. East Anglia, very wealthy at that time, had been significant in the spread of Christianity in England; in addition, monastic sites had been very important in trade and industry generally. It seemed very likely that the Norman church at Bawsey had been grafted on to a pre-existing monastic settlement. The coastal location also opened up the possibility that the site had been used as a port. If so, we could expect to find evidence of a waterfront with industrial buildings, such as had been discovered in excavations of similar monastic sites – for example, at Brandon in Suffolk where there were two churches on an island site linked to the mainland by a causeway.

The magnetometry results from Mick's 'confused area' north of the church contributed to speculation about the presence of some sort of harbour or waterfront facilities nearby. The results indicated what may have been an entrance to the enclosure here, begging the question: why have an entrance on what would have been the seaward side

of the enclosure, so that people coming to the site by land would have had to circle right round the boundary ditch to reach it? The existence of a harbour at this location was one possible explanation, and at 3pm, it was decided to open Trench 3 there to try to answer this and other questions. By the end of the day, this trench had revealed a land drain, various large pieces of 13th-century pottery, miscellaneous debris of human occupation, including large quantities of shells and animal bones – but no ships!

Trench 1 had also produced a lot of medieval pottery, bones and other finds. The enclosure ditch that had showed up so clearly on the aerial photograph was readily identifiable on the geophysics results, too; it turned out to be a massive affair, 5 m (16 ft) wide, with a small earthwork on its inner side. There was no sign of it having been constructed for defensive purposes (indeed, it appeared to have been quite shallow), which added to the speculation that it had once formed a boundary to a monastic settlement. The presence of 13th-century pottery fragments

(Above left) The arch in the Norman church before reconstruction. *Mick Aston*
(Above right) The completed arch, held in place by a wooden framework while the mortar dries. *Mick Aston*

THE THOMAS TILE

The tile unearthed by TIME TEAM bore the name 'THOMAS' ranged across its back in two rows of three letters. The blockmaker responsible for it had made the common mistake of forgetting to cut the stamp in reverse, with the result that the name appears in reverse image on the tile. According to one expert, tiles of this design had been included among some found in the floor of the monastic chapter house at Castle Acre, in central Norfolk, and the name might therefore be that of an officer or benefactor of that priory. There had been three priors named Thomas at Castle Acre between 1337 and 1428, but the one who was likely to have been commemorated on our tile was Thomas de Wigginhall, whose term of office ended in about 1376.

The 15th-century tile floor found in the chancel of the Norman church. *Mick Aston*

indicated that it had still been open at that date, but further digging was required to get a firm idea of when it had been first created.

In Trench 2 in the church, meanwhile, Neil Holbrook and his diggers had uncovered the foundations of the apse, which would have been linked to the tower by a large stone barrel vault. They had also come across a variety of finds, including our first human remains. Although Margaret Cox donned her 'spacesuit' to avoid contaminating any samples removed for DNA testing, the bones – including a skull – turned out to be disturbed remains from the 1930s' excavation. This minimised their archaeological value, but not the sense of awe that we felt at once more coming face to face with some of our ancestors.

Other finds from within the church included a 14th-century tile (*see box*). According to Andrew Rogerson, this would have been made nearby. In 1843, a medieval kiln was found about 400 m (1,315 ft) from the church, but the finder did not record its location and it was lost until 1928. In that year, tile rubbish tips were rediscovered by the owner of the land, who invited the Duke of Rutland to examine them. He didn't find the kiln, but two years later he purchased the land in order to excavate some of the rubbish tips. In all, he recovered 530 complete tiles and 350 fragments, which are now in the Rutland Collection at the British Museum.

The tile was just one of scores of finds that had been accumulating at the incident room during the course of the day. The field walkers and metal detectorists, in particular, had made large numbers of discoveries from various periods, and a special trip had to be made to the local DIY superstore when it was realised that the 20 people responsible for cleaning the finds had only one plastic washing-up bowl between them! Some of the most interesting finds included: a middle-Saxon *sceat*, a small coin minted in Holland around AD 700-715; a pair of Saxon tweezers dating from about 900; and various fragments of Thetford ware (*see* pp16–17) with potters' stamps from the late Saxon period. Together with information from previous finds made on the site, which had been recorded by the local museum, these were being plotted on a model of the site to see if any significant patterns emerged.

The day ended with an examination of the geophysics survey results of an area to the north-east of the church. They revealed, said John Gater, 'an amazing series of ditches – some straight, some curving – boundary ditches, a possible trackway, and then, outside the ditches, an area of "noise" and strong signals'. This last area could well indicate an industrial site where iron and bronze metalworking, tile works, kilns and so on may have been located in the past. Particular interest was shown in John's magnetometry readings, which might point to the existence of a bell pit, where bells would have been cast for the church. There was clearly a lot of digging to be done the next day.

Day Two

Exciting though some of the previous day's discoveries might have been, Mick announced that he would rather have firm evidence of a single building from the pre-Norman period than a 'bucketful of finds'. This was because it is buildings that often help to place finds in their archaeological context and tell us how a site was actually used in the past. TIME TEAM's search for pre-Norman buildings, however, was a real needle-in-a-haystack affair. Because most Saxon structures were timber-built, often the only indication of their presence is a slight discoloration in the soil, marking the postholes where such buildings would once have stood.

The task here was made all the more difficult, first, because of the sheer size of the site and, second, because of the nature of the geology – fine dark sand and flint lumps, 'funny stuff to dig', in Mick's words, and difficult to interpret. So, in an attempt to speed things along, Mick authorised the slightly unorthodox archaeological approach of using a mechanical digger to strip the topsoil from a large area of ground to the south-west of the church. This stripped soil was then thoroughly scoured by metal detectorists. Their extensive use this weekend marked another break with archaeological orthodoxy, since many archaeologists regard metal detectorists as little better than vandals who damage historic sites and fail to record their finds properly.

On this occasion, however, the use of large-scale surface stripping was justified by the fact that the topsoil had already been churned over by ploughing in past years. And the metal detectorists used at Bawsey were all members of the West Norfolk Search and Recovery Group, who have possibly the best reputation in the country for working with archaeologists. Andrew Rogerson meets with members of the group each month, collects what they have found (along with details of the location of each find) and takes the artefacts to the local museum for recording before returning them to the members at the following month's meeting. In this way, large amounts of valuable material have been made available to other archaeologists and historians.

As the day progressed, new trenches seemed to pop up all over the place. Trench 1 became Trench 1a, with Trench 1b being dug a short way off, also on the line of the enclosure ditch. Later in the day, a further huge mechanically dug trench (1c) was cut northwards here, followed later still by Trench 1d, another long trench going westwards. The idea was to try to pick up the line of the main enclosure ditch as neither the aerial photograph nor the geophysics survey (for which the ground in this area was too wet) had been able to locate it precisely. Finds from these trenches indicated that the ditch was probably Saxon in origin, dating back to the 8th century and surviving until the 13th.

Trench 4 was opened at the location of the postulated bell pit. And then, in the late morning, just north of the topsoil clearance area, Trench 5 was begun and soon provided what appeared to be the first evidence of one of Mick's elusive buildings. The diggers uncovered the bottom of an oven virtually identical to the one that had been built in our reconstructed Saxon village. Evidence of the wicker poles that would have been used as a frame (and then covered in mud 'daub') could be seen in the holes circling the heat-hardened oven bottom. Nearby was what looked like the remnants of a wall of the domestic dwelling that would have contained the oven. Both oven and dwelling dated from the 12th century, judging by the pottery found there.

One possibility considered the day before by Mick and Dr John Blair of Queen's College, Oxford was that there may have been more than one church on the site. This was quite common at early monastic settlements, such as at Glastonbury and Canterbury, although the more common popular perception is of single, grand structures such as at Rievaulx and Tintern. The most likely location here for any additional church buildings would have been on the slight ridge adjacent to the surviving Norman ruins. The geophysics results here revealed encouraging lines apparently leading away from the ruins to the east. Trench 6 was opened to explore this further, but the diggers' hopes were raised only to be dashed when a line of stone turned out to be bedrock. Trench 7 was later put in at right angles to Trench 6, but it too revealed no sign of the hoped-for second church.

Trench 3 – the 'confused area' that some had previously suggested was the location of an entrance or even a harbour – was no longer thought to be either. The diggers *had* found large quantities of shells, but their presence could have been the result of fertilising the land with kelp (seaweed) or even using them to lime the soil. Other finds here included a big sherd of Ipswich ware dating from between AD 720 and 850.

The whole site was producing a wide variety of finds – from the field walking and metal detectorists as much as from the trenches. These included lots of Roman roof tiles from the surface stripping, which had been going on all day, and a large number of crazed flintstones concentrated on another part of the site. These are known as 'potboilers' because it is thought that the crazing was produced as a result of the stones being heated in a fire and then dropped into cold liquid to heat it.

Sandi Toksvig, our other guest presenter, who had been overseeing the assembling of the finds in the incident room, said that so much material had been coming in that the finds washers were suffering from 'dishpan hands'! The finds included: a superb late Saxon silver penny from the reign of Eadred (who lost the kingdom of York to Eric Bloodaxe), dated 946-955 and struck at a mint at Norwich; a complete Saxon hooked tag, with a circle and cross motif, unusual because most are found broken; and, from Trench 4, a Roman floor tile with paw prints of a cat that had trod on it before the clay had dried. More archaeo-

(Above) The oven base surrounded by wicker pole holes, found in Trench 5. *Mick Aston*
(Right) Fieldwalking north of the church at Bawsey St James, with Sandi Toksvig in the foreground. *Mick Aston*

logically significant in terms of our work this weekend, the same trench had also yielded a big lump of 'bloom' from the bottom of a furnace (*see* p55) used for smelting.

Again, some of the finds were indicative of the presence of a high-status settlement on the site. Among these was a silver-inlaid ornamented strap end from a Saxon textile or leather belt. One of the craftsmen at the Saxon village produced an impressive copy of this, along with pewter replicas of the middle-Saxon *sceat*. The latter were distributed at the evening feast as we all tucked in to such delicacies as roast pork, Saxon nettle omelette, leek and barley pottage and a cheese known as 'Stinking Bishop'. Thor Ewing, our roving minstrel with his harp, entertained us by singing the earliest known Anglo-Saxon poem – a tale told by an illiterate cowherd about the formation of the world. It seemed a suitable ending to a long day.

Day Three

Trenches and yet more trenches! The weekend was fast setting a new record for the number of these dug on a TIME TEAM investigation. Not content with the ten (including 1a, b, c and d) that had been opened by the end of Day Two, a further seven were opened today to investigate various 'anomalies' revealed by the geophysics survey. Trenches 8a, b, c and d were dug in the area to the west of the church, Trench 9 was opened between Trenches 3 and 5 to the north and Trenches 10a and 10b were dug to the north-east.

Gradually, the complex picture of the site began to fall into place. Trench 4, the site of our putative bell pit, turned up a considerable quantity of slag, heavily burnt stone and bits of iron and lead work, indicating that organised industrial activity had taken place on this site. But as we excavated deeper, the 'bell pit' turned into a quarry, which subsequently had been infilled with rubbish. Huge amounts of medieval pottery were retrieved from this, all of it dating from before AD 1180. We knew this because the pieces we found had been made locally at Grimston, 2.5 miles to the east, where they had started making glazed ware in about 1180; none of the finds included glazed ware. It was thought that the quarry dated from the building of the church.

Trench 5, which had fascinated Phil all weekend, seemed finally to be revealing its mysteries. It appeared that there had been three main phases of activity here. The earliest had involved human burials, which could be Saxon. These had been replaced by the domestic oven and cobbled wall foundation, which could be connected with the 12th-century church. And then, later still, the site had been used for burials again.

This trench had a final *coup de grâce* to deliver. At around 6pm, with only a short time to go before the end of investigations at Bawsey, a remarkable complete skeleton was discovered. It lay underneath the 12th-century settlement, alongside fragments of 10th- or 11th-century pottery. And the cause of death of the man buried here was obvious even to the untrained eye: he had been lopped across the forehead with a sharp-edged sword, which, had cut a neat slice of bone, still *in situ*, from the top of his skull. Such a wound could only have been inflicted by an expert swordsman. An adjacent skeleton bore additional signs of late-Saxon swordplay, with its forearm having been broken in two, just as yours would be if you raised your arm in defence against someone attacking you with a sword.

We also got crucial dating evidence very late in the day from our excavation of the large boundary ditch. This was in the form of an 8th-century Saxon loom weight (a piece of clay with a hole through it, which would have been hung on a loom to keep the down-threads taut while weaving across them).

This date tied in with the expert analysis of the finds, over 300 by now, from both the trenches and the field walking finds. The fact that there were virtually no finds from the early Saxon period summed up how little had been going on at the site then. Things had started to get really interesting from around AD 700–720 onwards, which was the date of the Ipswich ware finds, large quantities of which had been turning up in one of the trenches opened that day. Found all over East Anglia (there are around 500 finds sites in Norfolk and 200 in Suffolk) and as far away as York, Kent and Oxford, Ipswich ware was the standard pottery for the region. It is easily recognisable as the only English pottery of that period that was fired in kilns.

Other evidence of middle-Saxon occupancy of the site came from the discovery of coins, pins and other

The burial of the skeleton with the slice through the skull, found in Trench 5 at the end of Day Three. *Mick Aston*

artefacts dating from the same period. Meanwhile, the fact that 11 styli – slender, pointed instruments used for writing primarily by monks – had been found on the site added to the likelihood that it had been a Saxon monastic settlement. The evidence for widespread industrial activity on various parts of it also fitted in with this theory.

The picture we had, then, was of what had probably been a very special site, which had enjoyed various phases of occupation and use. The Norman church in its heyday would have been a thrilling architectural import, shining in its gleaming white render on the top of the hill, its interior ablaze with colour and pictures of great splendour, and magnificent bells in its great tower.

There would have been an earlier timber church here too. The problem was to find firm evidence of such a structure, which would involve surface stripping a very large site and looking for postholes and timber slots.

And we also knew that this site had been in use earlier still. There had certainly been Roman buildings of some sort here, as we knew from the relevant building materials we had found, although we had uncovered no evidence of their original location. And we knew, too, from past finds that there had been very wealthy people here in the Iron Age. One of our trenches, moreover, had uncovered a working/occupation surface with lots of bone and burnt material, flintwork, implements such as scrapers and other finds. So it looked as though we also had a prehistoric settlement of some sort, dating from the Bronze Age, around 1500–2000 BC. Survivals of this kind are extremely rare in Norfolk because any remains usually get ploughed up, blown away or otherwise destroyed.

Overall, the site did not yield a picture of one clear-cut settlement from any particular period. The more holes we had dug, the more we had found. The most unexpected development, according to Mick, had been that almost every hole we had excavated had had something different in the bottom of it; and the extent of industrial activity, in particular, had been far greater than expected.

It all added up to a lot of further work compiling records, updating maps, maintaining archives and studying the finds. Mick said that archaeologists have an unwritten rule: one day out in the field equals ten days back in the office and laboratory. The scale of this weekend's operation meant that a lot of people would be kept very busy for a long time to come.

Check out the Time Team Live 98 *site on the Channel 4 website* (see *p113*).

Final thoughts from Mick

Bawsey was an extraordinary site for us to investigate and, I think, important for two main reasons. First, it was a very good example of something that is common in British archaeology - a site that belongs not to any one period but which has been occupied either time and time again or continuously. Such a site is a palimpsest – that is, it represents a piece of countryside reworked and reused by different generations. Much of the English landscape is like this – we might think we have a Roman or medieval site, but it turns out to have had prehistoric and other activity as well.

But the second reason was closer to my heart. Bawsey showed very clearly the problem we medieval archaeologists have at the moment – how do we recognise an early medieval monastery? For sites dating from about AD 1100, in the middle of the Middle Ages, it is a lot easier. English Heritage abbey sites you may have visited – such as Tintern, Roche and Battle – all have very similar plans with cloisters. However, earlier sites are different, often only distinguishable by finds – including styli – but this gives rise to much speculation and argument among archaeologists! I am still not sure that we have a Saxon monastery at Bawsey, though I would like to think we do!

(Top) 'Residents' of the Saxon village being filmed. *Bob Swain*
(Above left) Some of the finds installed on the timeline in the incident room. *Bob Swain*
(Above right) Victor sketches a skull in Trench 5 just before it disintegrated. *Bob Swain*

KEMERTON

WORCESTERSHIRE

WHAT MIGHT HAVE HAPPENED

As the family sat in the darkness of the hut, they could hear the drip of the rain as it fell from the sodden tips of the straw-thatched roof. The weather seemed to be getting worse, each year wetter than the last. The local tribes had become more protective of their good territory, the drier land above the valley flood plain. There were more raids and the people looked towards the large hillforts for protection.

Around the village, more of the children were practising with their sling shots as the men cut new spears. In the hut, the woman arranged the clay containers away from the wet areas; the pots holding the precious salt could not be allowed to get damp. If the troubles came closer, as she was sure they would, the family's supplies would be important to their survival.

Victor's reconstruction of the Iron Age settlement at Kemerton.

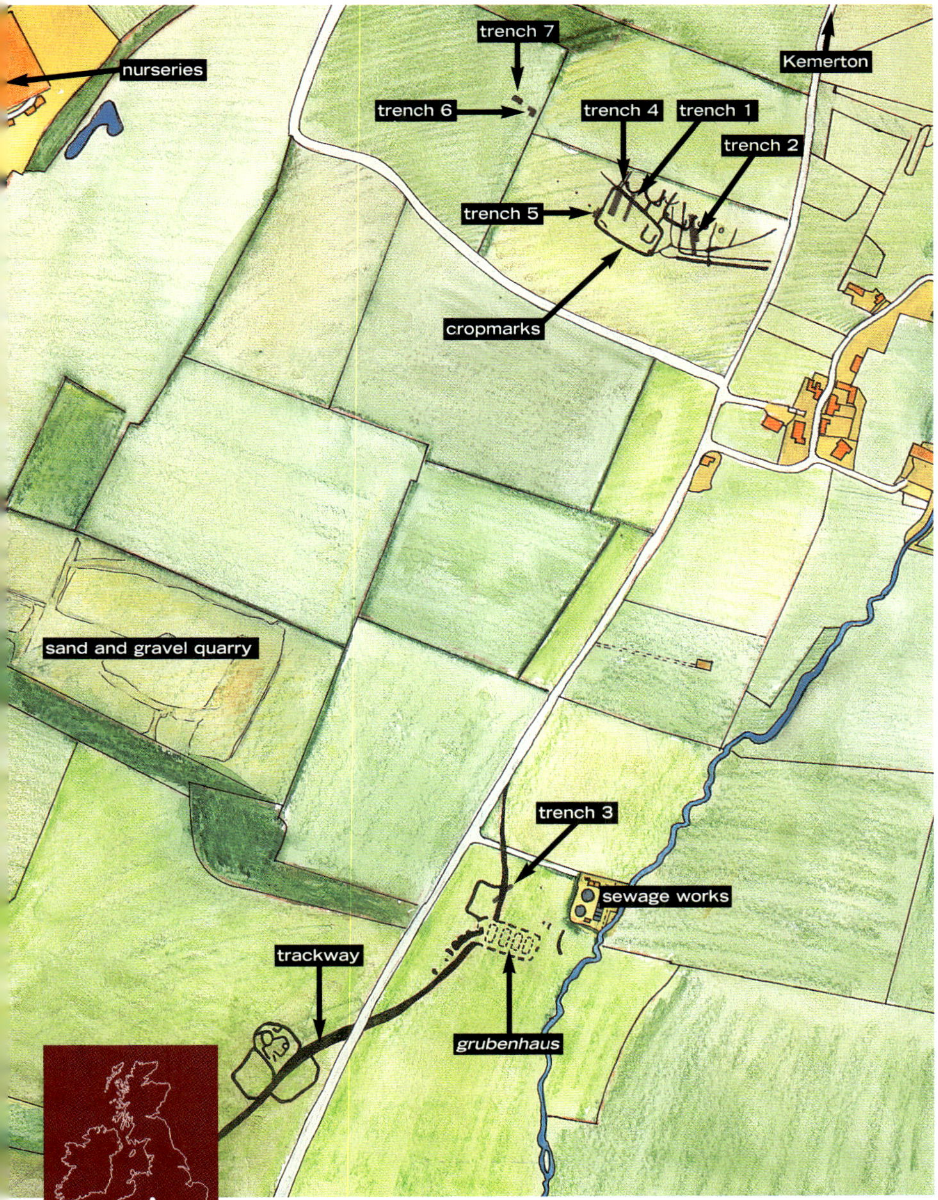

WHY WE WENT THERE

In 1990, freelance aerial photographer Jim Pickering was flying over south-east Worcestershire recording archaeological sites when, over the village of Kemerton, he photographed for the first time an extraordinary series of **cropmarks**, which were invisible on the ground.

What made this discovery so exciting to the archaeologists was the fact that other, important finds had already been made nearby. In 1984 and 1985, in an area a few fields to the south of the cropmarks, excavators had discovered evidence of possible late Neolithic occupation, an early Bronze Age ring ditch, middle to late Bronze Age cremations, middle Iron Age pits and enclosure ditches, late Iron Age and early Roman ditches and an Anglo-Saxon *grubenhaus* – a small hut for living or working in.

Three years after the aerial photograph came to light, the Worcestershire Archaeological Service excavated an area where the expansion of a sewage works was proposed. They found Anglo-Saxon deposits from a 5th–8th century AD rural settlement, including postholes, stakeholes, pits and a small amount of pottery. Because of the relative rarity of Anglo-Saxon remains in this part of Worcestershire, this site is considered very important. As a result, a decision has yet to be made on the final outcome of the sewage scheme.

Finally, in 1994-96, a quarried area a short distance from the sewage works was investigated and found to contain the most extensive and comprehensive evidence for late Bronze Age settlement identified so far in the county. The archaeologists found the remains of domestic settlement and associated trackways and field systems, and the artefacts recovered represented the largest amount of domestic Bronze Age material found in the Midlands. The pottery, in particular, was deemed to be of 'national significance'.

This part of Worcestershire appears to have been extensively occupied since the late Stone Age, but it was the possibility of discovering even more about the Bronze Age and Iron Age settlements that interested the county archaeologists. They contacted TIME TEAM with a proposal to do a joint assessment of the fields in which Jim Pickering's cropmarks appeared, near the village of Kemerton.

One legacy from the Iron Age was just to the north of us – Bredon Hill, one of the most important hillforts from that era in the country (*see box*). The site we were going to excavate – in which the cropmarks had been seen – comprised a number of fields, particularly one in which a crop of turnips was just beginning to show. In addition, down by the sewage works was a cropmark of a

(Above) The distinctive cropmarks at Kemerton. *Jim Pickering*
(Right) Some of the Bronze Age pottery found during the 1994–96 excavations at the sewage works. *Mick Aston*

BREDON HILL

The Cotswold hill on which this promontory fort is situated was the spot from where the poet A E Housman surveyed what he called the 'coloured counties'. The fort is protected by cliffs on two sides and by two ramparts and ditches across the southern end. The outer rampart is made of drystone and dates from about 300 BC; the inner one, consisting of dumped clay, was constructed in *c.* 150 BC. Inside were round houses and a number of storage pits.

The fort appears to have been attacked and destroyed early in the 1st century AD, possibly by Celtic raiders before the Roman invasion. The gate was burned and the remains of over 60 young men were found, cut to pieces, around the inner entrance. There is also evidence that a row of heads or skulls was displayed on poles above the gate.

Conderton Camp, also on Bredon Hill, is a short way to the east of the hillfort. The first phase of this small, oval enclosure – *c.* 300 BC – consisted of a single stone rampart with a ditch, enclosing an area of 1.2 hectares (3 acres). On the east and west was a counterscarp bank, and the entrances were on the north and south. At this stage, it may simply have been a cattle enclosure. Then, in the 1st century BC, a drystone wall was built across the spur, isolating an area of 0.8 hectare (2 acres) inside the original enclosure. This seems to have contained a village with a number of round houses and storage pits. The entire settlement was abandoned before the Romans arrived.

trackway that appeared to be of great antiquity. No trace of it is now visible on the ground, but once it would been a 'hollow way' with a ditch on either side, created by people walking and moving cattle and sheep along it over many, many years. Although it had not been dated, most of it had been scheduled, but there was a northern spur that had not been and which we could investigate.

Adrian Darby, the owner of the farm on which we would be working, is a great conservationist, and although he was enthusiastic about helping us, he was also quite adamant that we should not damage the land. To avoid this, we were required to keep all the top soil separate from any deeper layers of earth and to replace it in the right order when we finished and were 'making good'. While this would involve particular care taken by the operators of our mechanical diggers, it was an effort certainly worth making to find out just who had lived here and when.

Day One

Two trenches were planned for the turnip field, but first, the geophysics team was rushed to the sewage works site to survey the northern spur of the trackway. Their results virtually mimicked the marks revealed by aerial photography. In the meantime, Trench 3 was opened up here and very quickly began to produce what we hoped would turn out to be Bronze Age pottery.

In the turnip field, as Mick the Dig directed the mechanical digger to take off the first few inches of topsoil of what would become Trench 1, a strange sight appeared in the sky. A small white airship rose almost silently over the field and then turned here and there in a defined pattern. It was directed by one man with a radio link, who was being advised by another watching the closed circuit television picture from the onboard camera. This experimental aircraft was acting for us instead of our usual helicopter.

Archaeologist Francis Pryor, best known for his work at Flag Fen, a Bronze Age ritual site in Cambridgeshire (see 'Greylake' in the *Time Team 98* booklet), was able to tell Tony some of the broad differences between the Bronze Age and the Iron Age in Britain. During the 1,500 years between the start of the Bronze Age (*c.* 2000 BC) and the Iron Age (*c.* 500 BC), humans and their way of life changed a great deal. While Bronze Age people had ceased to be nomadic, settled and begun to change the landscape to suit themselves, the much greater population during the Iron Age meant that land was increasingly parcelled up, divided into territories and farmed more intensively.

This change in land use was caused by a change in diet. Whereas Bronze Age people got most of their food from animals – cows, sheep and pigs – their Iron Age counterparts found it more economically sensible to have arable farms: they ate meat but they also ate wheat and barley. Land devoted to these cereals could feed far more people than land used to produce meat alone. These choices of diet were reflected in the

THE OLDEST FIND

While Phil was supervising the work in Trench 3, he suddenly reached down and picked up from the gravel what, to the uninitiated, looked like an ordinary small stone. In fact, it was a major event for TIME TEAM: the oldest find they have ever discovered.

It was part of a Palaeolithic (Old Stone Age) hand axe, a tool probably used for butchering meat. It was made of flint, an uncommon stone in this part of Britain, and so may have been 'imported' from a considerable distance. It had been broken due to 'frost', but not the kind of frost that we all experience on a winter morning; in fact, the last time that it would have been cold enough to have broken the flint was during a glacial period. Similar flint tools have been found elsewhere in the Midlands that date from 500,000 BC, and Stone Age people stopped making this kind of tool in about 50,000 BC. So this hand axe could date from any time between those two dates.

landscape – more intensive farmscapes in the Iron Age and much evidence of livestock in the form of trackways in the Bronze Age. This was why Francis was so interested in our trackway, which he reckoned was quite a substantial one.

Back in the incident room, Stewart was closely examining aerial photographs and old maps of the area. He had marked the trackway running in a north-east/south-west direction and compared this to the other roads and boundaries in the area, which for the most part had a distinct north/south direction. He was looking for other small roads, paths and hedges that ran in the same direction as the trackway, since they could be evidence of much older features. He was also working on the hypothesis that these north-east/south-west features were territorial boundaries – ditches, dykes and trackways – of the farmsteads that had supported one or other of the Iron Age settlements on Bredon Hill.

By the time lunch was over, Trenches 1 and 2 were well underway. The positioning of Trench 1 proved to be unfortunate: half of its long length was 'lost', having been dug into by a medieval plough furrow; there were, however, interesting if indistinct features in the other half. Trench 2, on the other hand, showed evidence of small ditches that might have been created as rainwater ran off the roof of a thatched round house. However, the few bits of pottery unearthed so far were Roman – not exactly what we were looking for.

The same could be said of Trench 3, the promising sewage works site over the trackway. What we had hoped were bits of Bronze Age pottery were probably not, said Derek Hurst, a pottery specialist working for Worcestershire County Archaeology Service. But he was anything but disheartened for he was fairly sure that these were some of the very few pieces of Saxon ware ever found in Worcestershire and certainly the largest sherds yet discovererd.

In addition, he said, it looked as if a rectangular feature in the trench was remains of another *grubenhaus*, a very rare find in this part of the world. As its Germanic name implies, this form of dwelling or working space was extremely common in mainland Europe and, in the 6th to 8th centuries, when the Saxons began to invade and settle in England, it was frequently found in East Anglia. But as one travels west, they become fewer and further apart, until in Worcestershire, only about 10 miles from the Severn, then probably the border with Wales, these *grubenhausen* could be seen as pioneer settlements. To the county archaeologists, this discovery alone made the TIME TEAM excavation a great success.

But where were the Bronze Age finds and features we had expected? Moans like this prompted Mick to remind everyone that we should never arrive at a site with a predetermined idea of what we would find. 'What we may have found here,' he insisted, 'is a perfect example of an English landscape that has been lived in and worked on for thousands of years, by successive generations of people, extending right back to the Old Stone Age and on up to the present day.'

Promptly at four o'clock, an RAF Tornado GR4A streaked over the site at the end of a regular aerial reconnaissance sortie (*see box*) in this area from 13 Squadron, RAF Marham in Norfolk. The aircraft had an infrared camera in its belly underneath the cockpit (replacing the cannons), which could pick up differences in temperature on the ground. According to Sergeant Paul Stratford, a photographic interpreter, heavy rain and then the sun drying the

AERIAL RECONNAISSANCE

The following are the technical details of the Tornado Infrared Reconnaissance System (TIRRS) that operates out of 13 Squadron, RAF Marham, near King's Lynn in Norfolk.

Sensors: infrared linescan and two side-looking infrared sensors optimised for low-level reconnaissance.

Coverage: Swathe 3 nautical miles wide from 60 m (200 ft) above ground level; up to 600 nautical miles of continuous linesearch.

Recording method: videotape – one hour of continuous imagery for each sensor.

Key features: low-level, day/night, poor weather tactical reconnaissance capability; real-time viewing, replay and event marking from the cockpit; automatic edited highlights on tape for rapid exploitation.

(Top) Evidence of the *grubenhaus* (including a posthole) in Trench 3. *Mick Aston*
Box: The infrared image taken by the Tornado over Kemerton. *RAF*

ground quickly would constitute ideal conditions: features such as buried walls and ditches would retain more moisture than the rest of the soil and therefore would appear darker on the final photograph. Unfortunately for us, although it had rained heavily the night before, the sun had proved elusive and so the results were not as clear as they might have been.

As the day drew in, the archaeologists debated which direction the dig should take from here. One camp wanted to close down Trench 3 (after it was recorded) as it was taking us in a direction that we didn't want to go. But another faction wanted to continue excavating it as long as there was still something interesting to be learned. However, there was always the possibility that a shortage of labour might lead to its closing down.

New geophysics results had shown up the anomalies underlying the cropmarks in the turnip field even more clearly and had added some new ones. Carenza suggested 'surface stripping' a huge area – 20 by 40 m (66 x 131 ft) – to the west of Trench 1 to get a general idea of the archaeology, then concentrating on various features within it, such as ditches and pits where pottery sherds and other debris might be found.

There were a number of problems with this, however. For one thing, would the farmer who owned the field agree to the disposal of such a large part of his turnip crop? After discussion and negotiations, he was still not happy with the scale of the work. Then we found out it was impossible for the mechanical digger to shift that amount of earth and not mix up the topsoil with the rest; the only way he could do it was by excavating strips that would be, at the most, 7 m (23 ft) across.

This was finally agreed as an alternative, with two strips covering the most interesting parts of the geophysics results – one where an intriguing pit appeared to be, and another where there was 'noise' of a settlement and the corner of two enclosure ditches. And excavation would continue in Trench 3. But all this would have to wait until the next day.

Day Two

It had rained overnight, but the turnip field wasn't as waterlogged as we had feared. We now had five trenches. Trenches 4 and 5 had been put in to cover the most interesting geophysics anomalies, and although they weren't as big as Carenza had wanted, they still presented a huge task to the diggers. 'Look at that,' said Pete Bellamy, gesturing over to Trench 5, which was an intimidating 6 x 30 m (20 x 98 ft). 'That would normally take us at least three weeks to assess!'

Solid evidence of settlement in this area was beginning to come to light. In Trench 2, supervised by Carenza, there appeared to be a hearth and some signs of iron-smelting, as well as two post holes and some intriguing curved features. The trench needed to be widened to discover whether these last were two intersecting ditches or formed a circle, but the mechanical diggers were still engaged with the new trenches to the west. In one of these, Trench 4, the archaeologists were enthusing about the clear signs of a ditch.

Soil scientist David Jordan was well on his way to digging 100 small pits throughout the turnip field, from which he was taking soil samples. These he would take back to the incident room where an *ad hoc* laboratory had been set up. What he was looking for were the various levels of phosphates in the soil. Phosphate levels are high where people and, especially, animals live in some concentration; the mineral gets into the soil through excreta, the remains of fires, food rubbish and particularly bones. Human bones are usually found in only one or two places (cemeteries and other burial places), but animal bones have a tendency to be strewn around where people have lived. David would be able to identify the centres of occupation and their limits through the different levels of phosphates in the soil samples.

Next to a barn across the road from the turnip field, four children from a local primary school met up with Guy Apter of History in the Making, historical and environmental education specialists. Their assignment was to go into some local managed woodland to find a suitable ash tree and other materials to make an ard – a prehistoric plough – based on the Donnerupland Ard from Scandinavia. They needed a tree with a bend in it, but their choice was restricted by the fact that almost all the trees in the wood were straight. In addition, the slightly bent tree they did locate turned out to be full of knots and not quite wide enough, which could mean that the final product would snap. But they were willing to give it a try at the end of our final day.

(Top right) Surface stripping at Kemerton. *Mick Aston*
(Centre right) Soil scientist David Jordan in the incident room discovering the phosphate levels in the turnip field samples. *Mick Aston*
(Bottom right) The primary schoolchildren who helped to make the ard. *Mick Aston*

After lunch, work continued in the trenches, with diggers painstakingly removing thin layers of soil to reach indistinct features that would have disappeared with more severe handling. The ditch in Trench 4 was now quite recognisable, the darker soil that gradually filled up the ditch showing against the light-coloured natural gravel to either side. A small section had been cut into the centre and pieces of middle Iron Age pottery were being unearthed. In Trench 5, by far the largest on site, ditches were being discovered as well as postholes.

While the diggers were searching for dateable material that could be held in the hand, Stewart and Francis were looking at the broader picture. As well as the trackway, which appeared to be from the Bronze Age, they had noticed on the aerial photographs a line of pits near the trackway, each about 2 m (6.5 ft) square and about 2 m away from each other. These 'pit alignments' are almost invariably territorial markings from the Bronze Age. They could simply be the places from which dirt for an earthen bank was excavated, but it is also known for such a pit to have held one end of an entire tree trunk so that it stood up like a totem pole. A line of these must have been quite striking in the distant past. Stewart had also identified faint traces of a north-west extension of the trackway in existing hedges and roads, even in the middle of Kemerton, all leading towards Conderton Camp on Bredon Hill. Perhaps the ancient peoples who settled in this area used the track-way to herd their stock to safety there?

From these map and photographic investigations, it appeared that, while we were finding a satisfactory number of artefacts from the Iron Age right up to the Anglo-Saxons, our evidence of the Bronze Age would prove to be almost solely within the landscape itself.

Volunteers from the South Worcestershire Archaeology Group (SWAG) - who had also swelled the ranks of our team of diggers - had been **field-walking** in fields to the south and west of the turnips. In the western field, a healthy accumulation of prehistoric flint and Iron Age finds had been discovered in one particular sector. Derek Hurst plotted these on a map and then showed it to John Gater, who compared it with the geophysics survey of the field.

Surprisingly perhaps, the focus of the fieldwalking finds did not correlate with what was a spectacular result from geophysics. What had been a faint cropmark on one of the aerial photographs came out loud and clear on the geophysics survey: a D-shaped feature about 20 m (66 ft) across with a defined entrance and a few pits inside. This could easily be an Iron Age enclosure or even a Bronze Age one. And the lack of correlation between the finds and this result was actually quite intriguing, according to Malcolm Atkin, the Worcestershire county archaeology officer; the spread of finds to the west of the feature meant that there was probably a lot more to discover in the future about this area. First thing the following morning, we would be putting in two trenches (6 and 7), one across part of the entrance of the feature and the other across the back of it.

Malcolm also reassured us about the validity of TIME TEAM three-day excavations. His unit, he said, would have tackled the site in very much the same way to make an assessment – which was really all TIME TEAM could do in the time. Features such as ditches, pits and enclosures would be revealed, recorded and then covered up again for more thorough investigation in the future.

At the end of the day, it was decided that Trench 3, where excavation had been continuing more or less undisturbed by the cameras, would finally be shut down. Malcolm said that that whole area had produced extremely interesting results. First, there was the likely Bronze Age trackway, although no dateable finds had come to light. Then there was the Anglo-Saxon settlement from which such rare artefacts for the county had been uncovered. And finally there was also an Iron Age enclosure – so the site more than lived up to Mick's prediction that this landscape would show evidence of almost continuous occupation over thousands of years.

Day Three

As the morning progressed, Carenza became increasingly puzzled. It was not that her Trench 2 was not producing wonderful features that gave a vivid picture of life in the Iron Age – far from it. For instance, a curving line of dark soil about 25 cm (10 in) across had proved to be a drainage ditch made by water dripping off the roof of a round house. This must have once had a diameter of at least 5 m (16 ft) – more than enough room for a large family.

But what was making Carenza scratch her head was the contents of a pit outside this ditch. It was about 1.5 m (5 ft) long, 0.75 m (2.5 ft) wide and 0.45 m (1.5 ft) deep. If Carenza were asked to identify this in an empty state, she would have said it was an Anglo-Saxon grave of a child of about 10. However, no human remains were found in it. Instead, there were the remains of what appeared to be a wooden structure with metal reinforce-ments. Inside this box (or whatever it was) were artefacts including a Victorian flower pot, a large number of pieces of plaster and three sherds of Roman pottery that fit together beautifully to form the bottom of a bowl. According to one of the experts on site, the metal pieces looked as if they had been buried for no more than a couple of hundred years. Carenza couldn't imagine how all these

Carenza and the 'drip gulley' of the Iron Age house in Trench 2. *Mick Aston*

things had been deposited in this way.

In Trench 4, meanwhile, Robin Jackson, a county field archaeologist, had found bits and pieces that all added up to a virtually complete Iron Age kitchen. There were pottery sherds that showed signs of calcium on the inside, just like a 'furred-up' kettle – evidence of having been frequently used to boil water. There were also 'pot boilers' – rocks that were heated and which some think were put in water to heat it – as well as parts of querns, stones on which food was crushed. In addition, there were pieces of *briquetage*, a very special type of pottery that was used exclusively to hold salt.

ENVIRONMENTAL EVIDENCE

Liz Pearson, the county environmental archaeologist, processed soil samples extracted by the diggers from features in the trenches. Using a wet-sieving/flotation method, she was able to recover food and agricultural waste, which would tell us more of the human activity on the site.

She was able to show how the crops grown by the inhabitants of this area had changed over the centuries. During the Bronze Age and Iron Age, they had cultivated barley and emmer wheat – an ancient form of the cereal. Elsewhere in Britain, another type – spelt wheat – gradually became more common during the late Iron Age, and further work on the samples may show whether this happened at Kemerton.

Results from the *grubenhaus* revealed that the local Saxon farmers had made a radical change to bread wheat. There were two main reasons for this. Bread wheat is 'free threshing' – that is, easier to separate the grain from the chaff – and its higher gluten content made for a more elastic dough and lighter bread. At Kemerton, the evidence for bread wheat had been found in a dwelling of early to mid-Saxon date, but elsewhere in the country, it generally became predominant no earlier than the mid-Saxon period.

Work on Trenches 6 and 7 was being carried out at a furious pace as the hours slipped away. Trench 7, which crossed the back of the enclosure, produced very few artefacts, but the opposite was true of Trench 6 at the entrance. Here, a great quantity of Bronze and Iron Age pottery was uncovered, presumably dropped as people passed in and out of the structure. But best of all was a piece of bronze that would have come from either a shield or a scabbard – solid evidence that this must have been a high-status dwelling site. That it was placed some distance from the round houses on the rest of the site was not unique; a number of other examples have been found of a 'head man's' house being set away from the rest of the community, and this certainly has been the habit of the powerful in the centuries since.

Francis visited Carenza's trench, where he was able to paint a word picture of the round house that must have stood there, given the evidence of the oval ditch that would have circled it. This ditch also showed that the house had been constructed of flat, upright planks, and it would have been topped by a slanting thatched roof. A fire would have been lit in the centre of the house, with smoke gradually trickling freely up through a hole in the roof. (Modern experiments had shown that a chimney in a round house would have caused such a fierce blaze that the building would have caught fire.) It is likely that a dog would have been kept by the entrance for protection (gnawed bones have been found in this spot in other excavations), and the food would have been stored in racks by the wall. The residents would have been able to sit at their door and look out on their animals penned in enclosures bound by ditches to keep them in and predators out. They would also have been able to watch the sun set from here and remember their ancestors.

This had probably been a small settlement, despite our finding features of quite a few round houses and enclosures. One house would have been built and a family would have lived in it, and when the children grew up, they would have erected their own houses nearby. But when the occupants of the first house died, their home would have been abandoned, and this pattern would have been repeated over the centuries.

The people who had lived here would probably have used an ard similar to the one that Guy and the schoolchildren had just finished. To test it, a pair of young oxen – named Reeves and Mortimer – were hitched to it and, as we held our breath, the plough went into action. It worked perfectly.

By now, Carenza had come up with a solution to the puzzle of the pit in Trench 2. She now reckoned that this was a Roman grave that had been opened by a Victorian antiquarian who had removed the bones (antiquarians were particularly

Top left) Diggers hoe gravel to expose features in one of the big trenches. *Mick Aston*
(Top right) Carenza and the Roman bowl bottom from the mysterious pit in Trench 2. *Mick Aston*
(Above) The piece of bronze from a shield or scabbard, found in Trench 6. *Mick Aston*

interested in skulls) and left the rest of the contents. Before the hole was refilled, it attracted some 19th-century rubbish, including the flower pot. As for the metal pieces, the jury was still out – an iron Roman brooch found near the pit appeared to be in the same state as the metal bits found in the grave, so they might be contemporary.

David Jordan arrived on the site full of excitement. His analysis of the phosphates on the site had shown that the levels were very high where the cropmarks appeared and dropped off dramatically beyond them. This was firm proof, he said, that this had been a settlement of some duration. These were also some of the most concrete results that he had ever had.

The geophysics team were enthusiastic, too. Their final survey showed some extremely strong anomalies between Trenches 1 and 2, where the cropmarks had been sparse and faint. This indicated that the settlement had once spread right across the field.

A major finding was Stewart's discovery that a series of probable Bronze Age boundaries oriented south-west/north/east had become part of an Iron Age territorial system. Then, during the Anglo-Saxon period, the orientation had changed to north-south. The evidence for this was in Trench 3, where we had seen the trackway change to this direction at a point where the Anglo-Saxon *grubenhaus* was found.

Mick's prediction had come true. In these peaceful Worcestershire fields, overlooked by Bredon Hill, people had for millennia been born, worked the land and died, some perhaps as long ago as 500,000 BC. As the sun began to set and we watched the oxen pulling the ard across the turnip field, we had just an inkling of what it must have been like to have lived in those distant times.

Final thoughts from Mick

In the past, we thought we knew all the early sites, surviving either as earthworks or as stone monuments, and that early people had lived mainly on the hills between dense marshy or forest-filled river valleys.

The recognition of vast areas of cropmarks from the 1960s onwards totally changed our perception of how and where prehistoric and Romano-British farmers lived and worked. It is now clear that the big river valleys, full of gravel, were very important settlement areas at all times and that perhaps 90% (or more) of these sites are lost to us.

Cropmarks give us a chance to find these sites and I have wanted to do a programme on them for years. Kemerton provided a superb example of the sort of evidence we can recover.

Finds from the D-shaped enclosure in Trench 6: *(top and above left)* Iron Age pottery; *(top right)* a saddle quern. *Mick Aston*
(Above right) Reeves and Mortimer the oxen hitched to the prehistoric ard. *Mick Aston*

TURKDEAN

GLOUCESTERSHIRE

WHAT MIGHT HAVE HAPPENED

The ceremony to bless the genus loci *had been memorable and, in these troubled times, gave the whole family a feeling of peace. The investment in the shrine had certainly been worthwhile. The builder had combined new colours in the plaster with additional features, and had even reused an ancient stone in the foundation, which they all believed would give the site good luck. The light from the lamp threw their shadows against the wall and was reflected in the new brooches their daughters wore, bought to mark the occasion.*

A libation of wine was poured over the altar and the ceremony was completed. Although they may not have the grand baths and endless mosaics of some of their neighbours, this shrine offered them a place of peace that would give them hope for the future.

The garish – but historically accurate – altar created on site. *Mick Aston*

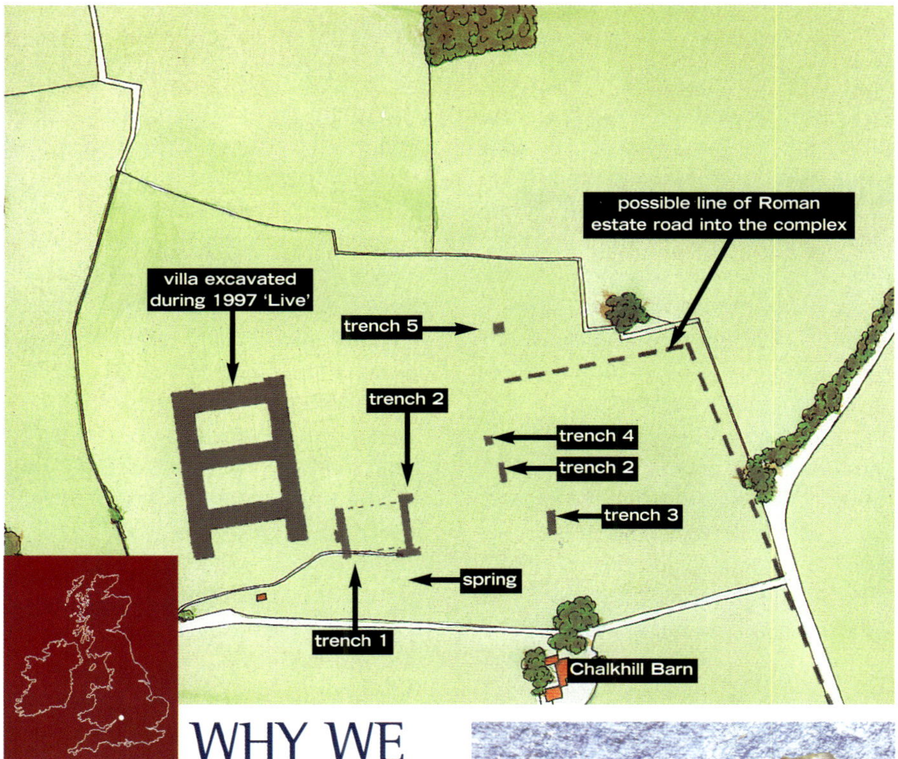

WHY WE WENT THERE

As we approached the farm near Turkdean, we all had a sense of *déjà vu*. It had been only a little over a year since we had said goodbye to that lovely setting of undulating hills and turned our backs on what had been one of the most exciting excavations that TIME TEAM had ever carried out, not least because it had been our first 'live'.

What had brought us here in the first place was a spectacular set of **cropmarks** that only appeared every few years when there was a sustained spell of dry weather. A series of geophysics surveys revealed even more: what appeared to be a Roman villa with at least three ranges of buildings. Excavation produced prizes virtually with the first spadeful. There were rooms with decorated plaster walls, a finial that once capped a roof, evidence of metal-working and – the favourite finds of the dig – a plunge pool in a bath house and a brooch bearing the message (in Latin) 'Use and be happy'!

However, this excavation raised almost as many questions as it answered. Was the complete villa ever standing at one time, or was one range of buildings abandoned as another was erected? Why was the bath house placed right in the middle of the central range, far from the residential rooms? (Did the Romano-British occupants rush across the courtyard in

their towels to have a bath?) Why was an industrial area so close to the living quarters?

But it was the final geophysics results that really amazed us. They showed yet another range of buildings extending to the east up the hill towards a spring. This completely changed our perception of the site. Rather than being a villa at the centre of a farming community, could this instead be a palace or even a temple complex, with a shrine devoted to a water deity at the spring?

When we had left Turkdean on that late summer afternoon, we had thought that whatever secrets the site might hold would be for others to unravel in the future. However, those final geophysics results haunted us, and fans of the series

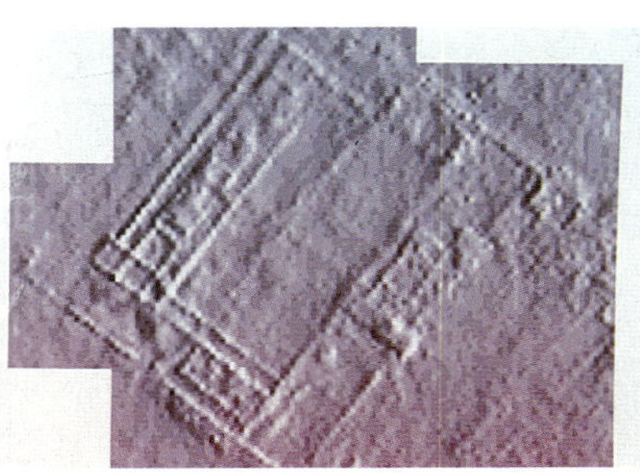

would not let us forget Turkdean: of all the digs that TIME TEAM has carried out, this one was the most commented upon by viewers. So when it came to plan this year's programmes, we broke a rule that we had held to for five years – this time we would return to a site, albeit a very special one.

Day One

The weather also seemed to be echoing the past – just like last year, it was cold, windy and dripping with rain. However, this time our incident room was not in a draughty barn but in a heated village hall in Notgrove about a mile and a half away from the site.

Tony was joined in the warmth by Mark Corney, the TIME TEAM lecturer in landscape archaeology at Bristol University (stepping in for Mick while he films), and David Neil, formerly of English Heritage and an expert in Roman villas and mosaics. Over the previous months, the thinking about the Turkdean site had begun to change, and the devising of alternative theories had been spurred on by the results of another geophysics survey that had been carried out a few weeks earlier – 'We're giving you the gold service,' said John Gater. According to Mark and David, these results showed that it was far more likely that the anomalies that we had seen before were evidence of the expanded community that had once supported the villa, and not of a temple complex or other sort of ritual site.

According to David, when sites like Turkdean are discovered, the only part of them that is usually extensively investigated is the villa building itself. The rest – the farmsteads, workers' huts, slave quarters, industrial spaces – are left untouched. What could make this Turkdean excavation special was the fact that we would be looking closely at these frequently ignored areas – which, after all, had been occupied by the people who generated the wealth to support the high-status villa.

Two areas on the geophysics survey initially intrigued the archaeologists. Running east-west, there appeared to be an aisled building, a structure consisting of a nave (a large central room) flanked

(Top) The enamelled brooch found at the previous year's excavation.
(Above) The fantastic geophysics survey results of the large villa that became the focus of the 1997 'live' broadcasts. *Mick Aston/GSB Prospection*

by a relatively narrow corridor on either side, and which sometimes had domestic rooms tacked on to one end. People may have occupied all parts of it, using them as residences or working spaces, but often livestock would reside in one of the sections of the building. In addition, to the east of this was a lot of geophysical 'noise' that, if predictions were correct, would reveal a great deal of industrial activity. It was decided to place Trench 1 at the west end of the aisled building and Trench 2 in the centre of this 'noise'.

In Trench 1, Phil and his crew of about a dozen diggers quickly uncovered a series of walls. However, they only

abutted at their junctions rather than being built into each other. This, according to Mick, meant that they might have been constructed at different times, so what may have started off as a structure with a single open space inside was eventually divided up. Just before lunch, David and Phil began poking into the south-west corner of the trench and soon announced that they had found another wall, which was followed by another and then another. Elsewhere in the trench, a white layer of decayed mortar or plaster was evidence of wall collapse, but in the 'room' next to this, the walls appeared to continue down for a significant distance.

Progress in Trench 2 was slower. Carenza soon came down on what seemed to be a floor with traces of iron slag (*see* p. 55), as well as a wall, possibly collapsed, extending east–west across the trench. Unfortunately, further excavation revealed an area of redeposited building material. According to Mark Corney, the presence of the slag on top of this rubble suggested that the industrial waste could be of quite a late date. As the afternoon progressed, the diggers cleaned the rubble in the trench and recorded it, and at the end of the day, they were poised to remove it to discover what lay beneath.

A number of coins were found in these trenches and, as in the previous year, they mostly dated from the 4th century AD. They included, in Trench 1, an example from c. 335 commemorating the founding of Constantinople. Trench 2 was dated by a *minim* – a late Roman bronze coin from the 4th or early 5th century – although a piece of Samian ware pottery found nearby could mean that that part of the site had been occupied at least 200 years earlier. In addition, three tessarae (mosaic pieces) were discovered, including a white one that indicated that there might have been a decorated mosaic rather than a plain one. This made a total of five tessarae

that had been found on the site – 'At this rate, if we keep coming back every year,' joked one of the diggers, 'we'll have a mosaic in about a century!'

Another area on the geophysics results that seemed promising was a great white 'blob' about 10 m (33 ft) in diameter that was very likely to indicate industrial activity involving heating or burning – perhaps a kiln? Late in the day, the mechanical digger was sent further up the hill from the other two trenches to investigate this anomaly, which seemed to be located on a platform scooped out of the bedrock. However, after the mechanical digger had removed soil to a depth of about 1.5 m (5 ft), Trench 3 had produced nothing but a few animal bones, charcoal and small pottery fragments. It was proposed to dig a slot through the middle to see if we could find out the source of the 'blob'.

As well as continuing to dig deeper in all the existing trenches the next day, it was also decided that we would tackle one or more of the springs that dotted the hillside. Every large villa complex had to have an adequate source of water in order to function, and some of the activities carried out at Turkdean in the past may have been sited near one of the springs. But there was also the possibility that we might find a small temple or shrine, even though, as Mick admitted, the archaeological community tends to regard those interested in such sites as part of the 'lunatic fringe'!

Day Two

A group of children from the nearby Cold Aston primary school arrived mid-morning on the site, perhaps more eager to meet their hero Tony Robinson than to find out about our excavations. Nevertheless, they were taken on a tour of this windswept Gloucestershire hill.

They first encountered Trench 3, where Pete Bellamy and another digger were working in isolation, trying to fathom what they had. Although they (and the mechanical digger) had dug quite deeply, they had only really reached the top of the archaeology. But Pete had enough information to come up with a hypothesis: he was sure that this had been a lime kiln. They had reached a solid layer of the charcoal that had once burned the stone, part of a process that could turn it into fertiliser or mortar. However, there was something missing: a limestone quarry would normally have been in the immediate vicinity. This led Pete to surmise that the 'quarry' for this kiln had been the Roman buildings on the plateau below, and therefore this kiln was medieval. During the Middle Ages, stone would have been robbed out of the villa and its surrounding structures and fed into the kiln. So when one of the children asked where the villa had gone, we were able to say that it had probably first gone into

(Above left) Trench 1 at an early stage. *Mick Aston*
(Above centre) Fragments of wall plaster found in Trench 1. *Mick Aston*

the kiln and then it had become part of some of the medieval buildings in the neighbourhood.

A little way down the hill, the children came upon Carenza in Trench 2. Here the rubble was finally being removed, but the archaeology was still hard to make out. Was that a wall on that side? Was that squarish hole a posthole? It would be some time before anything was comprehensible.

To the north of Trench 2 was a new excavation over what we thought was a spring. However, Trench 4 turned out to contain the junction of two channels of a culvert through which water flowed swiftly, eventually exiting (we thought) at the spring near the the aisled building in Trench 1. Although no dateable finds were excavated, there was a strong possibility that this culvert was Roman, said David Neil. Similar working Roman conduits had been found at the villas at Chedworth and Woodchester. Unfortunately, so far we hadn't found the spring head. A possibility was excavated even further to the north-east, almost at the top of the hill, at what was designated Trench 5. But this contained only modern rubbish and so was quickly closed.

The children scrambled down the hill to Trench 1 – what was fast becoming known as the 'top trench' because of the interesting archaeology that was coming out of it. One part, excavated to a depth of about 1.5 m (5 ft), had produced a surprise. It appeared that the substantial wall remains were standing on foundations laid on top of an earlier structure. From the finds, the top building was dated to the late 2nd or 3rd century, and certainly not later than AD 240, and the lower one was obviously earlier. The latter may have been a wooden structure built into a slot in the ground.

Both buildings appeared to have been high status: the upper one had once been faced with red-painted plaster, and in the bottom of the trench, David Neil discovered a fragment of a red terracotta *bipedalis* tile that, as its Latin name suggests, would have been about 2 ft (0.6 m) square when whole. This would have come from either a hypocaust (the Romans' form of underfloor central heating) or a bath house, and was further evidence for the relative high-status of the structures in this trench. This led to speculation about who had once lived in them. One suggestion was that it may have been here that the builders of the large villa had originally lived. Alternatively, David Neil thought that it might have been the home of the villa owner's bailiff, who would have managed the estate.

Finds expert Lindsay Allason-Jones from the University of Newcastle had earlier identified a child's earring found in this trench, and more substantial discoveries had since been made. These included three matching sherds from a 2nd-century mortarium (on which food ingredients would have been crushed) and a piece of a hefty millstone made of Yorkshire millstone grit.

As the children left to go back to school, the mechanical digger set to work to the south-east of Trench 1, where a spring was busy burbling away. After two false starts on supposed spring heads up on the hill, we weren't taking any chances. This trench, No. 6, would be tackled in earnest after lunch.

No sooner had the archaeologists been fed than they changed their minds again. Phil had another look at the northern, deepest end of Trench 1 and decided that it contained the remains of only one building. However, the new thinking allowed for an even more exciting scenario - and a suggestion that this site had been occupied for a considerably longer time than we had once thought.

The slot in the ground had probably been a boundary ditch of some kind and, over time, had become filled with silt and rubbish, the latter including the *bipedalis* tile. All this was levelled into an earth platform that was found to contain sherds of 2nd-century Severn Valley ware and a narrow piece of dressed red limestone that suggested that a building decorated with red lines had once stood somewhere on the site. A narrow layer of blackened earth could have been turf that had been burned – quite a significant finding. It meant that the site had been occupied early in the Roman period (as seen from the early debris in the soil beneath the black layer); then the land lay fallow and became grassed over. This was then burned and the aisled building erected on top, supported by massive foundations sunk in places to more than 1 m (3.3 ft).

No floors were found, but a clue of what they may have looked like came from the bank of the nearby stream: dressed flagstones found there may have been part of a dismantled floor. Finds including coins indicated a 3rd-century date for this residence, and other objects suggested that it may have been occupied at least to the early 5th century. Internal wall plaster was also found in a number of colours, including green, black-blue and yellow, further raising the building's status.

Chris and John, comprising the geophysics team for this dig, had marked out the eastern end of what was now generally accepted as yet another villa on this site, revealing exactly how substantial it had once been. Trench 7

(Above left) The culvert in Trench 4. *Mick Aston*
(Above right) The piece of 2nd-century mortarium found in Trench 1. *Mick Aston*

was dug all along this line. There appeared to be an entrance in the wall found here, but disapppointingly, the south-east corner nearest the spring seemed to have collapsed in a haphazard fashion and any link with the spring had been lost.

Trench 6 had been dug right next to the spring. While a good amount of pottery fragments, including a tiny Oxford ware cup and an unusual shallow bowl, were found in it, no structures – and thus no shrine – were discovered. From the stream itself, Tim Hand – our metal detectorist, who had found most of the interesting metal finds the last time we had visited Turkdean – pulled out substantial pieces of a Polden Hill brooch and a trumpet brooch, both probably dating from the 1st century. Lindsay reckoned that these very early finds were made of bronze, although the calcium deposited on them by being in the stream gave them a silvery colour.

When we had excavated the large villa at Turkdean a year ago, we had been dealing with a structure built and lived in during the 'golden age of Roman villas' in the 4th century AD. Now we had the chance to look at what life was like at the time when the Britons were learning about Roman ways following the invasion of AD 43. While here in the countryside, villas were being constructed and farms were beginning to produce the grain that would support the Roman military establishment in mainland Europe, in the cities created by the invaders public buildings were being erected, and up in the north there was a great deal of military activity as the Romans tried to secure the northern frontier.

As we gathered near Trench 1 at the end of the day, Lindsay stated that, with a building complex this extensive, there had to be something really special in the way of interior decoration that remained to be found. Meanwhile David was closely studying the geophysics survey of the villa, trying to predict where a mosaic floor might be located – perhaps an impossible task since much of the villa structure appeared to have been 'robbed out' down to below floor level. What was certain was that the next day we would be concentrating on the interior of the villa in an attempt to find out more about how the residents had lived.

Day Three

'What I'd like to know,' said a digger in Trench 1, 'is how the Romans here dressed to keep out the bloody cold!' The rest of his complaint was whipped away by the bitterly cold wind. However, most of us were able to forget the prematurely wintery weather as the villa emerging from the soil in front of our eyes produced an increasing number of surprises.

Trench 7 had been substantially widened and extended a short way to the south so that it now took in Trench 6, and this was the number now given to this part of the excavation. The digging had revealed the outlines of two tower rooms, one at either end of the eastern side of the aisled building. These two-storey structures would have flanked the entrance to the house, still visible in the stonework that our diggers were now brushing down, and they must have ensured that any 3rd-century visitors would have been suitably impressed by their first view of the villa. The widening of the trench had also unearthed a wall that was likely to be the other end of one in Trench 1, giving us the outline of three sides of the building.

Back in Trench 1, Roger Box, whose reporting of the cropmarks had led to the discovery of the large villa, had been digging *outside* the western end of the villa when he began to pull out substantial pieces of internal wall plaster in a variety of colours. David Neil was called over and confidently labelled this as a cellar. The plaster – and especially the blue colour, which was expensive and rare – could mean that it was used as an underground semi-religious chamber, perhaps similar to one found in Lullingstone in Kent, where there is a wall painting of three nymphs holding their breasts out of which water spurts! Given the quality of the plaster that Roger was finding, it was finally decided to stop excavating, cover the plaster in a thin layer of sand and refill the trench. This would preserve it for future archaeologists who, after weeks of delicate work, might be able to recreate the plaster as it had been before it fell from the wall.

A shout from Carenza in Trench 6 led everyone to crowd around one of the stones inside the walls. As Carenza drizzled dirt over it and then gently brushed it off, the letters 'FIL' appeared. This was quite a find: it is extremely rare for inscriptions to be found in villas, even one that was relatively crudely cut and was, said David, probably a form of graffiti.

It reminded Guy de la Bédoyère, our expert on Roman history, of something and he spent an hour out of the wind in one of TIME TEAM's Discovery Land Rovers poring over a reference book of Roman inscriptions. He emerged pointing at a picture of a Roman milestone. Certainly the writing on this looked remarkably similar to our graffiti, but Simon Esmond Cleary, the author of *The Ending of Roman Britain* who was visiting the site for the

(Above left) Crane view of Trench 1. On right is the deepest part where evidence of a burned layer was found. At the top is the cellar where the possible ritual chamber was discovered. *Mick Aston*
(Above right) David Neil cleans up some foundations. *Mick Aston*

afternoon, said that the stone on which our inscription was carved was much too insubstantial to have been part of a milestone. At the end of the day, Phil and Carenza gently dug the stone out of the surrounding rubble so that it could be examined more thoroughly at a later date.

Stewart had been continuing his work (started during the 'Live' the year before – see *Time Team 98*) on how the country-side here had been divided up by the people who had lived here over the centuries. Walking the landscape and examining maps and other references, he had tracked down roads mentioned in the *Anglo-Saxon Chronicles* in the immediate area, and had found traces of Roman roads running along the ridges between the valleys, as well as the well-known Roman road called the Foss Way that passes through the landscape only a short distance away. By looking at all these and the present boundaries of the farms at Turkdean and nearby, he was able to delineate the boundaries of the estate of which our Roman villas were a part. As an added extra, he also discovered gaps where, from the lay of the land and kinks in the boundaries, it is likely that at least two and possibly four more Roman villas wait to be discovered in the immediate neighbourhood. Here were targets for a whole army of archaeologists of the future!

The search was still on for the origin of the spring that flowed down the hillside. To the north-east of the new villa, high up on the hill, there was a depression in the ground surrounded by gently rising ground – in effect, an amphitheatre. This could easily have been the shrine site, with a simple wooden structure and trees to mark it, but it would not have survived. The view down the hill to the two villas, large and small, would have tied in the religion practised there to home and family, both extremely important to the Romano-British who probably lived there.

Within the depression on the hillside, which Stewart thought must have once been a quarry (the stone from which may have fed the lime kiln on the opposite side of the hill in earlier times), the previously closed Trench 5 was reopened and dug deeper. At first, it appeared to be simply another

(Top left) The interior of the Lullingstone villa, with the cellar chapel area *(centre left)*. The newly found villa at Turkdean may have had an underground ritual chamber similar to this. *Mick Aston*

(Above centre) The 'FIL' stone was found in the right-hand part of the trench. *Mick Aston*

(Above left) Phil and Carenza next to the 'FIL' stone, shown in situ. *Mick Aston*

In the spring where the dye was showing, Alan the metal detectorist had made another wonderful discovery. He had found a third Roman brooch, this time a beautiful fan-shaped one, complete except for the pin at the back. On it were at least a dozen triangles of bright enamel in red and orange in a chequered pattern. Lindsay, our finds expert, had had a closer look at the two brooches that Alan had found earlier. Both, she said, appeared to have been deliberately snapped in half and then possibly flung into the spring, which could have had ritual connotations.

The answer to the digger's question at the beginning of Day 3 came in the form of Roman re-enactor John Harris. The well-to-do Romano-Briton

culvert, but further excavation finally revealed it to be the spring head, with water quickly bubbling up through the ground. To test whether this fed the spring next to the new villa, a harmless blue dye was put into the water. This was detected in the culvert in Trench 4, but we waited in vain for the dye to appear in the water emerging by the villa. Then there was as shout from someone at another spring a short distance away: blue dye was staining the water there. So it appeared that springs criss-crossed the hillside and we had yet to find the one that would have supplied the new villa.

of the 3rd century would have faced the bitter winds that were chilling our bones dressed in a warm thigh-length woollen cloak. This would have covered a woolen tunic bound at the waist with a red leather belt that incorporated sheaths for two knives. His lower half would have been covered in woollen leggings tied at the waist, with a long strip of cloth wrapped from ankle to knee around each leg to form puttees. The outfit was completed by leather shoes, the soles studded with nail heads.

All day, stonemason Giles Macdonald had been carving, from a block of Portland stone, a small altar similar to Roman ones that had been found near springs. At the same time, Chris Owen had been attempting to create colours from natural materials – unfortunately, his experiments with blue came to nothing, even with the distinctly non-Roman use of a gas torch. The result – which, though true to history, was far too garish for most of us – was baptised with wine as we toasted the dig and the gorgeous sunset that lit our last look at Turkdean.

Final thoughts from Mick

It was a strange feeling going back to Turkdean, but in some ways, it was a lot easier as, this time, we were not doing a 'live' series of broadcasts as well!

Excavation usually produces as many new questions as it answers and so it turned out at Turkdean. While it is now clear that we have another large house as well as the accommodation found in 1997, it is still not clear – at least to me – how the site actually operated in Roman times: a series of houses, houses of different dates, an estate centre, a farm complex, a religious complex or a stately home. All are still possibilities, I feel!

(Top left) Crane view of Trench 6. The outline of one of the two tower rooms can be seen clearly on the left, as can the paved entrance in the middle.
(Above left) The fan-shaped brooch found in the spring. *Mick Aston*
(Above right) Carenza dresses in appropriate Romano-British dress to match those of re-enactor John Harris. *Mick Aston*

NEVIS

WEST INDIES

WHAT MIGHT HAVE HAPPENED

It would be his last meal in the Great House. He had ordered the best Bristol wine and his favourite Gloucester cheeses to be brought to him. He had his finest glassware on the table and the deep red of the wine shone with the light from the candles. He now had a moment to himself as the sun set across the distant sea. Through the windows, he could see the cane fields where the slaves still laboured to get the last crop in. For them, the future was uncertain – the new owner had a very bad reputation. A fair price had been paid, but he couldn't help feeling a twinge of guilt about the fate of the people he still thought of as the sinews of his plantation. He had grown to admire their skill and the ease with which they had learned the art of sugar making.

Still, within weeks he would be back in England, to his properties there, which offered some security at least. Despite the falling price of sugar, he had invested well at the height of the market. For his family and himself, the future would be less dependent on the doubts and uncertainties of the West Indies trade, but for the workers who still toiled in the fields below, he feared the worst.

A sugar plantation in Jamaica, from *Le Magasin Pittoresque*, 1837. *Mary Evans Picture Library*

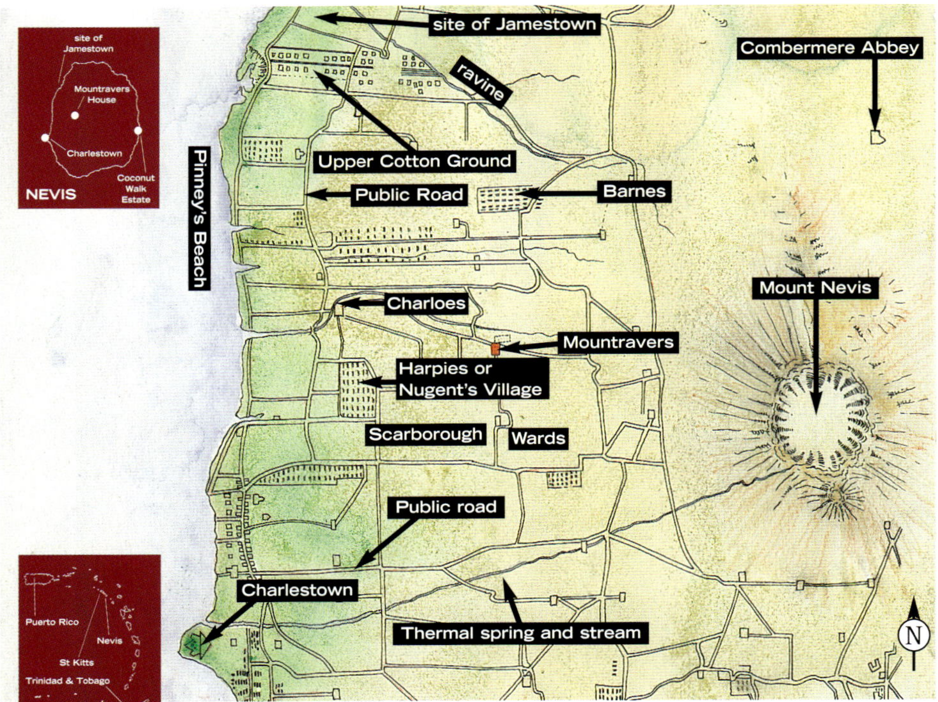

WHY WE WENT THERE

'We'll call it "TIME TEAM's Tropical Adventure"', series producer Tim Taylor had said, only half-joking. And as we crawled out of a flotilla of eight-seater Islander prop planes, bleary-eyed and instantly smothered by the heat and humidity of the Caribbean island of Nevis, we certainly felt that we had entered the unknown. This wasn't going to be like any other TIME TEAM dig.

But why were we here? Well, in a survey carried out among purchasers of the *Time Team 98* site reports, we had asked two questions: had they liked the series' two previous 'abroad' programmes (in Majorca and Maryland), and would they be happy to watch two programmes devoted to the same dig – a financial necessity if we were to go 'abroad' again. The viewers had overwhelmingly answered 'Yes' to both. So the next problem was to settle on a place. Croatia, Crete and Galicia in northern Spain were all candidates at one time or another, but then we were contacted by David Small, a historian and part-time teacher in Bristol.

David had been investigating the Pinney papers at Bristol University. John Pretor Pinney (1740–1818) had ended his life as an extremely wealthy resident of Bristol, but the source of his riches lay thousands of miles to the west, on the tiny volcanic island of Nevis, one of the northern-most of the Leeward Islands in the eastern Caribbean and now an independent nation together with the larger island a mile or so across the Narrows: St Kitts.

Nevis is only 26 miles in circumference, and its centre is dominated by Mount Nevis, a volcanic cone rising to 985 m (3,232 ft). It was first populated by people from Central America in about 5000 BC, followed by at least two other waves of migration. In the last few centuries BC, the Arawaks moved in from South America: a highly cultured society, they produced distinctive, fine red-painted pottery and beautifully carved ritual items, jewellery and other objects. In about AD 1000, the Arawaks disappeared from the West Indies and their place was taken by the Caribs, also from South America. They were a tough, warlike people who raided far and wide in their logboats – in fact, the word 'cannibal' is derived from the Spanish name for this nation. Although they, too, produced pottery, theirs was much cruder than the Arawaks'.

In 1493, on his second voyage to the New World, Columbus sighted two islands separated by a channel. One he dubbed St Christopher (after himself, some say) and the other, with its almost permanent crown of mist and cloud, he called (despite the hot climate) *'Nuestro Señora de las Nieves'* - Our Lady of the Snows! Over time, the first name became abbreviated to 'St Kitts' and the second was anglicised to 'Nevis'. Columbus never set foot on either of the islands.

In 1623, a group of colonists landed on St Kitts and founded what would become the first successful English colony in the Caribbean. They made an agreement with Tegreman, the Carib chief, to allow them to plant tobacco. By 1626, relations between the settlers (now including some French) and the Caribs had deteriorated: in one encounter, six Carib war canoes holding over 400 men attacked the colonists. This was followed by a surprise night attack by the settlers,

Main map: detail of map of 1871
(Above) Nevis, with Mount Nevis and Pinney's Beach. *Mick Aston*

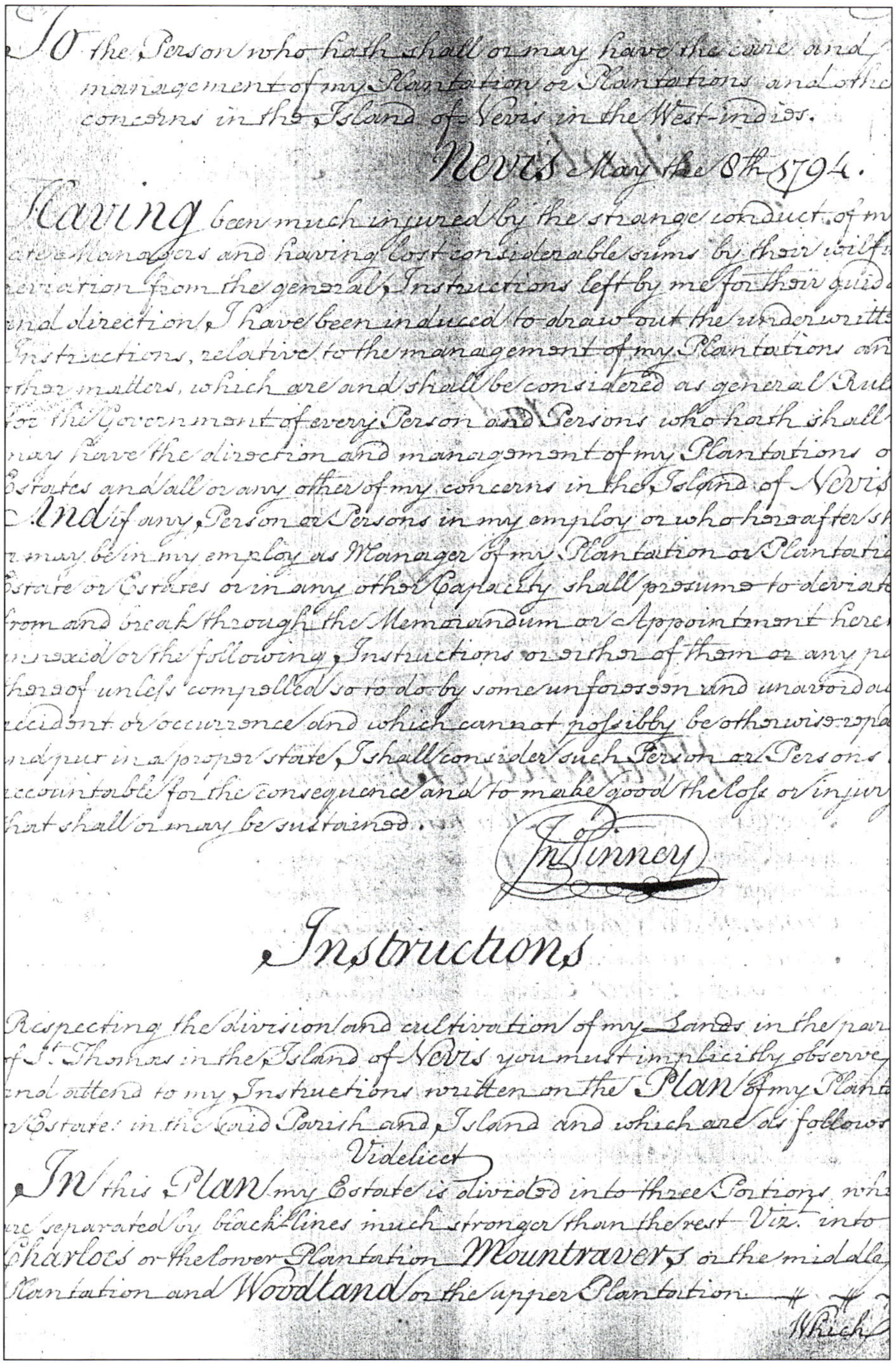

To the Person who hath shall or may have the care and management of my Plantation or Plantations and other concerns in the Island of Nevis in the West-indies.

Nevis May the 8th 1794.

Having been much injured by the strange conduct of my late Managers and having lost considerable sums by their wilful deviation from the general Instructions left by me for their guidance and direction, I have been induced to draw out the underwritten Instructions, relative to the management of my Plantations and other matters, which are and shall be considered as general Rules for the Government of every Person and Persons who hath shall or may have the direction and management of my Plantations or Estates and all or any other of my concerns in the Island of Nevis. And if any Person or Persons in my employ or who hereafter shall or may be in my employ as Manager of my Plantation or Plantations Estate or Estates or in any other Capacity shall presume to deviate from and break through the Memorandum or Appointment here annexed or the following Instructions or either of them or any part thereof unless compelled so to do by some unforeseen and unavoidable accident or occurrence and which cannot possibly be otherwise replaced and put in a proper state, I shall consider such Person or Persons accountable for the consequence and to make good the loss or injury that shall or may be sustained.

Jno Pinney

Instructions

Respecting the division and cultivation of my Lands in the parish of St. Thomas in the Island of Nevis you must implicitly observe and attend to my Instructions written on the Plan of my Plantation Estate in the said Parish and Island and which are as follows Videlicet

In this Plan my Estate is divided into three Portions which are separated by black lines much stronger than the rest Viz. into Charlocs or the lower Plantation Mountravers or the middle Plantation and Woodland or the upper Plantation — Which

who killed an estimated 2,000 Caribs, including Tegreman, although some survivors managed to escape to other islands.

In 1628, the English spread from St Kitts to Nevis and established a colony at Jamestown, which has since disappeared. By this time, it appears that there was no indigenous population on the island – perhaps wiped out by the previous years' attacks or even by disease introduced by Columbus and his crews to the West Indies.

Between 1672 and 1698, when the Royal African Company had the monopoly for providing slaves, Nevis became a market for their sale to the other Leeward islands. Those forcibly taken from their homes in Africa (of whom some 10–20% died on the 'Middle Passage' before they ever got to Nevis) were greatly prized because they made possible the new bonanza crop – sugar cane.

On Nevis itself, the slave population increased from 3,849 in 1678 to 10,000 in 1778 – nine black people for every white person on the island. Once on Nevis, about 40% of the arriving slaves died while becoming 'seasoned' to the island and others took their own lives

PRODUCING SUGAR

From October to January, the ground was prepared by creating 'holes' (actually square depressions in the soil) in which to plant the sugar cane. The canes were then planted and manured, and the 'holes' gradually filled in. After 13–14 months, the cane was mature, and around Christmas, the previous year's crop was harvested (*above*). The cut cane was carted to a mill to be crushed. Initially the mills were powered by oxen, but later the animals were replaced by wind (*below*) and then steam. It was dangerous work for the slaves; if a worker's fingers got caught in the mill, it was usually necessary to amputate the entire arm.

The cane juice would run directly from the mill to the boiling house (*below*), where, in intense heat, it would be ladled into a series of coppers (boilers). The final one was the hottest, to encourage the sugar to crystalise, or 'strike'. The sugar was allowed to cool and then scooped into barrels and taken to the curing house where the molasses drained out. The latter would be taken to the still to be turned into rum.

The trade in sugar from cane began to decline on Nevis fairly quickly. The growing of a single crop depleted the once-rich soil, and in the mid-18th century, yields began to decrease. In addition, the American War of Independence (1776–83) meant the loss of important markets on the American mainland. However, it was the introduction of sugar from the sugar beet (the result of a competition initiated by Napoleon) in 1822 and the emancipation of the slaves in British colonies in 1834 that sounded the death knell for the trade. Today no sugar cane is grown on Nevis.

(Top) John Prater Pinney's instructions to future managers of his plantation on Nevis, written because of the 'strange conduct' of previous managers, which had cost him a great deal of money. *Reproduced by permission of the Librarian of the University of Bristol.*
Box: (*top*) Slaves cutting sugar cane; (*centre*) slaves grinding cane in a windmill; (*above*) slaves working in the boiling house.
From William Clark's *Ten Views of the Island of Antigua*, 1823, *British Library*.

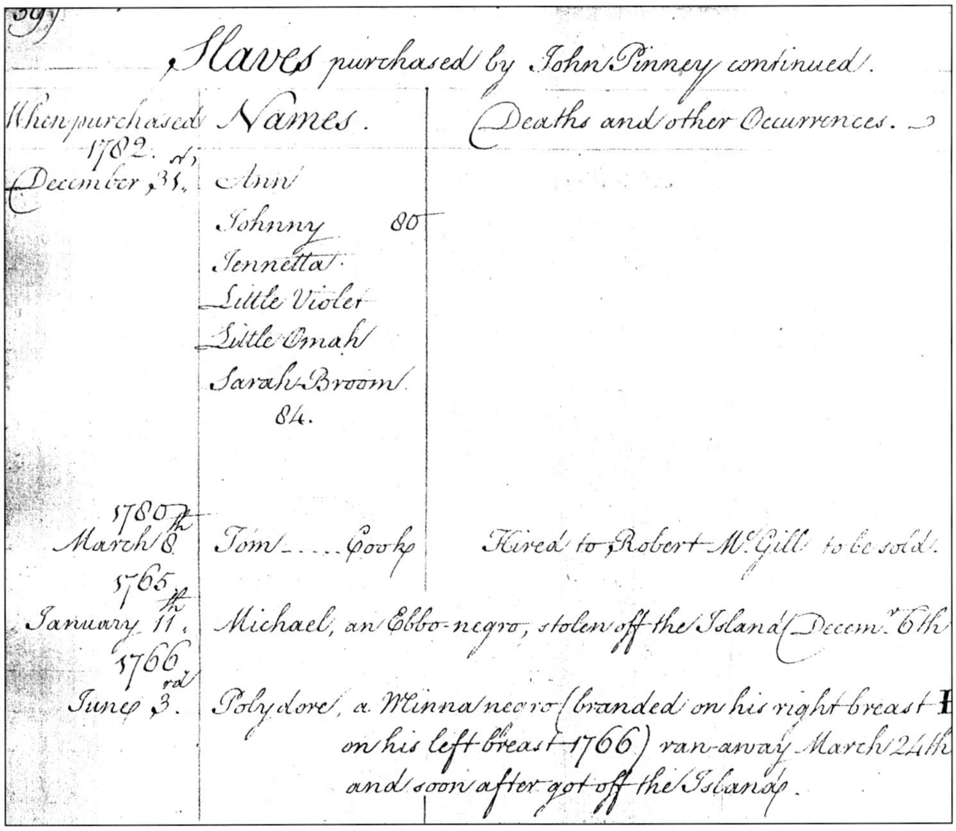

39

Slaves purchased by John Pinney continued.

When purchased	Names.	Deaths and other Occurrences.
1782. December 31.	Ann	
	Johnny 80	
	Jennetta	
	Little Violet	
	Little Omah	
	Sarah Broom	
	84.	
1780 March 8	Tom ..... Cook	Hired to Robert McGill to be sold.
1765 January 11.	Michael, an Ebbo-negro, stolen off the Island December 6th	
1766 June 3.	Polydore, a Minna negro (branded on his right breast I on his left breast 1766) ran away March 24th and soon after got off the Island.	

or (on pain of death) stole small boats to sail back to Africa. The result was that the birth rate did not keep up with the death rate and it was necessary to import slaves continuously to maintain their numbers. West Indian sugar production – which involved back-breaking, hot, filthy work (*see box on p91*) – was extremely important to the British economy: in the 18th century, it contributed more wealth to British coffers than any other part of the empire. And Nevis was so successful that it was known as the 'Queen of the Caribees'.

One English family that greatly benefited from the sugar boom was the Pinneys. In 1685, the 24-year-old Azariah Pinney took part in the ill-fated Monmouth Rebellion, the aim of which was to place the Protestant Duke of Monmouth (Charles II's illegitimate son) on the throne. When the rebellion ended ignominiously at the battle of Sedgmoor, Azariah was captured and initially sentenced to be hanged. However, his sister paid a ransom and he was released on condition that he leave Britain for at least 10 years. He chose Nevis for his exile, arriving with £15, a Bible, six gallons of sack and four of brandy. It was a dangerous place; 60% of those who landed there – free and slave – died within five years from gastrointestinal disease, tetanus, malaria or yellow fever. But Azariah did well and by 1705 he had become the co-owner of the 87-acre Charloes plantation, among other properties. He died a very wealthy man in 1719 or 1720 and was succeeded by his son John, who only outlived his father by a year or so. However, John's marriage in 1708 had brought the 161-acre Proctors estate into the family; this was amalgamated with Charloes and renamed Mountravers.

John's son John Frederick was brought up in England and only came to Nevis in 1739. He stayed a mere three years, and thereafter refused to return, even though the estates had begun to fall into decay. The unmarried John Frederick chose as his heir a cousin, John Pretor, on condition that the latter took his surname.

It was this John Pretor Pinney – perhaps the most successful Pinney of them all – on whom the TIME TEAM investigations centred. Having inherited Mountravers and the other estates on Nevis in 1762, he arrived on the island two years later, when he was 24. He made a religion of accounting, detested debt and had a superb grasp of business, and by the time he left Nevis in 1783, he had made Mountravers – eventually comprising 393 acres, extending from the top of Mount Nevis on down to the sea – one of the most successful estates in all the Caribbean, producing about 30,000 kg (66,000lb) of sugar annually and 32,8000 litres (7,000 gallons) of rum.

On his combined estates on Nevis, Pinney had about 200 slaves; a male slave was then worth about £50, a woman £37 and boys and girls about £14 each. Despite an initial negative reaction to the practice of buying and selling human beings, he eventually found a justification. In a letter dated 2 March 1765, he wrote: '... I was shocked at the first appearance of human flesh, exposed for sale. But surely God ordained them for ye use and benefit of us; otherwise his Divine will would have been made manifest by some particular sign or token.'

Among the planters on Nevis, Pinney was more considerate of his slaves (whom he called 'the sinews of a plantation'). At the time, it was considered normal on Nevis for one slave to produce about one hogshead of sugar per acre annually, but at Mountravers, the slaves produced only about 60% of that amount. Pinney may have preferred not to work his slaves to death, even if it meant less profit, but he may have also been persuaded to adopt more humanitarian working practices because a steady amount of work was more efficient. He ordered that one of his managers 'must not use severity, for I will not suffer any human being, committed by providence to my care, to be treated with cruelty.' However, whips, necklocks and branding irons were definitely used on occasion – Pinney instructed his manager to avoid using it them in front of guests at Mountravers, particularly abolitionists.

In 1808, Pinney began the sale (finalised in 1816) of Mountravers and other properties to Edward Huggins for £35,650 (about £1.75 million today). Huggins took physical possession in 1809. He was a very different type of slave owner, with a reputation for great cruelty it was said that his slaves had tried to kill him five times. In 1810, to punish some of the Mountravers slaves for refusing to manure fields during the

Part of John Pretor Pinney's inventory of slaves purchased by him from his arrival on Nevis in 1764 to his departure in 1783, including one 'stolen off the island' and another who ran away. *Reproduced by permission of the Librarian of the University of Bristol*

night and attempting to run away, he and his two sons marched about 20 of them, men and women, into the Charlestown market place and flogged them. The first was whipped for 15 minutes; one woman received 291 lashes and three others over 200 each; and one woman died of her injuries. However, when Huggins was prosecuted for cruelty, he was acquitted by a jury packed with other planters.

Edward Huggins greatly altered the Great House at Mountravers. Next to the original two-floor wood-built house of the Pinneys, he added a large wing 'three storeys high with vast windows and dramatic arches, in a superb situation, surrounded by a moat ... It had a ballroom and a staircase wide enough for three ladies in panniered dresses to descend together.' Over the years, the property changed hands a number of times, until in 1946 it was bought by Walter Wade, who sold a great deal of the stonework from the Huggins wing and other buildings. In 1993, the Great House and 14 acres of the former Pinney's estate were bought by Bill Pinney, distantly related to John Pretor Pinney, with the object of restoring the property to its former glory.

But we were faced with ruins at Mountravers, covered with thick jungle vegetation that would need machetes to cut through it. We wanted to see if we could put together the stone jigsaw to find out how the plantation worked from the perspective of both the white owners and the black slaves. Later we would expand our investigations to two other sites: the 'lost' capital of Jamestown and the Amerindian site at the Coconut Walk estate on the west side of the island – a tall order given that we had only six days!

Day One

While most of the visitors to this lovely island were holiday-makers who could laze away the day, this certainly wasn't true for TIME TEAM. The diggers had to be up at 5.15am so that they could have breakfast and arrive at the Mountravers site by 6.30. There were two reasons for this gruelling schedule. First, in October on Nevis it gets dark at 5.30pm, so shortening a typical TIME TEAM day by almost three hours; and second, because of the heat and humidity, it was important that the diggers had regular rest periods and a two-hour break for lunch during the hottest part of the day – further limiting the time when work could be done.

The drive to Mountravers took almost 20 minutes, the four-wheeled vehicles barely making it up the extremely pitted and rutted road. Our incident room at the site was to be in the stables just to the south-west of the Great House ruins. The stables, which had been partially rebuilt by Bill Pinney, were rumoured to have been the home of the camels that, in 1778, John Pretor Pinney had brought to the island. (The experiment had not been a success.)

The diggers were joined by Winston Crook. A former actor (including a role as a thug on *EastEnders*) born in Birmingham of Nevisian parents, he had come to Nevis about seven years before to set up a mountain bike club and a windsurfing school. For us, he had rounded up a posse of 'machete men' who were soon hard at work hacking away the jungle from around the Great House. The diggers started work immediately, digging Trench 1 out of a possible midden (rubbish pit) next to what had been the kitchens.

Hardly any soil had been removed when substantial fragments of pottery were recovered, as well as some extremely fancy bits of glass, including the base of an elegant goblet. We had also found pieces of the heavy glass bottles that would have held the wine served in that goblet; one of these fragments had the words 'GLASSWORKS BRISTOL' on the base. We had been hoping to find pottery since John Pretor Pinney had written that he had ordered china from Wedgwood in Stoke on Trent. Because of our excavation in Burslem, we had very good contacts with ceramics experts, and one of them, David Barker, was expected on Nevis the next day. It was then that we would find out if we had some 18th- and/or early 19th-century Wedgwood. There was also a clay pipe among the pottery fragments, for which we anticipated getting a good date.

Over breakfast, Stewart had said that finding the slave quarters on the Pinney estate would be one of the most difficult things he had ever attempted. He had only two obscure references to the site – unearthed by David Small from the Pinney papers – to go on.

The 'machete men' had by now cleared away the undergrowth from around the midden and in the cellar of the Great House, where Trench 2 had been begun.

(From top) The road up to Mountravers, with Mount Nevis in the distance; aerial view of Nevis, with Mountravers surrounded by jungle on the upper right; the broken bottle base with the words 'GLASSWORKS BRISTOL' moulded into the glass. *Mick Aston*

Here TIME TEAM encountered nature that was truly red in tooth and claw. As digger Barney Sloane stuck a pick-axe near one of the walls, a donkey spider about 12 cm (5 in) in length scuttled out of the vegetation. Even Winston – who had the responsibility of capturing and removing the brown shaggy arthropod that bore a worrying similarity to a tarantula – said that it was a particularly large one. Mick the Dig, TIME TEAM's own arachnophobe, had hurried away before hearing that verdict.

Before lunch, the diggers had to decide who was going to go into the cellar under the counting house next to the Great House. It was here, in this stone-roofed building, that John Pretor Pinney had kept his valuable papers and cash safe from storms, fire and robbers. Victor had already located what he thought were collapsed wooden wine racks. However, our resident artist hadn't been aware that large chunks of masonry had been falling from the ceiling in recent weeks and he shouldn't have entered without a hard hat. But that wasn't the only thing that made the counting house cellar such an 'interesting' location: it was also supposedly the home of a multitude of fruit bats and, perhaps, scorpions. But that didn't put off our intrepid diggers for, in a letter, Pinney said that, when he had feared that the French would invade, he had buried some valuable documents in a large pot in the cellar and he wasn't sure that they had ever been removed!

Meanwhile, Stewart (dressed for the jungle and now the spitting image of Indiana Jones), David Rollinson, our local historical adviser, and Joseph 'Charlie' Woodley, a former surveyor's assistant on Nevis, had all gone, machetes in hand, to search for the remains of an animal mill. Preceding windmills on Nevis, these were circular buildings with a mill in the middle into which raw sugar cane would be fed to be ground up and the juice extracted. The mill was powered by oxen yoked to a pole that turned the roller as the animals walked in a circle around the machine. The sugar cane juice would flow downhill to a boiling house.

The existence of this mill had come to light when we received photographs of a map of 1801 that had been owned by an American woman who, on her death, had left it to the government of Nevis. This showed a plantation known as 'Stuart's', which was right next to Pinney's estate and may have been owned by him at some point. The animal mill certainly appeared to be contemporary with him, and it could prove to be the only evidence of this part of the sugar-making process that we would find on the island, although there were still a number of windmill bases left. But to get to it, not only did Stewart, David and Charlie have to hack their way through hundreds of metres of jungle, but they also had to approach the area via the golf course of the exclusive Four Seasons resort, which provided a couple of golf carts for the purpose.

After lunch, Barney and Mick the Dig drew the short straws and were assigned to dig in the counting house cellar (Trench 3). 'It was like the Black Hole of Calcutta,' Mick said later. It was a miserable job in a space about 4 m (13 ft) square and only 1.2 m (4 ft) high. The sweat literally poured off them, and in the space of only a couple of hours, the two of them drank about 12 litres (21 pints) of water. As they removed the rubble, they saw that half the floor was still covered in good quality red tiles; the remainder consisted of very loose soil. It appeared that the cellar had been occupied by human squatters at some time, as well as by unidentified animals. No bats or scorpions revealed themselves, but there was a substantial termite colony in one corner and a very large land hermit crab, which Carenza promptly adopted and christened 'Pinney'.

The cellar posed a problem. Was the red tile floor the only one, or was there

an older one below? To find out – and to try and locate Pinney's pot – the next day they would have to remove the rest of the rubble and then the tiles. Since the soil was so loose, it might be possible to force a stick through at regular intervals to see if it hit another floor (or even the pot). John Gater also agreed to assess the cellar to see if it was suitable for a **resistivity** survey, but he wasn't hopeful.

Late in the day came news of a great triumph for Stewart's team. By measuring angles and distances from the 1801 map, they had calculated what they thought was the distance of the animal mill from the still extant ruins of Stuart's plantation house. This had given them the approximate area where the mill could be. On their first venture into the jungle, they had immediately located

(Above left) The Great House ruins after the jungle had been cleared away. Mick the Dig rests at the entrance to the counting house cellar. *Mick Aston*
(Above right) Stewart watches Mick the Dig work outside the counting house cellar. Note the counting house's stone roof, built for added security. *Mick Aston*

the road to the mill shown on the map, and hacked their way down it the previously calculated distance. They had then split up and, 15 metres (50 ft) apart, began hacking three separate lines through the jungle. It was David Rollinson who shouted that he had found something. There, completely buried in undergrowth and hidden from the air by the tree canopy, was a building with walls up to 3 m (10 ft) high. As they examined it, they concluded that it was a boiling house. In order for the sugar cane juice to flow into the boiling pans, the animal mill would have to be at a higher level. And after they had ascended a slope, there it was, seemingly in as good a state of preservation as the boiling house.

According to David, the animal mill had been abandoned and never turned into a steam mill, a relatively common practice. This meant that we would be able to see it as it had been in Pinney's era, frozen in time.

Over dinner, plans were made to tackle the mill, which would involve a great deal of clearing of undergrowth before we could really assess its structure. Stewart, David and Charlie could not stop smiling – this had been a true discovery, for no one had been aware of such a structure until TIME TEAM had come to the island!

Day Two

David Barker, keeper of archaeology at Stoke Museum, had arrived late the night before and now had his first sight of the pottery fragments found in the upper layer of the supposed midden. It was all English, of a 'good but not too posh' standard and from about 1830–40, when the Huggins family had owned the plantation. What was unusual was that it was all of a similar date – why throw away a great many pieces of good china that were about the same age? David was unable to ascertain from which English pottery any of it had originated, except for one tiny piece that bore the name 'WEDGWOOD'. But although we were mildly disappointed that we hadn't yet discovered anything contemporary with Pinney, it was early days yet – and we hadn't really dug down that far into the midden.

The morning was considerably brightened by the appearance of Albert Powell at the site. An amazingly spritely 85-year-old Nevisian, he had left the island in the 1930s and had lived and worked all over the world. However, as a child in the 1910s and '20s, he had been a constant visitor to Mountravers where his aunt had worked as a laundress, and he was able to help Victor envisage how the place had looked in its heyday.

Albert told us how carriages had once driven up to the house on a road that ended at the west (main) entrance to the house, where there were tall bamboos growing. There were also fruit and ornamental trees – including royal palms in the back, along with a beautiful flower garden – and guinea fowl and wild turkeys used to nest in (and drop their eggs from) some of the trees on the south side. At that time, the estate had been virtually self-supporting, growing its own food and producing milk, pork and chickens, as well as such exotics as nutmeg and cinnamon. Those had obviously been halcyon days for Albert – 'I almost burst into tears when I came back in the 1960s and saw what they had done to the house,' he said sadly.

Having examined the counting house cellar, John had almost immediately decided that a resistivity survey – which was all that he and Chris Gaffney had to offer here on Nevis – would simply not work. Mick again drew the short straw and began excavating part of the floor.

Pete Bellamy had more or less finished excavating Trench 1. This contained not only the midden – which never produced anything older than 1840s, except for the still undated clay pipe – but also retaining walls and terraces dug into the slope.

Meanwhile Barney and Caroline Barker were recording the cellar floor of what had been the original Pinney house. Part of this was flagstone and the rest was covered in brick, perhaps indicating two separate rooms. The fairly low-ceilinged room was quite narrow, but there could have been other rooms beyond it that hadn't been cleared by our invaluable 'machete men'. According to the few old photographs we had, on top of the stone-walled cellar had been a wooden house, reached by a wide inviting staircase; one end of this house had

Medicine from Africa

Ecologist Jim Johnson, a former American Peace Corps volunteer who had worked in Nevis and then decided to stay on, wanted to show Tony some of the plants on the estate that are known to have originated in Africa. These had been brought to the island for or by the slaves themselves, their owners having recognised that the Africans' own medicine suited them better than the white man's. The following are the plants commonly found at Mountravers, along with their probable uses:

Aloe *(Aloe vera)*: soaps, shampoos, tonics, burns

Baby bush *(Kalanchoe* species*)*: burns, bruises, tonics

Baobab tree or dead rat tree *(Adansonia digitata)*: ornamental, food, water storage

Castor beans *(Ricinus communis)*: castor oil

Cupid's paint brush *(Emilia fosbergii)*: ornamental, aphrodisiac

Cusha or kasha *(Acacia* species*)*: livestock feed, charcoal, reliquaries and carvings

Flamboyant tree *(Delonix regia)*: ornamental (Nevis's national tree)

Gale-of-the-wind *(Phyllanthus* species*)*: medicinal

Gardenia or crape jasmine *(Tabernaemontana divarica)*: ornamental

Jamaican akee *(Blighia sapida)*: food

Jumbie beads *(Abrus pecatorius)*: sedatives from seeds, liquorice from roots and leaves

Manciport or mammey apples *(Mammea americana)*: fruit

Mountain yam or 'air potato' *(Dicorea bulbifera)*: food

Nettle vine or cowitch *(Tragia volubilis)*: cold and allergy symptoms

Pencil tree *(Euphorbia turucalli)*: ornamental

Periwinkle *(Vinca alba, Vinca rubae)*: blood pressure, sugar problems

Rabbit's food or lion's mane *(Leonotis* species*)*: heat and skin rashes

Torch bush or seaside sage *(Croton* species*)*: burning, colds

Washer woman *(Mormordica charantia)*: medicinal teas for non-specific illnesses, washing animals

been connected to the grandiose three-storeyed structure erected by Edward Huggins. It was these ruins that Bernard and Jane Thomason were now surveying, precariously gripping their theodolite while straddling the eroding walls.

Albert, having wandered over to the table where the finds washers were removing the soil from the pottery fragments, exclaimed in recognition. He pulled out a large sherd of coarse brown pottery and said that this had once been part of a small butter churn – as a boy, he had been required to push the central plunger up and down for 30–45 minutes at a time to produce butter for the Pinney estate cook. Then he picked up a piece of curved blue-patterned china and proclaimed that this was exactly like the soup bowls used 'in my day'. David Barker pointed out that this meant that the owners of the estate in the 1920s were still regularly using china that was 80 years old! 'Ah,' said Albert, 'but since it was so difficult to get the china from England, they took great care with it, so it lasted.'

Stewart asked Albert for his assistance to find the road to Scarborough's, another neighbouring estate, one of only two clues to the location of the Mountravers field slave village – according to David Small, John Pretor Pinney had written that his slaves resided near this road. And he had also said that he wanted to plant lemon and lime trees (which have fearsome spines) along the boundary with the Ward estate and that this 'hedge' was to be near his own slave quarters. Stewart hoped that, by locating the place where the road and the boundary met, and

using the clues he'd obtained from the aerial photographs and an early 19th-century map, he would be able to track down traces of the slaves' village.

Meanwhile, Carenza had been looking at an old photograph that purported to show a 'slaves' dungeon' quite near the Great House. After 'machete man' Rudy had cleared away some jungle a little way down the slope from the stables, she decided that this could be the place and began to excavate. But already David Rollinson and others were beginning to ask why anyone would have put a 'slave dungeon' so close to the house, although David Small pointed to references of this structure in the historic record. As for the location, when Stewart returned that evening, he pointed out that the photograph on which all this excavation was based actually showed the 'dungeon' behind a pipe running between the stables and the enormous cistern to the south of the house (which was 5.5 m/18 ft deep, with only 2 m/6.5 ft showing above the surface). Carenza's 'dungeon' site was well in front of this line.

Jenni Butterworth and Caroline had been called on to work at the animal mill, around which the 'machete men' had done an enormous amount of clearing. But by the time they got there – quite late because of filming requirements and the other tasks for which they were responsible on site – they had only enough time to reveal a few courses of bricks. However, they fully expected to spend the next day devoted to this relic of early sugar cane production.

Day Three

Jenni and Caroline (and Stewart, David Rollinson and Charlie) were to be disappointed. The leaders of TIME TEAM's tropical expedition had decided to pull almost everybody back and concentrate on the main buildings at Mountravers, which were to be substantially cleared by Winston and his 'machete men'. The only exceptions were Stewart and Charlie, who were to continue their search for the slaves' village.

As they disappeared into the jungle, David Barker and Pete discussed the strange phenomenon of a load of 1830–40 pottery being smashed and buried at the same time, as had happened to our fragments from the midden. Then Pete remembered that there had been a terrible earthquake on Nevis at just about the right time. It had hit the island on 8 February 1843, levelling much of the capital Charlestown and devastating many estates. This could explain why there was so much breakage of ceramics of about the same age.

The clay pipe: the results

The expert to whom David Barker sent Victor's drawing of the clay pipe found in the midden decided that the 'EB' was indeed beneath a crown, and this led him to think that the pipe might have been made by Edward Bird, a pipemaker who, originally from Surrey, had moved to Amsterdam, married and worked there until 1665. There had been a considerable export trade in his wares, especially to the Caribbean. His son, also called Edward, had continued the work until about 1683.

However, in the clay pipe trade, makers' marks seem to have been particularly valuable – and transferrable. Two pipemakers in the Dutch town of Gouda also seem to have used the EB mark. In 1683, pipe merchant and maker Adriaen van der Cruis took out a complaint against Jacobus de Vrieut because of the latter's use of the EB mark, claiming that he, van der Cruis, had held the rights to it since 1672. The complaint was upheld.

Because of this confusion with the EB mark, the expert decided that it was impossible to be specific about the identity of the maker of the Mountravers pipe, but the crown indicated a Gouda source and a date of between 1700 and 1720 – still much earlier than the other artefacts found in the midden.

(Top) Work begins on clearing the site of the animal mill, while Victor tries to envisage its appearance in the past. *Mick Aston*

Now we were just beginning to find things that were older than this seemingly constant dateline of 1830–40. Mick emerged from the counting house cellar grasping a piece of slipware bowl that David Barker assured us could be dated to about 1760. The clay pipe from the midden was also expected to be quite old. Victor made drawings of the entire pipe and a detail of the maker's mark: 'EB' surmounted by a crown or an eagle with outspread wings. David was going to fax this to an expert back in England to get confirmation of the date (*see box*).

Stewart and Charlie hacked their way laboriously through the jungle, following as best they could the ruined wall alongside the road to Scarborough's. (Doug Dreger, the sound engineer working with the camera man to film this Herculean task, later said that this had been one of the hardest assignments he had ever had – and he was accustomed to filming all over the world, including Borneo!) Finally Stewart checked his map and his compass and announced that he was fairly sure that they had arrived at the intersection of the road and the boundary to the Ward estate, and to one side should be the slave village.

However, to be absolutely sure that they had not been misled by the jungle, Stewart got into a helicopter with Mick and sent Charlie and researcher Julian Hudson back into the undergrowth to where he, Stewart, thought the intersection was. Then, when the helicopter was directly above them, Julian and Charlie let off a smoke flare. The intention was for it to rise above the trees so that Stewart could pinpoint the exact spot. However, to Charlie and Julian's dismay, the smoke spread *under* the tree canopy and they thought that Stewart would not be able to see it. (They didn't know that, from Stewart's vantage point, the light from the flare had shot out like a laser beam.) As the helicopter went round for another look, the two of them scrambled up trees and, almost at the top, began to shake the branches furiously so that they would be seen. They certainly were – and when the helicopter came closer to let them know, they were almost blown to the ground!

Meanwhile, Pete was now recording Trench 1, prior to shutting it down. Other than the pipe, there had been nothing older in the midden, but from other evidence on the site, it was becoming apparent that the terraces he had found were 19th-century.

Carenza had had a fresh look at the photograph of the slave 'dungeon' and had begun to attack the remnants of a structure to the east of the cistern. She was assisted by Sue Francis, who was usually employed on TIME TEAM creating computer reconstructions of finds but offered to help because we were so short-handed. They uncovered, among other things, a substantial stone window frame and the remains of a barrel-vaulted roof (which exactly matched the old photograph), as well as evidence that this building had been blown up by Walter Wade.

When David Rollinson was called upon to investigate, he said that the roof was of a particularly strong construction and this more than anything else said 'hurricane shelter' to him. Perhaps this was where the

Pinneys had sheltered during the three huricanes that had hit the island in 1772. However, David Small disagreed, pointing out that, while there was a reference to a 'dungeon' in the Pinney papers, there was none for a hurricane shelter.

But it was Barney in Trench 2 in the Great house cellar who was the star of the afternoon. After coming up with nothing particularly startling, he had begun to dig a small pit in the middle of the trench and soon was bringing up 17th-century artefacts predating the Pinney occupation of the site. Then, as he carefully trowelled down, an extraordinary sight greeted him: the characteristically gruesome face of Cardinal Robert Bellarmine! The entire face was on the broken neck of a jug that would have been made in Flanders in about 1680 – the cardinal had been the great persecutor of the reform party there and these jugs were intended to ridicule him.

This was not the first time that TIME TEAM had encountered Cardinal Bellarmine – the last occasion had been at the Richmond Palace site the previous year (*see Time Team 98, p9*) – and the jugs were common not only in Europe but also in the New World. But what made the grim-faced prelate so special to us now was the evidence he provided for sustained settlement at this particular place high up on the slope of Mount Nevis.

And that ended our excavation of Mountravers Great House. Except for some recording, the archaeological work there would finish now. But we had learned a great deal about the house and some of its associated structures, and would leave detailed records of our findings for future archaeologists on Nevis to carry on the work. Meanwhile, Stewart would get one more day to see if he could find any hard evidence for the slave village. However, because these settlements were so very poor – especially compared to the slave owners' establishments – they had very little to leave behind, perhaps only some stones on which wooden huts would have been built, hearths and very basic pottery. Stewart reckoned that we had a less than 1% chance of finding anything, but it was worth a try.

Over the next three days – the second half of our six-day 'tropical adventure' – we would be turning our attention to two disappearances: the Amerindians who lived on the island thousands of years before the British arrived; and the first colonial capital of Nevis, Jamestown.

(Above centre) The neck of the Bellarmine jug found in the Great House cellar. *Mick Aston*
(Above right) Carenza begins to dig in the right place to find the slave 'dungeon'. *Mick Aston*

Day Four

Nevisian legend has it that, in 1680, a huge earthquake hit the island and the then capital Jamestown – a few miles north of the present one, Charlestown – had been swallowed up by the sea following a tidal wave. It was even said that you could hear the church bell toll from under the water on certain nights. However, Stewart had reservations about this disappearance.

He took Tony and David Rollinson on a tour of Fort Ashby, thouht to be one of the forts placed to defend Jamestown. It was difficult to see that this had once been a half-moon-shaped battery, since a café (now derelict) had been built on top of the substantial stone structure. However, when they made their way round the back, to the side facing the Caribbean, they could see that, amazingly, the four cannons were still in place. (We discovered later that only recently been put back.)

David said that this particular fort had been built at the beginning of the 18th century because of fears of an invasion by the French. The only documentary evidence for a fort on this site were two maps drawn by a French spy in 1703 and 1706.

Stewart pointed out that it was highly likely that the present Fort Ashby had had a predecessor. The maps showed seven defensive structures, all within musket shot range of each other and two of which were intended to protect the colonial capital from seaborne invaders. The southern-most appeared to be in the same place as Fort Ashby and the northern-most was a mile or so up the coast at Cades Bay. However, since these would have been right at the water's edge, how could Jamestown have been swallowed by the sea? Indeed, one of the French maps showed a settlement (*'petit bourg'*) a short way inland behind both a battery and a horseshoe-shaped fort. Stewart was fairly sure that if we investigated the field on the opposite side of the road from Fort Ashby, away from the sea, we would probably find evidence of Jamestown. Meanwhile he was going to try to make a positive identification of any remains of the forts that appeared on the maps.

John and Chris had been carrying out a resistivity survey in that field during the three days we had spent up at Mountravers. It had been extremely hard work – with almost no wind, the heat had been almost unbearable, and the ground was covered in tussocks, fallen palm trees and coconuts, all of which made surveying especially difficult. However, at the end of Day Three, they had come up with some intriguing results, which were now to be tested by our diggers. Carenza was responsible for a trench across a 'rectangular anomaly' which could be a building. Mick the Dig was to investigate another large anomaly and Phil and Kate Sloane a smaller but quite strong one.

Although there was a bit of a breeze, the sun was searing even though it was still early morning. Mick Aston tried to make it less difficult for the diggers by weaving a shelter of palm fronds around the upturned base of a palm tree that had been felled by Hurricane Georges only a few weeks earlier. While Carenza's trench was producing little at this early stage, Mick the Dig and Caroline were soon revealing a mortared stone platform with four notches for postholes along one side. It was generally accepted that would probably have been a wooden dwelling of some sort. Mick the Dig was the first to produce a find – an early bottle base – but more were to come. Perhaps the most exciting were another clay pipe bearing the initials 'EB' and some pottery sherds which had once been part of another Bellarmine jug. These finds could be dated to about 1680, which showed that Jamestown had existed on this site at what was thought to be the time of the earthquake. Late 17th- and 18th-century pottery was also found in Phil and Kate's small trench.

Joan Robinson, who with her husband David runs the Nevis Historical and Conservation Society, pointed out that babies were recorded as having been born in Jamestown and there were other documents showing that land had been sold there for many years after the earthquake – in fact, right up to the mid-19th century. At some point – perhaps because of a fear of being inundated by the sea during the 13 hurricanes that hit the island during that timespan – Jamestown was abandoned in favour of Cotton Ground on a nearby hill: there are no records of the two places existing at the same time.

Meanwhile, we were also looking at a very different site on the opposite, windward, side of the island, at Coconut Walk, another sugar plantation. This was a complete change from the humid, jungle conditions we had encountered at Mountravers and at the putative Jamestown site. Here, except for beds of prickly pears, the vegetation was sparse and the few trees had been contorted by the wind. The shoreline was littered with driftwood and bits of coral that had broken away from the reef offshore. And to our delight, there was a constant stiff breeze that relieved the heat, although it tended to make us forget that the sun could still burn.

It was here that pre-Columbian Amerindian pottery could be found scattered all over the ground. We had organised a **fieldwalking** group of students from the nearby Gingerlands High School, who collected within the 5 m (16.5 ft) squares of a grid laid out with string and plastic stakes; all the pottery sherds, pieces of coral and bits of flint they could find in each square had to be put into separate bags, which bore the grid square numbers. The presence of flint came as a surprise: there is none on volcanic Nevis – in fact, it is thought that virtually all the flint found in the Caribbean originated from a tiny island off Antigua. As Phil had a brief look at some of the lovely pieces in a wide variety of colours, he said that Nevis had gone up ten times in his estimation because of the flint!

Fort Ashby viewed from the seashore. Note the stone base with the remains of the (now defunct) café on top. *Mick Aston*

While the students were investigating their squares, Chris and John carried out a geophysical survey of the area. They had adjusted their equipment so that their signals would penetrate the ground by only about 25 cm (10 in) to avoid as much as possible encountering the volcanic bedrock, which, because it had once been extremely hot, could send out extremely strong signals that would hide any anomalies caused by human activity. The technique appeared to work well and Chris and John thought they had found lots of human activity 'noise' and one very strong anomaly that just might be a kiln. Exactly what these signals might mean would be investigated by excavation the following day.

Back at what was now agreed was the lost colonial capital of Jamestown, a different tack was being tried. Mick, Carenza and local archaeologists dug a series of about 20 'shovel pits' – small holes only as wide and deep as a shovel – radiating north from Mick the Dig's stone platform. The contents of each were sifted and the number and type of finds noted. The result was that we now thought that our excavations were right at the southern margin of the former capital; finds from the 18th and 19th centuries became increasingly numerous as one went north.

While all the work was going on at Coconut Walk and Jamestown, the search for the slave village on the Mountravers estate was continuing. While Stewart was busy at Fort Ashby, David Small and Charlie Woodley started the difficult task of trying to find some evidence that the slaves owned by the Pinneys and Hugginses had actually lived here. To their astonishment, they were quickly rewarded, finding fragments of pottery and beads. Stewart then joined them in the hunt, and they found terraces on which houses would have been situated, the ruins of an overseer's house and a water cistern.

At the end of the morning, the three of them brought back their finds for David Barker to examine. Among other things, there was a sherd of Oriental porcelain and some stoneware, and all the artefacts came from a period spanning the mid-1700s to approximately 1840, six years after the slaves were emancipated.

This was a fantastic find for Stewart, David Small, David Rollinson and Charlie had found the only known location of a field slave village on Nevis and one of the very few in the Caribbean. They had also shown that the old maps that they had used could be relied on to give accurate measurements. However, it is also fair to say that, without the two clues from the Pinney papers, nobody would have known where to start looking. As a result, there were many beaming faces at the end of the day.

There was discussion about what to do next. Some of the archaeologists felt very strongly that it would be wrong simply to say that we had found the village and then abandon it, but wiser heads prevailed. There simply wasn't time left to do a massive clear-out of that part of the jungle, which would be necessary if we were going to find anything significant. In addition, the remains of the village were so fragile and so few that any further archaeological work would have to be undertaken very carefully and thus very slowly. All we could hope is that someone would eventually use our work to do a proper investigation of the slave village.

(Top) Victor's reconstruction of Nevis's first capital, Jamestown.
(Top left) The Amerindian site at Coconut Walk, with the lime kiln in the distance on the right. *Mick Aston*
(Above left) One of the shell beads found on the site. *Mick Aston*
(Above right) Phil points in delight at a large pot base simply lying on top of the sand at Coconut Walk even though it is hundreds of years old. *Mick Aston*

Day Five

First thing in the morning at Coconut Walk, Phil opened up a small trench over one of John and Chris's anomalies. A couple of inches below the surface he came up with an incredible find: a post-hole. The distinct dark circle of soil was all that remained of a wooden post, the rubble that had once held it in place and any soil that may have fallen into the depression when the wood had rotted. This indication of an Amerindian settlement was extremely rare, and it boded well for the rest of our investigation of the site.

We had been joined by John Fuller, a barrister on Antiqua who is an expert on the Amerindians of the Caribbean – the Arawaks who lived there until about AD 1000 and the Caribs who succeeded them. Within a few minutes of his arrival, he reached down and picked up a small egg-shaped piece of terracotta. At first sight, this appeared to have a 'sad face' scratched into its surface: two eyes and a frowning mouth. Then researcher Julian Hudson turned it on its side and it suddenly became a shark! This, according to John Fuller, had been one of the handles of a pottery container.

Soon all eyes were firmly on the ground, and those who weren't engaged in digging trial trenches over the geophysics team's anomalies were searching for more evidence among the thousands of plain (but ancient) pottery sherds that littered the shoreline. Charlie Woodley, liberated from the jungle, found two superb polished stone axes, and John Fuller showed us a shell in which a hole had been drilled so that it could be worn on a thong around the neck as a bead. But best of all was a cylindrical white stone bead that an Amerindian had somehow managed to drill right through – even though these people had no metal. John said that this was early Arawak and therefore extremely old, whereas most of the other finds dated from the period AD 600-800. It had either been handed

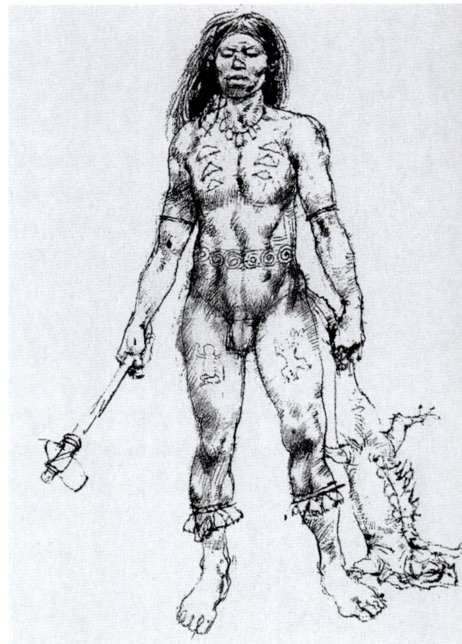

down from generation to generation or been saved by someone who had found it at another, older site.

Meanwhile, Stewart had found plans to the coastal forts in the island archive in Charlestown. From the information he gleaned from these – and with help from David Small and his partner Christine Eickelmann on the historical references to the defences – he decided that the missing horseshoe-shaped fort and the Cades Bay fort were one and the same. From an inventory carried out by one of the island's governors, he learned that Fort Ashby had been preceded by what was called Moreton's Fort, the plan of which coincided exactly with that of Fort Ashby. Having located these two points, he was then able to say with some certainty where the remains of Jamestown lay.

In the excavations in the field opposite Fort Ashby, which were now being recorded and closed, the diggers had come up with finds dating from about 1680 to the mid-19th century, but there weren't many of them. Stewart and Mick decided to look at a coconut grove to the north, in the

(Top left) Phil and the first posthole at Coconut Walk. *Mick Aston*
(Top right) Victor's idea of what a Carib warrior would have looked like, complete with prints applied to the body with carved blocks.
(Above right) The two polished stone axes found by Charlie Woodley. *Mick Aston*
(Above centre) The Amerindian pot handle - 'sad face' or shark? *Mick Aston*

direction Stewart expected the Jamestown settlement to have spread. Here he found the remains of five standing buildings, each two or three courses of stones high, as well as a plentiful supply of pottery and clay pipes. When David Barker examined these, he found the same date spread as in the southern field.

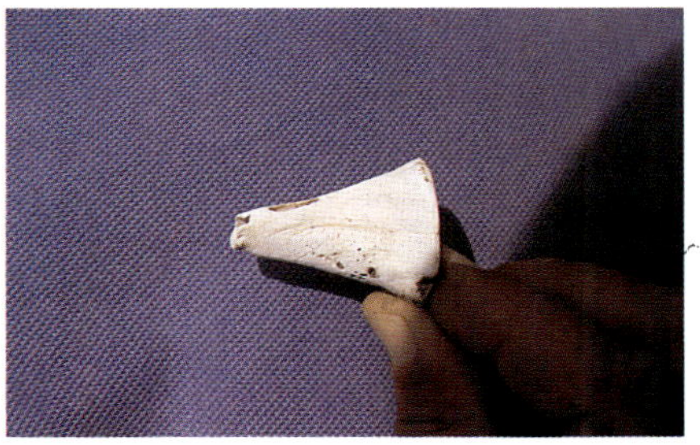

Even more exciting was the realisation that one of the buildings was very large - about 8 x 12 m (26 x 39 ft) - and Stewart found a hole on the outside of one wall in which a post would have been inserted. David Rollinson was certain that this was a 17th-century warehouse, similar to ones still to be found in Charlestown and on St Kitts. The posts on the outside would have held up the roof for ventilation. This was quite a discovery - in the late 17th and 18th centuries, such a substantial structure, which in Jamestown's case would have held the sugar on which the island's economy depended, would have been one of the principal buildings of the capital.

The cast and crew at the Amerindian site travelled up into the hills to the Golden Rock Plantation Inn for lunch. Here we were able to see many intact buildings that had once comprised a sugar plantation, including a counting house that, it was said, was the twin of the one at Mountravers. We were also able to watch in awe as a huge cloud bank swept in from the south and produced a horrendous downpour – the tail-end of Hurricane Mitch on its way to ravage Central America.

After lunch, when the rain had settled down to a drizzle, Barney set to work expanding the posthole trench, while Julian put together a gridded plan of the site, marking the major landscape features and significant finds. It was intended that the relative spread of the sherds collected by the students the day before would also be entered on this. To this end, the fragments in each bag were laboriously counted. Unfortunately, when this task was finally completed, the archaeologists had come to the conclusion that nothing on the shore surface was *in situ* – everything had been washed around by the storms and hurricanes to which this part of the world is so prone.

After their initial success with the posthole, John and Chris were to be disappointed with the rest of their results. A series of small trenches over what had appeared to 'sure things' – even a possible kiln - revealed only volcanic bedrock. The extreme temperatures that had formed Nevis in the first place had created strong magnetic anomalies that, despite the geophysics team's best efforts, could not be avoided.

As the sun began to set, Stewart travelled the short distance to Cades Bay in search of the northern end of Jamestown. It is likely that it was this fort that disappeared following an earthquake – a cannon had been found offshore and scuba divers and snorkellers have reported seeing objects on the seabed. But the earthquake and subsequent tidal wave probably occurred in 1690 and not ten years earlier – there is no record of an earthquake then but there is for the later date.

By the time Stewart arrived, it was already too dark to see anything. But a chance encounter with a local resident gave him a clue for the next day. Tyson, who lived opposite the Inn at Cades Bay, said that there were structures buried in his garden, as well as pots!

Day Six

Rain during the previous afternoon and during the night had left the trenches at Coconut Walk looking like little swimming pools, despite the fact that they had been dug in sand. In the large posthole trench, Barney created a small drainage ditch at one corner to remove the flood. This trench, which had to be dug extremely carefully given the fragile remains we were looking for, had produced two more main postholes and, in the dark marks in the sand, evidence of other (unknown) activity.

From the positioning of the postholes, it appeared that we had found the remnants of a hut. According to John Fuller, this would usually have been octagonal with a roof thatched with palm fronds and the sides made of a decorated woven material. Both hammocks and food would have been hung up within the hut. The cooking fire would have been just outside the door, and this would have been protected by a woven windbreak so that the fire wouldn't be extinguished by the strong trade winds that are common on this side of the island. The location of the fire by the door meant that the inside of the hut would have been full of smoke. This was

(Left) A *zemi*, made from a conch shell (*see* p102). *Mick Aston*
(Right) Victor's reconstruction of the Amerindian hut, the postholes of which were found at Coconut Walk.

intentional – it helped to keep down the mosquitoes – but it also meant that the lungs of the Arawak residents would have resembled those of four-pack-a-day smokers! (This has been seen in the bodies of Eskimos who had lived in smoke-filled igloos.)

Sifting sand along the shore led to the discovery of the types of food that the Indians would have eaten. There were bones of the surgeon fish and different varieties of parrot fish, as well as iguana and the extinct tusked rice rat. They would also have consumed vast quanties of conches, but there were very few conch shells about because, on this part of the beach, a lime kiln had been built as part of the sugar plantation and the shells and coral had been burned in this for their mineral content.

However, we did find on the site surface several axes made from very large conch shells. And a conch was one of our last – and best – finds. Its conical top had been carefully ground away, leaving a flat, smooth edge. John Fuller told us that this was a *zemi*, which had a ritual significance, often being attached next to hut doorways.

Meanwhile, on the other side of Nevis, Stewart had returned to Tyson's house at Cades Bay, this time during daylight. In the garden, he found the remains of two structures and pottery dating from the mid-17th to the 19th century. This supported the idea that he had found the northern extent of the 'lost' capital of Jamestown.

Following the 1690 earthquake, a massive tidal wave had ploughed half a mile inland at this point, according to a contemporary witness. This would have swept away the fort and probably some of the buildings at this end of the settlement, but the residents would undoubtedly have rebuilt more or less on the same spot, as they continue to do in other hurricane hotspots in the Caribbean. But over time, Charlestown down the coast became more important, and in the early 1700s, it was designated the capital of Nevis. Jamestown – so named because, it is said, the colonists who settled there had intended to go to Jamestown in Virginia – became increasingly less populated until, some time in the 19th century, it was abandoned altogether.

With nightfall fast approaching, the diggers from Jamestown joined the others at Coconut Walk for a final assault. They targeted two small areas right on the eroded edge of the beach. This was true 'rescue archaeology' for, within a few years, all of this part of the coastline will have fallen into the sea – the two places where we were digging now would probably not last the winter. This meant that we had had a very rare opportunity to look for the remains of this Amerindian settlement.

More pottery sherds were found, as well as the bones of fish and other animals that formed part of the Arawaks' and Caribs' diet. But although two burials, complete with grave goods, had been unearthed nearby by the Nevis Conservation and Historical Society, our last efforts produced only small finds.

In the short dusk, we loaded up the four-wheel-drive vehicles and returned to our hotel. There we found a steel band that had been working with producer Tim Taylor in our absence. So as Victor showed us his amazing panoramic drawing of what Jamestown would have looked like (*see* p99), and as we all toasted each other for having survived three of the most gruelling digs we'd ever participated in, we were serenaded by the steel band playing a curiously evocative version of the TIME TEAM musical theme!

Final thoughts from Mick

Nevis was an amazing experience and I think we all learned a lot from it. Most of us had never been to the Caribbean before, so it was all a new and exciting adventure.

In our brief time there, we saw a great deal of the island's wealth of archaeology. It was strange seeing many items – clay pipes, pottery, glass – that would be familiar on any post-medieval site, indeed in almost any garden soil, in Britain but here transported 4,000 miles to the other side of the Atlantic. Indeed, the contrast between our 8–10-hour journey via jumbo jet and the month or more of sea travel required in the 17th and 18th centuries could not have been greater.

The plantation houses and the sad stories of the slaves all had resonance with the owners' country houses in Britain – particularly for those of us in Bristol from where much of the trade was controlled and the wealth accumulated. A lot of what we know from Britain began to make a lot more sense.

By contrast, the Amerindian site felt very foreign, but I also found it immensely exciting and interesting. Few of us had seen so many finds at the surface on any other site anywhere. There was just so much pottery in huge pieces, together with conch and stone axes, beads and food remains in the form of shells and bones. If nothing else, this evidence reminded us forcibly that there had been people in the Americas before the Europeans arrived and that they had left behind a rich archaeology that we had been privileged to take a brief look at.

(Top) One of the Amerindian conch shell axes found at Coconut Walk. *Mick Aston*
(Above right) Drilled cowrie shell beads. *Mick Aston*

ARCHAEOLOGICAL METHODS

Aerial photography

Because earthworks can be so confusing on the ground, many archaeological sites have been found through aerial photography. Even if earthworks have been ploughed over, it is still possible to identify sites through scatters of stones, tiles and other debris, or through cropmarks (*see right*).

Aerial photography is also splendid for putting a site into context. Ancient field boundaries can suddenly become obvious, as can the strips of fields tilled centuries ago. Trackways and other features unseen on the ground can appear crystal clear on an aerial photograph.

Augering

Augering is a technique used by environmental archaeologists to look at deposits below the ground surface without having to dig trenches, *writes Jane Siddell of the Museum of London Archaeological Service*. In this, it is similar to geophysical prospection. Augering consists of driving a probe into the ground, and collecting a sequence of soils and sediments within the probe. This can either be done by hand with a small auger, or mechanised versions may be used. The probe is then removed and the contents may be examined to see what type of environment – marshy, for example – is represented in that probe.

The depth of drilling is accurately measured, and along with the Ordnance Survey co-ordinates, the results may then be located in three dimensions. The results can then be used in conjunction with historical surveys and geophysical plots, for instance.

The technique is quick and can cover large areas to examine how the sub-surface horizons change within the wider landscape – for example, to search for ancient courses of rivers and streams. It may also be used to locate specific horizons such as burnt layers.

Cropmarks

These are light and dark marks visible – particularly in aerial photographs (*see left*) – in growing and ripening crops, which reflect differences in the subsoil beneath. As crops, especially cereals, come to maturity, any parts that are short of water (because they are growing over, say, hidden stone walls or packed stone layers) will tend to grow less and ripen first, while areas of crops over pits and ditches will tend to remain greener a bit longer and be taller than the rest. These differently growing plants can, together, sometimes become ghostly outlines of former houses, barns and other structures, as well as ponds, walls and wells.

However, cropmarks can also be caused by the natural geology of the site, the weather at the time the crop was sown and/or is growing, and numerous other non-archaeological factors.

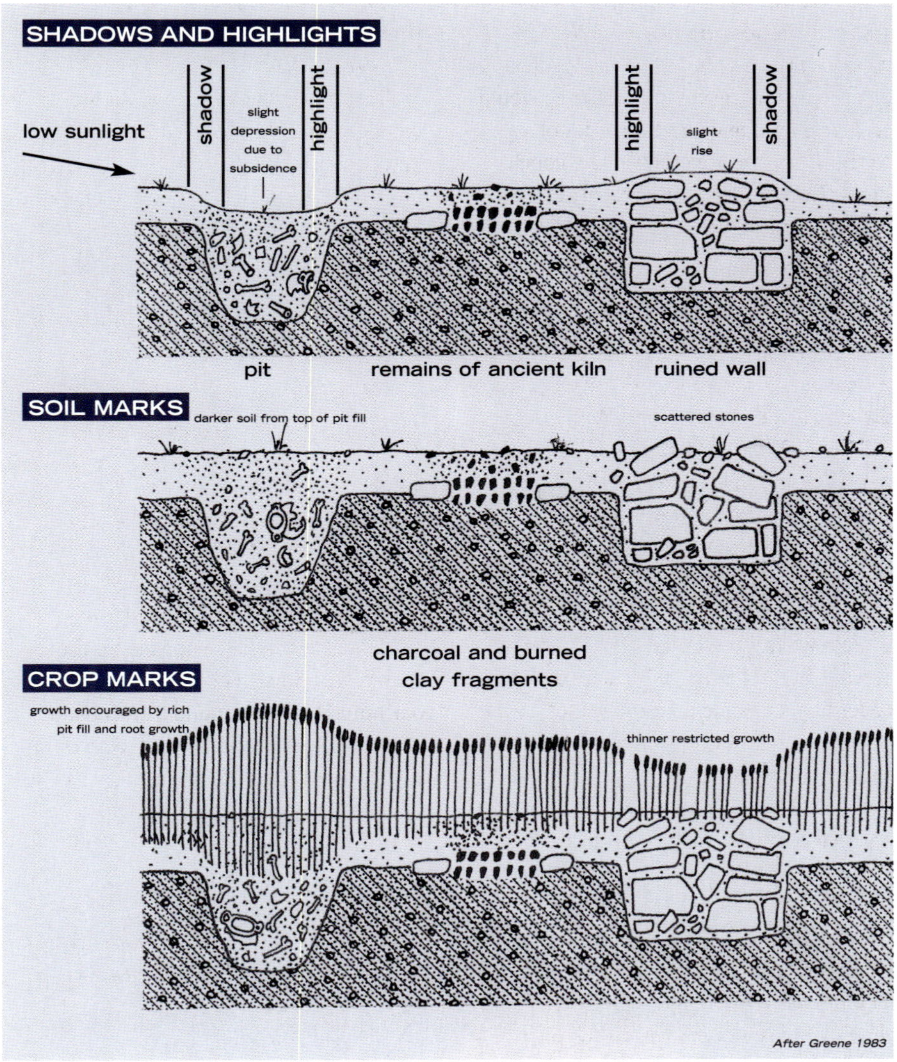

RAMAC/GPR

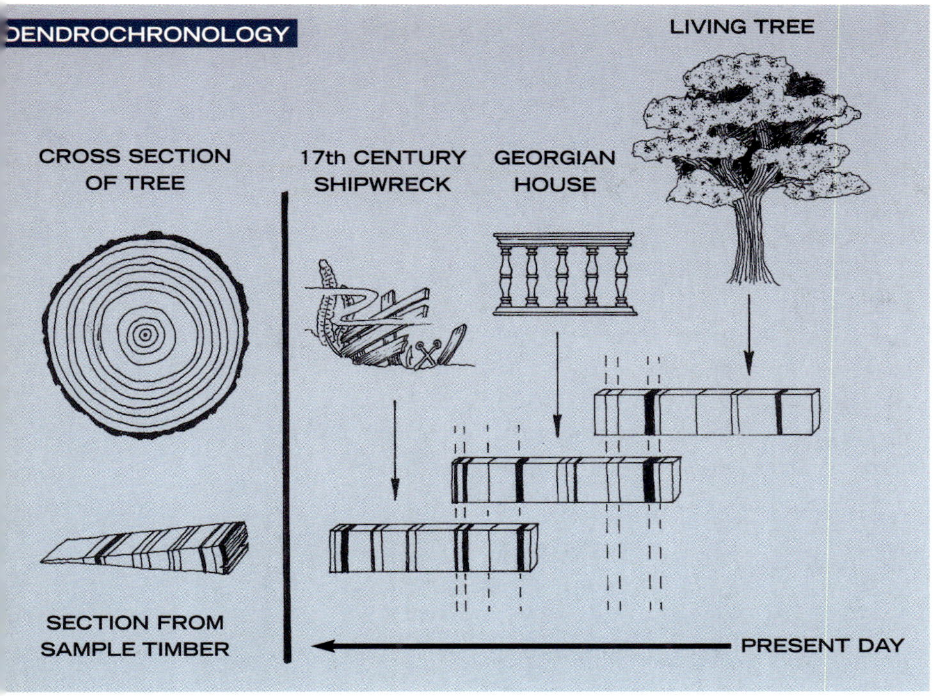

Dendrochronology

Dendrochronology or 'tree-ring dating' makes use of the annual pattern of growth shown by most tree species in temperate regions. Each year trees such as oak put on a layer of new wood under the bark. The thickness of that layer – the tree-ring – will depend on various factors. The genetic make-up of the tree and the type of soil in which it is rooted both play a role, as do other environmental factors, but generally it is climatic factors that determine whether the ring will be wide [conditions favourable for growth] or narrow [unfavourable conditions]... Therefore, examination of the annual growth rings of a tree will reveal not only its age, but also the fluctuating climatic conditions during its lifetime.

Within restricted geographical units, trees of the same species growing at the same time will show similar trends in tree-ring growth... In order to make use of the chronological information contained in tree-rings, long tree-ring chronologies have been constructed... The Northern Ireland chronology, for example, goes back to 5452 BC, while a German sequence from the Rhine area extends back to 8480 BC... [In England] there is now a continuous sequence that runs from the present back to AD 404, and another... covering 434 BC–AD 315... No English tree-ring sequence has been found that spans the 4th century AD. [From *Dendrochronology: Guidelines on producing and interpreting dendrochronological dates*, English Heritage]

Field survey and investigation

All human activities leave some imprint on the land, *writes Stewart Ainsworth.* Some are obvious, such as castles and cathedrals, some – such as hedges, fields and earthworks – less so. The role of the archaeological investigator is to identify the clues and traces left by the obvious to help find and understand the less obvious.

Evidence can come from many sources – maps, documents, aerial photographs – but mainly through looking at the ground itself and principally earthworks ('lumps and bumps'). These are the clues on the surface to what is below ground and tell us how landscapes evolved. By acquiring a wide knowledge of what archaeological monuments look like, the archaeological investigator can survey 'lumps and bumps', compare them to known sites and interpret them to reveal and understand the sites and landscapes built by and lived in by our ancestors.

Fieldwalking

An area or a site is divided into a grid, and fieldwalkers then move slowly through their assigned parts of it, picking up everything of interest from the surface – for instance, pottery sherds, beads, bits of glass, pieces of bone. These finds will tell the archaeologist a number of things. Remains of various ages may indicate that the site was occupied at different times and, if the remains are from different cultures, by different types of societies. If the density of finds decreases or simply stops, this can be a clue to the location of the site's boundaries.

The accuracy of fieldwalking can be affected by the state of the land. Ploughing can bring older finds to the surface. Erosion of steep terrains can lead to finds being buried much deeper than they should be or to them being washed away from their point of origin. And if a site has been occupied by a number of societies over time, it can be very difficult to discover evidence of the earlier ones among the greater number of finds from the later ones.

Ground-penetrating radar

Electromagnetic waves, *writes John Gater of GBS Prospection*, are transmitted into the ground and are reflected back to the surface when they 'hit' different layers of soil, tarmac, concrete or rock. The time taken to 'bounce' back gives an idea of the depth of the layers and a series of 'bounces' provides a detailed picture of the buried deposits through a vertical slice of ground.

Magnetometry

Archaeologists, *writes John Gater*, use instruments known as fluxgate gradiometers to measure minute anomalies in the Earth's magnetic field. These can result from the past activities of humans on an archaeological site and may indicate the position of buried pits, ditches, pottery kilns and areas of metal working.

Radiocarbon dating

This method of dating organic matierals found by archaeologists – for example, bone, antler, peat, marine and freshwater shells, wood and charcoal – depends on the fact that plants take up carbon dioxide gas from the atmosphere and incorporate it into their tissues. Some of that carbon dioxide contains the radioactive isotope of carbon: carbon 14 (C^{14}). When it dies, a plant ceases to take up C^{14} from the atmosphere and that already taken up decays at a known rate, allowing the time that has elapsed since the plant died to be measured. Animals and humans that eat the plant tissues take the C^{14} into their own bodies and so their remains can be similarly dated. After 120,000 years, so little C^{14} is left that it is difficult to get accurate results.

(Facing page) A ground-penetrating radar kit being used at Papcastle. *Mick Aston*

Resistivity survey

By injecting small electrical currents into the ground and measuring its resistance to the current flow, *writes John Gater*, it is possible to gain an idea of where buried wall foundations, floors, paths and roads are surviving. While these deposits result in high resistance readings, waterlogged ditches and pits will produce low resistance anomalies.

Seismic refraction

This is used widely in exploration geophysics, *writes Sue Overton of GBS Prospection*, but only has limited application in archaeology because of the relatively shallow depths usually involved. However, its strength lies in the fact that it does provide information about the depth of an archaeological feature or deposit.

The technique involves using a sledge hammer or a small explosive charge to emit a compressional energy wave into the ground. As this wave passes through the subsurface, there will be distinct changes in its velocity as it passes through different layers. At each interface, some energy will return to the surface. The time it takes for this energy to travel from the surface into the ground and back again is recorded by a line of sensors called geophones. This enables us to provide a vertical section through the earth. In this sense, the technique is similar to ground-penetrating radar (GPR); however, the latter is of limited use on 'wet' sites such as clay, whereas seismic survey is best suited to such conditions.

Stratigraphy

A 'section' cut through a site like a layer cake with a slice removed – can give a detailed look at the history of that specific area. This can range from the geology at the bottom, up through the layers that result from construction and occupation, with recutting of ditches, replacement of walls and the like, to the abandonment of the site and, at the top, the formation of soil with turf. The objects associated with the layers of a section – especially pottery and coins – can give good evidence of the date of occupation of the site

However, the depth at which finds are unearthed may not determine their age. This becomes clear when a site's stratigraphy – the order and relative positions of different layers (strata) in the soil – is studied, as in the example below.

(A) A church wall is built on top of foundations. Inside the church, a floor is laid, and outside is a grassy churchyard. Grave 1 is probably the same date as the church as it cuts into the same ground surface, but it may predate the church.

(B) Over time, a soil layer builds up against the wall in the churchyard, a variety of floors are laid in the church. Grave 2, which cuts through the built-up soil, must have been dug while the wall was still standing but some time after it was constructed.

(C) The church has fallen down and the wall has been reduced to a heap of rubble overlying the below-soil-level wall, the church floors and the wall foundations. Soil has accumulated on top of all this. Grave 3 has been cut through this soil layer and must be later in date than the collapse of the wall.

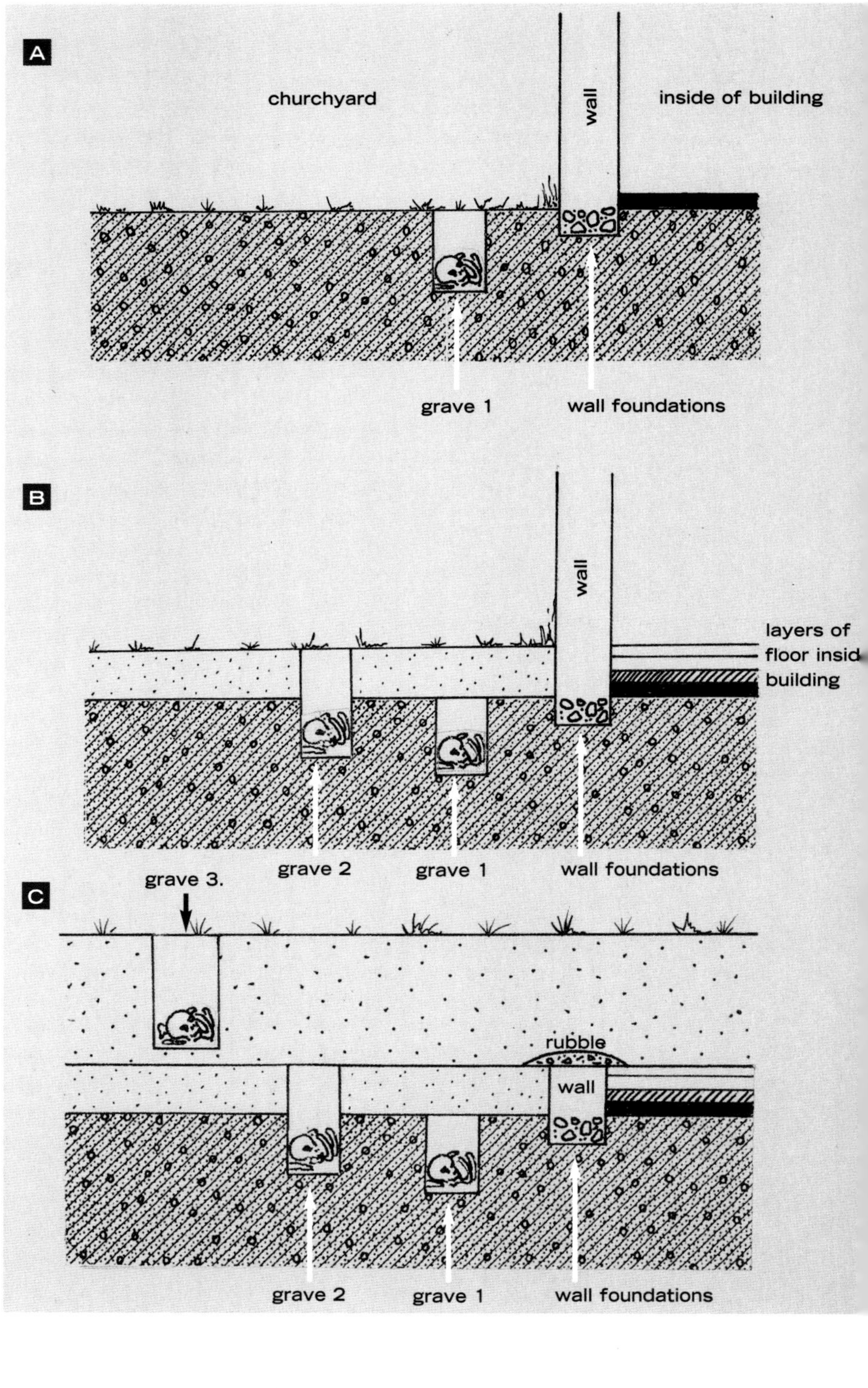

SITE UPDATES

SERIES 1: 1994

ATHELNAY & WEDMORE, SOMERSET

There was no excavation at the protected site at Athelnay, but the investigation continues. The farmer 'unearthed' a number of artefacts (worked stone, tiles, pottery, etc.) from corners of his attic. These are to be recorded, drawn and included in an article which will be published in the *Proceedings of the Somerset Archaeological and Natural History Society.*

Wedmore is a small farm site that was not included in the broadcast programme. The small evaluation trenches that TIME TEAM dug in an area of potential housing development provided useful information to the archaeological context of the site. Development permission has since been given, but an archaeological mitigation strategy is being agreed for the site. The priority will be to protect the stratified archaeological remains (early medieval and possibly some Roman).

LLANGORSE, POWYS

Archaeologists are still working on the reports on the finds from the long-term excavations, including the artefacts from the TIME TEAM investigations. A preliminary assessment of the slag and other metal-working evidence from the crannog has been completed. Llangorse has been getting lots of publicity, with a paper given on some embroidered textiles found during the 1990 season. Other finds from various excavation seasons, including the shale ring (now thought to be possibly lignite or kennel-coal), are now on display in the exhibition 'Courts and Kingdoms' at the National Museum, Cardiff.

Every effort is being made to protect Llangorse into the next millennium. 1993 was the final year of work on the crannog, and the remains have been preserved for future investigation. Recommendations from an erosion control study, commissioned by Cadw and the Brecon Beacons National Park, are under review.

The finds have all been drawn, and work continues on the forthcoming National Museum and University of Wales publication that will incorporate the results of the TIME TEAM investigations.

MUCH WENLOCK, SHROPSHIRE

The TIME TEAM investigation of the house and garden on Sheinton Street identified a mid-13th-century house with a stone-built solar and an aisled timber hall, which may have been the priory guest house. Excavation extended past the kitchens and uncovered a rear yard and a large medieval cesspit. Further investigation revealed a well-preserved cobbled courtyard and drain leading up to the back wall of the medieval hall. Further dendro-chronological samples gave a more precise date for the building (1254–90); one sample had nearly 400 rings, showing that the tree would have been planted around the time of King Alfred.

Later that year, building work on the other side of Sheinton Street preceded by archaeological evaluation revealed traces of lynchets (ancient ploughing terraces) that may be Anglo Saxon. This shows that Sheinton Street formed part of the Norman 'new town' built over farmland. Other work in the town in advance of redevelopment revealed plans of two other medieval halls, of smaller frontage dwellings and backland occupation. These findings broadly confirm the development model of the town suggested by TIME TEAM.

Mark Horton carried out some excavations in the area of the High Street, close to the presumed site of the medieval hospital. These produced worked stone and demolished structures, indicating a major stone building nearby, possibly the hospital itself, whose position has never been properly located.

All this work will form the basis of a study of the buildings and archaeology of the whole of Much Wenlock in the future. The dendrochronology dates have provided a good backbone for other Shropshire dates; some experts found the 1254 date hard to believe because it was so early. However, the dates have since been published in *Vernacular Architecture* 25 (1994). Reports on the archaeology of Much Wenlock are available from the Sites and Monuments Record at Shropshire County Council, Shire Hall, Shrewsbury, and the material has been deposited in the Shropshire County Museum Service.

A video of this programme THE NEW TOWN OF A NORMAN PRINCE is available. See page 114 for details.

RIBCHESTER, LANCASHIRE

There have been a number of small-scale evaluations and watching briefs in the village since the TIME TEAM excavations. Nearly all have produced interesting and significant archaeology that adds to the overall picture of the village in Roman times. One of the watching briefs chanced upon the edge of the ditch found by TIME TEAM.

Results of the TIME TEAM excavations

will form part of a forthcoming monograph by English Heritage on the Ribchester excavations, to be published in 1999. Most of the finds have been studied and are in safekeeping in Ribchester Museum, doubling the size of their collection.

A video of this programme ON THE EDGE OF EMPIRE is available. See page 114 for details.

SERIES 2: 1995

HYLTON CASTLE, SUNDERLAND

Following TIME TEAM's investigations, Sunderland City Council organised an earthwork survey of the whole area, more documentary research and a design strategy for reconstructing some of the Elizabethan gardens. The water features from gardens identified by TIME TEAM led to a grant from Northumbrian Water for a freshwater fishing lake in the grounds of the dene.

The city council's development of a park within the castle grounds is now complete. Work for this included a resistivity survey, the findings of which resulted in excavations. The archaeologists discovered a medieval cobbled road right in the middle of the proposed play area. The council redesigned the playground to incorporate the ancient road, and a footpath now follows the course of the medieval road across the area.

Another resistivity survey also revealed a cobbled courtyard right in front of the castle, and this too was incorporated into the design of the park. Landscaping has taken place near the west front. Archaeologists carried out some watching briefs and small trial excavations, in which they found some landscape features relating to the setting of the monument. Although the trenches contained no dating evidence, the features appear to date from the 18th century.

Open days were held at Hylton Castle in 1996 and 1997, with historical and medieval re-enactments that drew over 10,000 visitors. The castle is in the care of English Heritage, which has carried out some conservation work (on beetle infestations, etc.). The report on the TIME TEAM excavations - with a report by Beric Morley, the TIME TEAM buildings expert - is due to be submitted in 1999 to either the *Archaeological Journal* or *Archaeologia Aeliana.*

ISLAY, WESTERN ISLES

The stone-lined chamber on the top of the mound found during the TIME TEAM excavations was investigated further and found to contain animal bones, a fine Bronze Age flint arrowhead and a bone disk, which may have been a threaded toy. The chamber could have been a grave, but no evidence of burials was found. The finds are on display at the Finlaggan Trust Visitors Centre.

Next to the chamber, the archaeologists found two Bronze Age cairns. These are known to mark the burial places of important individuals, and there was evidence of a cremation burial here. It is possible that the cairns may relate to a regional power centre in the medieval period.

Dr David Caldwell and his archaeological team – accompanied by army engineers – returned to the site in 1997 and 1998. In 1997, they built a dam in the loch between the two islets, leaving a dry working area of 10 x 5 m. This revealed the midden that Tony had helped excavate underwater, and a couple of archaeologists were able to excavate the deposits in the dry, mainly by flotation and wet sieving. The midden was found to cover an area of 500 square metres, with a maximum depth of 1.5 m. The 13th-century coins sealed in the material gave an end date, and there was also 13th-century pottery, but there was no firm evidence for the starting date of the midden. The material remains included lots of animal bones, fishbones, insect remains and leather goods as well as exotic species such as almonds and walnuts.

The archaeologists were hoping for more samples of insect remains from the underwater midden, so in 1998 the army constructed another temporary dam to keep it relatively dry. Additional finds included metal mounts that seem to have been part of two dog collars (possibly from famous Scottish hunting hounds). The archaeologists also carried out a little work in the chapel and discovered evidence of an altar, a nice fragment of a medieval grave-slab and a late 14th-century Scottish coin embedded in mortar, which backs up the historical evidence for the chapel's date.

The TIME TEAM investigations led to a lot of public interest. Plans to develop the site are underway; one building has already been conserved and a tarmac road now provides access.

Quite a bit of post-excavation work still needs to be done, but by the summer of 2000, David Caldwell hopes to have completed the final manuscript, which will be published as a monograph. A report on the work at Finlaggan appeared in *Discovery and Excavation in Scotland* in 1998.

LAMBETH, LONDON

A permanent exhibition of some of the artefacts from the TIME TEAM garden excavations is now on display for visitors to Lambeth Palace. A full archaeological report on the investigations into Roman Lambeth and Westminster, including the TIME TEAM excavations, was published in *London Archaeology* (vol. 7, autumn 1995).

TOCKENHAM, WILTSHIRE

After TIME TEAM's departure, a small excavation, based on the geophysical survey results, was carried out to clarify the apsidal structure in the west wing and to see exactly how much survived. The apse appears to be polygonal with five exterior sides and a semi-circular interior. It once contained a magnificent mosaic floor constructed of very high-quality tesserae (mosaic pieces), which was totally destroyed 800-900 years ago. The high number of tesserae suggests that it would have covered the entire chamber and, had the structure survived, it would have been the third largest mosaic-floored hall in the country. The foundations had also been almost completely robbed away, except for the very bottom courses of local oolitic stone, the rest being just backfilled rubble. This supports the hypothesis that the walls were robbed out to build the earliest buildings in the village. Very little pottery was found.

The TIME TEAM report was published in the 1997 edition of the *Wiltshire Archaeological Magazine*.

WINTERBOURNE, WILTSHIRE

Archaeologists returned to this site following a new planning application for a building that has since been constructed. Four more Saxon graves were excavated; one contained an iron knife, but the rest contained no grave goods. The archaeologists suspect that they have uncovered only a small proportion of the cemetery, but no further work is planned. An assessment report is virtually complete and will soon be sent to English Heritage.

The report on the archaeology of the 80 or so burials found so far in the cemetery – comprising graves excavated prior to TIME TEAM, the TIME TEAM excavations and the latest handful of graves – is currently being prepared for publication. As soon as the material from the latest graves has been studied, the work will be written up and will hopefully appear in the *Wiltshire Archaeological Magazine*.

The most significant outcome of the TIME TEAM excavations was that the pond barrow, a last-minute discovery, was scheduled and thus protected. The TIME TEAM excavation finds will be kept in Salisbury Museum and the archive will be held there, too. A selection of archaeological finds from earlier excavations at Winterbourne Gunner are on permanent display in the museum.

SERIES 3: 1996

BOLEIGH, CORNWALL

The tops of the stones from the court-yard house exposed by the TIME TEAM excavations are still just about visible in Jo's garden next to the fogou. Jo has written a book about his esoteric experiences of living beside the fogou, interpreting it as having a religious or ritual purpose. TIME TEAM prefer to keep an open verdict until firm evidence relating to the fogous' function is found.

The geophysics team carried out a survey at the site of another fogou at Treveneague, which had been 'lost' for a century. The results of their survey were then tested by excavation to see whether the anomaly found did relate to the fogou. The trench showed that the fogou was still there beneath a field of cabbages but that much of the building stone had been robbed out. Accurate information about its precise location has now been added to the Sites and Monuments Record.

The material from these excavations has been studied and is now being drawn for publication. The excavation report has been written and will be published in *Cornish Archaeology* in the near future.

LAVENHAM, SUFFOLK

A report on the TIME TEAM excavations was written for the Suffolk County Council Archaeological Service series. A wonderful brooch that was found has been conserved ready for display, and the rest of the finds have been fully archived. No archaeological work has taken place on the Iron Age site since the TIME TEAM excavations as the farmer has been investigating the medieval remains on the farm.

The TIME TEAM weekend brought together Gilbert Burroughes and John Shepherd, a glass specialist from the Museum of London, for the first time, and they have continued the glass-furnace experiments started in Lavenham. In 1996, they built a furnace of a slightly different design, but still as close to surviving archaeological remains as possible. They found that, with the right size and shape of kiln, they could reach a similar temperature and melt glass without the use of bellows, as it created enough draught by itself. This amazed Gilbert who, as a potter and an expert on furnaces, didn't believe that such a kiln could achieve those temperatures.

Early in 1999 they hope to do the final experimental run, to improve the kiln fractionally and to maintain the fire for 2–3 days to get all the bubbles out of the glass. Glass-blowing experts are standing by for the go-ahead to attempt to make precise replicas of Roman glass vessels using this furnace, although they will use modern glass rather than recycling more Roman glass.

NAVAN, CO. ARMAGH

After TIME TEAM left Navan, excavations at Ballydoo continued. Archaeologists found lots of Early Christian glass fragments, including barley-sugar glass rods that indicated glass-working or manufacture. Armagh is historically the ecclesiastical centre of Ulster, but Ballydoo is only the second Early Christian site outside the city to have been excavated – a rare example of a site of this period that has not been destroyed by later buildings.

The geophysics team returned to Navan to carry out another survey for Jim Mallory of Queen's University, Belfast and his excavation team. The survey showed that the double ditch at Creeveroe extended more than half a kilometre further south, going over the hill and down the other side.

In 1997, cross-sections through the three main ditches at Haughey's Fort produced Bronze Age pottery. The 1998 excavations, led by Jim Mallory and Chris Lynn, targeted the fort's main ditch for dating evidence. Excavations at Tara, one of the other 'royal' sites, dated its big enclosure ditch to the early Iron Age, but Navan's could be anything from Neolithic to Iron Age. A cross-section revealed it to be 3.5 m deep, V-shaped and waterlogged at the bottom. A large squared block of oak was found right at the bottom, which dendrochronologists were able to date to possibly 95 BC (the date of the building on the mound). The block was charred on just two sides, suggesting that it may have been part of a structure. When the building on the mound was excavated, the lack of surviving wood debris had been noted. This timber could be from that building – the debris may have been cleared up and put into the ditch. A note on this is due to appear in the next volume of *Antiquity*.

The main report on Dudley Waterman's excavations at Navan Fort between 1963 and 1971 was published in 1997 as a Stationery Office monograph. The report on the excavations with TIME TEAM will soon be published in *Emania*.

STANTON HARCOURT, OXFORDSHIRE

Kate Scott and the Earthwatch volunteers have been busy in the Oxfordshire gravel pit ever since TIME TEAM left. Following the TIME TEAM precedent, they used a digger to excavate long parallel trenches right through the site, recording finds along the way, in an effort to get as big a picture of the site as possible before time runs out. As the area is being transformed into landfill, the excavation site is constantly shrinking and is now only an acre. The good news is that Kate and her volunteers should be able to keep working until May 1999 and Kate has been given enough funding to take them up to that deadline and on into the writing-up process. The excavations continue to produce new and interesting information and a variety of artefacts, but by far the largest category of finds consists of mammoth bones, making this the largest UK collection of remains of this variety.

The archaeologists have found even more stone tools, bringing the total number of artefacts to 21, all in different states of preservation. As some were found in the lowest silt deposit, Kate is fairly sure that most were from the land surface rather than washed down the river. One in particular – a black flint trimming tool – had very few signs of having been rolled in the river, which suggests that it wasn't in it for very long and hadn't travelled far.

Many more large bones have been discovered in the last three seasons, bringing the total to nearly 1,500. These include an entire bison skull complete with both horns, a spectacular lion jaw and the semi-articulated hind-quarters (vertebrae, ribs and pelvis) of an elephant carcass. This last was lying in a sandy area at what appeared to be the margin of the river, suggesting that it had not been washed down river and had hardly moved.

It has been a constant battle to keep up to date with the post-excavation work on so many finds. However, research will continue for another few years after the end of the excavation itself, and this will be followed by publication.

TEIGNMOUTH, DEVON

Chris Preece, the archaeologist on the TIME TEAM excavations, left the Church Rock shipwreck project and a new archaeologist has been assigned to the diving team. The site is currently buried under about 4 m of sand, but in 1998, Simon Burton carried out a sonar sub-scan and discovered a further part of the wreck, possibly a ballast mound. TIME TEAM worked on the stern timbers; this could be the rest of the wreck. Winter gales may pile on more sand or a single gale could remove the whole lot. It is now simply a waiting game for the sands to shift again.

Following the broadcast of the TIME TEAM programme, there was a record increase in visitor numbers to Teignmouth Museum. A report on the TIME TEAM excavations was sent to the Advisory Committee to Historic Wreck Sites at what was once known as the Department of National Heritage.

TEMPLECOMBE, SOMERSET

After the TIME TEAM investigation into the Templar preceptory, no further work was carried out, but the findings from the excavation and surveys will be useful to archaeologists when considering future planning applications. The report on the TIME TEAM excavations has been written and submitted for publication to the *Proceedings of the Somerset Archaeological and Natural History Society*.

When a number of houses were built under planning permission that predated the TIME TEAM excavations, a local archaeological society (SESAS) carried out a watching brief in the area identified by Carenza behind the high medieval wall. This revealed some more medieval features (the stone footing of a wall that seemed to line up with a TIME TEAM geophysical anomaly) and a little medieval pottery (mainly 12th–13th century, plus a little post-medieval) but no preceptory. Martin Savage and Hazel Read of St Alfred's College, Winchester have written an interim report on the pottery, and a site report appeared in the *Somerset Archaeological and Natural History Society Proceedings Newsletter* 55; finds will in due course be handed over to Taunton Museum.

SERIES 4: 1997

BIRMINGHAM, WEST MIDLANDS

In 1997, Soho House Museum staged an exhibition, 'Breaking New Ground', based on the TIME TEAM excavations. These have been written up and will be incorporated with the results of other investigations into a volume of the English Heritage Archaeology series for publication in 2000.

The TIME TEAM excavations in Soho helped strengthen the case for the investigation and protection of a Boulton & Watt foundry in Smethwick, a mile away, threatened with a demolition application. As the foundry comprises rare examples of standing Boulton & Watt buildings, the feeling was that it would make little sense to excavate one set of buildings while demolishing another. All the threatened buildings are now listed and were upgraded from II to II* – that is, they are in the top 5% for added protection, a rarity for industrial buildings. The foundry is now to undergo a full investigation, including excavation in the near future.

GOVAN, GLASGOW

Steve Driscoll remains convinced that Doomster Hill is a court site (moot). Stewart interprets it as a castle motte protecting a fordable river crossing, with a settlement growing up around it. Steve believes that, were it a castle, there would be some historical tradition. Stewart says that moots are unusual and rare, whereas mottes are common. In addition there are many non-documented castles, some of which, such as siege castles, were used very briefly and quickly abandoned. The market-place trench produced nothing pre-14th century, so there is no dating evidence for a moot, which would have been extant about two centuries earlier, whereas an early 14th-century date is entirely consistent with castle-building in Scotland.

Excavations continued after TIME TEAM left. The extension of the churchyard trenches cleared up the picture dramatically. The church foundations, which were cut through by the dateable burial with the face-mask jug, themselves cut through two earlier burials. The dates of these, which will hopefully be ascertained by radiocarbon dating, would thus provide a *terminus post quem* for the building. The remains of the road also came up quite well but not enough of the stone structure it overlay was visible for identification.

There are plans for a major excavation in the future, possibly based on the Doomster Hill area, but the archaeologists are still looking for funding.

LAUNCESTON, CORNWALL

No further excavation work has been carried out in the sewage works or on the site where the body was found. The water main, whose repair prompted the discovery of the skeleton, is no longer in use because of the finds. The water supply to the houses south of the river has since been moved so that the area where further bodies may be located remains undisturbed. When the new water main was dug alongside Andy Reeve's neighbour's garden wall, a number of flagstones were uncovered, which Andy thinks may be part of the lazar house. He also found two granite troughs across the road, and some medieval pots at the far end of the site.

The excavation report has been submitted *Cornish Archaeology* for publication.

MALTON, NORTH YORKSHIRE

Since this is a scheduled site protected by English Heritage, there has been no further archaeological work since TIME TEAM's departure. Malton Museum has held a TIME TEAM exhibition, and Ryedale District Council's Derventio 2000 project continues to move ahead. A report on the TIME TEAM excavations has been sent to English Heritage.

NETHERAVON, WILTSHIRE

Wessex Archaeology continued excavating for a fortnight after the TIME TEAM left, taking the same trenches down a bit further and recording them. No mosaics were revealed, just a substantial edge in the terrace, a curved wall of an apse and lots of building material (especially roof tiles), which indicated the location of quite a large building. This enabled Duncan Coe (country archaeological expert) and Ian Barnes (MOD archaeological liaison officer) to develop a strategy for the protection of the site. The area has since been landscaped, but the site of the villa itself had material placed on it to protect it. All the information from the excavations has been added to the Sites and Monuments Record. An interim report has been written, post-excavation work is nearly complete and the final report will soon be submitted to the *Wiltshire Archaeological Magazine*.

A letter to TIME TEAM from a viewer stated that sackfuls of tesserae (mosaic pieces), apparently recovered during the original building work, were given to local schools. He had seen a collection of Netheravon tesserae, so it appears that the villa did have fine mosaic floors after all.

ST MARY'S CITY, MARYLAND

As a result of TIME TEAM geophysics and confirmatory excavation, it is now easier to work around St Peter's and probe-test for brick foundations just below the surface. Among recent discoveries was the gate to St Peter's – located exactly where Dr Forman (who excavated the site in the 1940s) had said it would be.

The 1997 excavations were based at the site of 'Stewart's fort'. The brick remains that had turned up at the end of Day Three turned out to be brick-fill in an unidentified shallow rectangular feature with wooden posts and lots of artefacts. Evidence of fencing linked it with a known plot of land next to the final geophysics survey area, which must have extended far more than was anticipated. Some test pits based on a line on aerial photographs revealed a long palisade trench in that area, which appears to be quite early and contained relatively few artefacts. Middle Street (one of main roads) cuts across it, but the archaeologists don't yet know what it is. This could be all that remains of 'Stewart's fort', and it awaits further investigation.

Other recent work includes an underwater survey that revealed a possible shipwreck, excavation of the 19th-century slave quarters and a search for a merchant's house of the 1660s and the first print-house; the latter revealed 17th-century printing type and many other artefacts.

SERIES 5: 1998

ASTON EYRE, SHROPSHIRE

After the TIME TEAM investigation, Dan Miles took further dendrochronological samples and was able to tie down the dates of the various structures even more accurately: gatehouse (1341–52), solar (1469–71), barn and extension to gatehouse (1612/13).

The building is still for sale and awaiting conservation and restoration.

DEYA, MALLORCA

Earthwatch volunteers continue to help Bill Waldren with his investigations on Mallorca. The results of TIME TEAM's participation will be incorporated into the overall post-excavation strategy for publication.

DOWNPATRICK, CO. DOWN

Part of the site – Carenza's three trenches in a row – was investigated further to look at the feature that had produced a blip on the magnetometry results. This turned out to be industrial, almost certainly something associated with construction and possibly a lime kiln. The archaeologists excavated down to the top of the sealed archaeology but didn't go into it.

John's geophysics results have appeared in a book by Fred Rankin on

Down Cathedral, giving the definitive history of the site. The other results will be published as part of the longer-term archaeological investigations by the DoE into Cathedral Hill, hopefully within three years.

The church remains keen to turn the flat area on top of the hill into a coach park, despite TIME TEAM having found Benedictine kitchens below ground. This proposal is still under consideration by the DoE, so there is a chance that the archaeology will be preserved.

GREYLAKE, SOMERSET

A Bronze Age socketed axe found after TIME TEAM left is now in Taunton Museum. A few more timbers were discovered next to the trench, which are probably from same structure and produced similar dendrochronological dates. A few more test pits were dug; these revealed few finds, which gives more information about the extent and direction of the structure. The water level is being monitored and post-excavation work is ongoing.

HIGH WORSALL, NORTH YORKSHIRE

The post-excavation report is well under way. Results of the TIME TEAM investigations have been passed on to English Heritage and will help them schedule the site. A note on High Worsall appeared in the November 1998 *Annual* of the Medieval Settlement Research Group, and Robin Daniels gave a lecture to the Low Worsall Society on the anniversary of the TIME TEAM weekend.

RICHMOND, SURREY

The turf was put back on the lawn and there are now no signs of our trenches. The post-excavation work is complete and the report has been written. It will hopefully appear in the near future in the journal *Post-Medieval Archaeology*.

SANDAY, ORKNEY

There has been no archaeological invest-igation on Sanday since TIME TEAM's visit. Elsewhere in Orkney, however, a chamber tomb was discovered when a tractor fell into it, a Neolithic settlement is being investigated and a Birmingham University team has been working on a church site.

TURKDEAN, GLOUCESTERSHIRE

See pp82–8 for TIME TEAM's further investigations. The delicate finds from the 1997 'Live' dig have been conserved and are being studied for the post-excavation report.

RESOURCES

GETTING INVOLVED

If the TIME TEAM series and this booklet have increased your interest and you want to become more than an armchair archaeologist, there are a number of organisations that can provide advice and information.

COUNCIL FOR BRITISH ARCHAEOLOGY

Bowes Morrell House, 111 Walmgate, York YO1 9WA, tel: 01904 671 417, fax: 01904 671 384, e-mail: archaeology@csi.com, website: www.britarch.ac.uk

A first step is to find out what is going on near you – there are local and regional groups all over the country. The best source of information is the CBA, members of which include individuals and organisations across the whole spectrum of archaeology, from professionals to amateurs.

The CBA provides information, advice and practical support to assist those who want to become involved in archaeology through fieldwork and/or by participating in meetings and events. It also publishes the popular news magazine *British Archaeology*, which ranges right across the subject – from prehistory to the archaeology of the 20th century, from conservation to legislation, and from education to the latest discoveries and newest ideas. It also contains campaigning editorials as well as features and reviews by some of the best writers and thinkers in the field.

Members and subscribers to the magazine also receive the CBA's information listings supplement *Briefing*. This provides details of forthcoming fieldwork opportunities, events and exhibitions, conferences, lectures, day schools, short courses, grants and awards, and new books.

Young Archaeologists' Club

The young person's section of the CBA, the YAC – whose president is TIME TEAM's Tony Robinson – is for people between the ages of 9 and 16, schools and families. YAC members can take part in club activities, join a local branch and go on field study holidays. Each member receives the club's quarterly magazine *Young Archaeologist*. It is packed with stories of recent discoveries, news, reports from junior correspondents, competitions, questions and answers, and things to make and do. To contact the YAC, use the same address as for the CBA.

CURRENT ARCHAEOLOGY

9 Nassington Road, London NW3 2TX, tel: 0171 435 7517, fax: 0171 916 2405, e-mail: tsubs@archaeology.co.uk, website: www.archaeology.co.uk

With six issues a year, this lively and popular colour magazine provides good coverage of news about recent finds, new books and topics of debate. Subscribers also get the extremely useful *Directory of British Digs*, full of details of forthcoming archaeological excavations. The annual subscription is £15.00, payable by cheque or credit card. For an extra £10.00 (£25.00 in all), you can get the latest six back issues plus the Directory. Those with Internet access can have a look at the *Current Archaeology* website, both for a foretaste of the magazine itself and for a mass of useful information about archaeology.

ENGLISH HERITAGE EDUCATION SERVICE

Portland House, Stag Place, London SW1E 5EE, tel: 0171 973 3442, fax: 0171 973 3443

In addition to caring for over 400 monuments, English Heritage has a superb Education Service that exists to help teachers - at all levels - make full use of the historic environment. Visits to historic sites are a recommended part of the National Curriculum - and educational visits to English Heritage sites are free. The Education Service offers guidance not only on sites' historical relevance, but also on the part that visits can play in subjects as varied as English, maths, science and geography. Schools can subscribe to a teachers' membership scheme. Contact the Education Service to obtain copies of the following free publications: *Windows on the Past* (which contains details of the teachers' membership scheme), *Visiting Historic Sites* and *Resources* (which describes a host of educational publications and videos).

HISTORY IN THE MAKING

44 The Roman Way, Glastonbury, Somerset BA6 8AD, tel: 01458 831 664

Historical and environmental education specialists who use the local environment as a classroom and its resources as teaching aids to bring education to life for children. Their work is cross-curricular, covering history, geography, science, design and technology, English, maths, art, music and archaeology.

RECORDS AND ARCHIVES

The recording of historic monuments is the function of Royal Commissions that cover England, Scotland and Wales. Their role is to survey sites and landscapes and to record standing buildings. In addition to producing many reference publications, they maintain libraries and archives, most of which are open to the public.

Royal Commission on the Historical Monuments of England (RCHME)
National Monuments Record Centre
Great Western Village, Kemble Drive, Swindon SN2 2GZ, tel: 01793 414 700
fax: 01793-414 707
e-mail: info@rchme.gov.uk
website: www.rchme.gov.uk
National Monuments Record enquiries:
tel: 01793 414 600, fax: 01793 414 606
The RCHME, which employs Carenza, Stewart and Bernard, gathers information on England's heritage and provides it through the National Monuments Record (NMR), an amazing archive containing over 12 million items. You can use the NMR to discover your local heritage - just like TIME TEAM does. By ringing the NMR or visiting the RCHME website and giving the name of your town or village, you can be supplied with aerial photographs, lists of local archaeological sites, and historic and recent photographs of buildings in the area. The service is free, although there is a charge for photocopies, photographic prints, etc., and for a fee, there is a five-day express service.

Historic Scotland
Longmore House, Salisbury Place, Edinburgh EH9 1SH, tel: 0131 668 8600, e-mail: enquiries.historic@dial.pipex.com
website: www.historic-scotland.gov.uk
To access information on Scotland's 40,000 listed buildings and 6,000 scheduled ancient monuments, write to the organisation or visit its website. Historic Scotland also publishes two free leaflets concerning the archaeological record in Scotland: *Managing Scotland's Archaeological Heritage* and *Scheduled Ancient Monuments.*

Cadw: Welsh Historic Monuments
Crown Building, Cathays Park, Cardiff CF1 3NQ, tel: 01222 500 200
Ring or write to obtain information on Wales' 20,000 listed buildings and 3,000 ancient monuments. Produces free leaflets on listed buildings, ancient monuments and grant aid.

INTERNET

Check out the Channel 4 Internet site on **www.channel4.com** for the dedicated TIME TEAM website (you can find it under 'Knowing'). Here you will find information about all the programmes in the series, books of general archaeological interest, links to related sites, expanded biographies of all the TIME TEAM members (including soundbites) and much, much more. There are also links to the two 'Time Team Live' sites, which were compiled 'as they happened' during the excavations at Turkdean in 1997 and Bawsey St James in 1998; they contain a great deal of background information and many photographs of the finds. Finally, in the TIME TEAM forum, you can swap opinions andinformation with like-minded TIME TEAM viewers.

FURTHER READING

Oxbow Books in Oxford specialises in archaeology and carries an enormous stock of books. They also issue regular free lists of new publications, and can supply all titles by post. Contact:
Oxbow Books
Park End Place
Oxford OX1 1HN
Tel: 01865 241 249
Fax: 01865 794 449
E-mail: oxbow@oxbowbooks.com
Website: http://www.oxbowbooks.com

CHANNEL 4 TELEVISION PUBLICATIONS

The reports in the following booklets – all A4 size and with plenty of colour – are accompanied by maps, photographs, computer reconstructions and lists of further reading. The booklets can be obtained by sending a cheque or postal order (payable to Channel 4 Television) to: TIME TEAM, PO Box 4000, London W12 8UF. All prices include postage and packing. Be sure to specify which titles you are ordering.

The Time Team Reports
From the 1995 series: The possible location on Islay of the Gaelic 'inauguration' ceremony of the Lords of the Isles. The parkland surrounding the 14th-century Hylton Castle near Sunderland. A Romano-British villa found in a Wiltshire village. The banks of the Thames where the Romans may have made their first crossing. A 6th-century Saxon cemetery near Salisbury. *36 pages, £3.50*

Time Team 96: The site reports
Roman pottery in Suffolk. Mammoths' tusks in Oxfordshire. The Knights Templar in Somerset. A rare Venetian wreck off Teignmouth in Devon.
A prehistoric 'fogou' in Cornwall. An ancient royal palace in Northern Ireland. *44 pages, £3.75*

Time Team 97: The site reports
Historic St Mary's City in Maryland (TIME TEAM's first foray abroad), one of the earliest landing points of the English. Matthew Boulton's manufactory among the back gardens of Handsworth, Birmingham. A 13th-century leper hospital in Launceston, Cornwall. Dark Age 'hogback' grave markers in Govan, Glasgow. A Roman fort, Norman castle and Jacobean mansion in Malton, North Yorkshire. A substantial Roman villa beneath an army training camp on Salisbury Plain. *48 pages, £4.00*

Time Team 98: The site reports
The privy lodgings of Elizabeth I at Richmond Palace in Surrey. A mysterious Bronze Age trackway in the Somerset Levels. A possible Viking burial site in Orkney. One of the most important undiscovered Roman villas in Britain, found in Gloucestershire. An enigmatic Beaker settlement on Mallorca. A grand medieval manor house hidden within an ancient farm in Shropshire. The ecclesiastical settlement in Co. Down where St Patrick may have died. A deserted medieval village in North Yorkshire. *68 pages, £4.95*

CHANNEL 4 VIDEOS

Two programmes from the very first series.

Time Team: On the Edge of Empire
Ribchester, Lancashire: an inhospitable location for the first century of Roman rule. The team finds traces of the ancient remains of fortresses beneath local fields. *£9.99*

Time Team: The New Town of a Norman Prince
Much Wenlock, Shropshire: an oak beam and some stone arches provide a surprising link with an early Plantagenet king. *£9.99*

All prices include postage and packing. To order, send a cheque or postal order (made payable to Disc Distribution Ltd) to: Time Team, c/o Disc Distribution Ltd, PO Box 27203, London N11 1WQ. Be sure to specify which video(s) you want.

GENERAL BOOKS ON ARCHAEOLOGY

Archaeology: An introduction by Kevin Greene (Routledge, 3rd edition 1995, paperback £17.99)
An accessible overview, usefully illustrated, of all the main issues in archaeology: methods of discovery, fieldwork and recording, excavation, dating and technology.

The Handbook of British Archaeology by L and R Adkins (Constable, 1982, paperback £14.99)
Diatom? Quern? Clactonian? These are all explained in this handbook, which has a chapter on techniques as well as ones on all periods up to the Middle Ages. Although it has not been updated since 1982, it is still an essential reference work.

THE TIME TEAM CLUB
The Time Team Club is an exciting and forward-looking organisation for those who follow TIME TEAM and want more information about the programme and about archaeology. Benefits for members include a TIME TEAM badge; *Trench One*, a quarterly magazine full of articles about the personalities and archaeological methods used on the programmes; a dedicated book club; and great competitions with prizes that include the chance to attend an actual programme shoot. Members also get exclusive discounts on TIME TEAM merchandise, as well as special offers and discounts arranged with various museums and exhibitions. There are also educational opportunities to extend members' experience and knowledge of archaeology.

To join, write to: Time Team Club, PO Box 7000, Cardiff CF5 2YU
or ring: 0990 446699
You can also join via the TIME TEAM website.

Interpreting the Landscape by Mick Aston (Routledge, new edition 1997, paperback £17.99)
An enthusiastic description of how the landscape around us has been created, and how basic archaeological fieldwork combined with local history studies can help us to appreciate our surroundings.

Techniques of Archaeological Investigation by Philip Barker (Routledge, new edition 1998, paperback £18.99)
The standard work on the techniques of excavation, now updated and expanded to cover the very latest developments.

PAPCASTLE, CUMBRIA

Hadrian's Wall in the Days of the Romans by Ronald Embleton and Frank Graham (Frank Graham, 1984, hardback £10.95)
This book receives full marks for its vivid evocation of military and civilian life on a Roman frontier. Crammed full of inspired colour and black-and-white reconstructions, it proceeds along the wall from South Shields to Carlisle.

Hadrian's Wall: History and Guide by Guy de la Bédoyère (Tempus, 1998, paperback £9.99)
This guidebook provides the perfect companion to an exploration of the wall. As well as providing details of each site and an overview of its social and military history, the author, a TIME TEAM expert, gives practical details of visible remains, their opening times and accessibility.

Life and Letters on the Roman Frontier by Alan K Bowman (British Museum Press, 1994, paperback £9.99)
Many aspects of daily life on Hadrian's Wall have been revealed by the incredible stock of writing tablets found at Vindolanda. This compelling book discusses the context of the letters and reproduces 38 of them with translations, allowing us a glimpse of life on a frontier post in the 1st century AD.

Roman Forts in Britain by Paul Bidwell (English Heritage, 1997, paperback 15.99)
A readable but detailed study of the legionary fortresses from the 2nd century AD onwards. The author, who has excavated all along Hadrian's Wall, discusses the function of forts, military buildings, supply systems, trade and everyday life.

Roman Forts in Britain by David Breeze (Shire, 1994, paperback £4.99)
A concise introduction to the Roman legionary fortress, with a select gazetteer of sites to visit.

THETFORD, NORFOLK

Discovering Abbeys and Priories by Geoffrey Wright (Shire, 1998, paperback £5.99)
The new edition of this user-friendly handbook clarifies the difference between abbeys and priories, traces the history of monasteries from Anglo-Saxon times to the Dissolution, and describes the different monastic orders. Considerable refererence is made to sites open to the public.

Life in a Medieval Abbey by Tony McAleavy (English Heritage, 1996, paperback £6.95)
Colourful picture book explaining monasticism in simple terms, from a 'who's who' of medieval monks to an evaluation of the political role of the church in medieval England. Distinguished from other guides by some brilliant reconstruction paintings.

Medieval Monasteries by Jeremy Greene (Leicester University Press, 1992, paperback £19.99)
A good overview of the archaeological evidence for monastic houses in Britain in the Middle Ages. Using literary as well as archaeological sources, the author discusses the building of monasteries, life within them and their eventual dissolution under Henry VIII, with frequent reference to important sites.

Norman England by Trevor Rowley (English Heritage, 1997, paperback £15.99)
The Normans left behind a rich legacy of buildings: castles, cathedrals, churches and abbeys. This well-illustrated book discusses these material remains in relation to the social and cultural changes that took place following the Norman Conquest.

The Normans in Norfolk by Sue Margeson, Fabienne Seillier and Andrew Rogerson (Norfolk Museums Service, 1994, paperback £7.95)
A very attractive and readable description of the Norman impact on Norfolk as seen through the material remains: castles, churches, artefacts. Written in French and English and packed with photographs and maps, this is an excellent introduction to the subject.

PLYMPTON, DEVON

The British House by Edmund Gray (Barrie & Jenkins, 1994, paperback £8.99)
This book charts the architectural development of the British house from the earliest prehistoric dwellings to the 20th century. It contains a useful list of open-air museums and smaller houses open to the public.

Houses and Cottages of Britain by R W Brunskill (Gollancz, 1997, hardback £30.00)
Previous books by the author have dealt with the exteriors of vernacular buildings (*see below*). This volume concentrates on the developmental history inside houses and cottages, and on how to separate out medieval remains included in a modern building.

Standards of Living in the Later Middle Ages by Christopher Dyer (Cambridge University Press, 1989, paperback £12.95)
Between 1200 and 1520, the inhabitants of medieval England had to contend with war, pestilence and rebellion. This book discusses how different social classes adapted to the problems of everyday living, from gathering taxes (for aristocrats) to surviving wet weather (for peasants).

Traditional Buildings of Britain by R W Brunskill (Gollancz, 1992, paperback £12.99)
The unrivalled introduction to vernacular architecture. With its clear diagrams and reference to existing structures, this is just the thing for budding 'house detectives' curious to find out about the buildings surrounding them.

CHEDDAR GORGE, SOMERSET

Fairweather Eden by Michael Pitts and Mark Roberts (Arrow, 1998, paperback £8.99)
Although based on the amazing discoveries of Palaeolithic remains at Boxgrove in Sussex, this book also provides an introduction to the development of Stone Age archaeology in Britain. Writing in an exciting, narrative style, the authors brilliantly capture the frustrations (as well as the excitement) of archaeological excavation.

In Search of Cheddar Man by Larry Barham *et al.* (Tempus, 1999, hardback £9.99)
Reveals all about recent insights into the discoveries at Gough's Cave in the Cheddar Gorge. Tells the astonishing story of the DNA link between one of Britain's earliest humans and a Cheshire school teacher. The author appears in the TIME TEAM Cheddar programme.

Prehistoric Europe, edited by Barry Cunliffe (Oxford University Press, 1994, paperback £13.99)
The best overview of prehistoric Europe available. Each chapter is written by an expert in the field, but the authors have all worked together to provide a seamless history of Europe from 700,000 years ago to AD 700. Many colour and black-and-white photographs.

Stone Age Britain by Nicholas Barton (English Heritage/Batsford, 1997, paperback £15.99)
Excellent, up-to-date introduction to major themes in Palaeolithic studies, such as the reconstruction of past environments, the peopling of Britain and the development of symbolic expression. Well illustrated and readable.

SMALLHYTHE, KENT

The Good Ship: Ships, shipbuilding and technology in England by Ian Friel (British Museum Press, 1995, hardback £25.00)
Looks at the technological developments in shipbuilding in medieval England from AD 1200 to1520. The author appears in the TIME TEAM Smallhythe programme.

Medieval Ships and Shipping by Gillian Hutchinson (Leicester University Press, 1994, paperback £18.99)
A readable and scholarly introduction to shipping and shipbuilding in Britain during the period 1066–1500.

Ships of the Port of London: vol. 2: 12th to 17th centuries (English Heritage, 1996, paperback £30.00)
Study of the archaeological remains of ships and boats used in the port of London. Reconstructs the design and use of the ships, employing evidence from the vessels, from waterfronts and from trade goods.

Ships and Shipwrecks by Peter Marsden (English Heritage, 1997, paperback £15.99)
A clear and concise overview of British maritime archaeology from prehistoric log boats and medieval seafarers to the early 19th century. For anyone interested in the construction, use and function of boats.

BURSLEM, STOKE ON TRENT

Beneath the Six Towns: The Archaeology of the Staffordshire Potteries by David Barker (City Museum & Art Gallery, 1991, 80p)
This pamphlet describes archaeological work at kiln sites around Stoke. Burslem is one of the oldest centres, starting production in the medieval period, while other kilns thrived from the 17th to 19th centuries.
To obtain a copy or for more information about the Potteries, contact: The Potteries Museum and Art Gallery, Hanley, Stoke on Trent ST1 3DW, tel: 01782-232323, website: www.stoke.gov.uk/museums/

Fieldwork in Industrial Archaeology by Kenneth Major (Batsford, 1975, paperback £3.95)
Written by an experienced amateur researcher, this little book suggests exactly how to go about studying the industrial past. Everything – from photography techniques to field survey recording standards – is covered.

Industrial Archaeology: Principles and Practices by Marilyn Palmer and Peter Neaverson (Routledge, 1998, paperback £25.00)
This book considers how much we can learn about our manufacturing past, using archaeology. The authors discuss how to use documentary evidence and field techniques to discover how ordinary people lived and worked, and how modern landscapes have been shaped by industrial society.

Industrial England by Michael Stratton and Barrie Trinder (English Heritage, 1997, paperback £16.99)
Absorbing guide to the changes in the economy and in manufacturing in the 18th, 19th and 20th centuries and their effects on the English landscape. Lots of good pictures and discussions of key sites.

Josiah Wedgwood by Richard Tames (Shire, 1995, paperback £3.50)
An authorative and informative account of Wedgwood's life and ceramics,.

The Potteries by David Sekers (Shire, 1998, paperback £2.95)
Explains how Stoke on Trent became the most important centre for pottery production, and describes manufacturing processes and working conditions.

BEAUPORT PARK, EAST SUSSEX

The Iron Industry of the Weald by Henry Cleere and David W Crossley (Merton Priory Press, 2nd edition 1995, paperback £24.95)
An extensively rewritten and extended edition of the definitive regional study of iron exploitation, this book covers Roman, medieval and post-medieval iron industries in the Weald, and provides a gazetteer of still-visible remains.

Life in Roman Britain by Joan Alcock (Batsford/English Heritage, 1996, paperback £15.99)
An excellent social history of life in Roman Britain covering food and drink, clothing, recreation, administration and religion. Richly illustrated.

Roman Bath by Barry Cunliffe (Batsford/English Heritage, 1995, paperback £15.99)
The illustrated story of the discovery and subsequent investigation of one of the most important spa towns of Roman Britain. The author, who excavated the site, shows how bathing rituals were closely connected with religious practice.

Roman Baths in Britain by Tony Rook (Shire, 1992, paperback £4.99)
An alphabetical gazeteer of Roman bath sites. Also contains useful chapters on the architectural development and construction of Roman baths.

REEDHAM, NORFOLK

The B-17 Flying Fortress Story: Design, production, history by Roger. A Freeman and David R Osbourne (Arms & Armour Press, 1998, hardback £35.00)
Operational histories of the 12,731 B-17s that flew in World War II, including the aircraft that crashed at Reedham. The evolution, testing, and performance of the aeroplane are also covered.

The Boeing B-17 Flying Fortress by Martin W Bowman (Crowood Press, 1998, hardback £25.00)
A detailed examination of the design, development and operational career of the Flying Fortress, from its earliest beginnings through its seven major variants.

Claims to Fame: The B-17 Flying Fortress by Steve Birdsall and Roger A Freeman (Arms & Armour Press, 1997, paperback £10.99)
The B-17 Flying Fortress was the most successful bomber in World War II and was held in great affection by its crews. Its claims to fame include the most missions flown, the shortest operational life, famous crew members, and the most damaged aircraft.

Final Flights: Dramatic wartime incidents revealed by aviation archaeology by Ian McLachlan (Patrick Stephens Ltd, 1989, hardback £14.95)
An account of the salvage of various aircraft crash sites in England by aircraft enthusiasts, as well as the stories behind the crashes. Although narrative sometimes triumphs over fact, everything is based on true stories that no fiction can match. The author appears in the TIME TEAM Reedham programme.

Twentieth-Century Defences in Britain: An introductory guide (Council for British Archaeology Practical Handbook in Archaeology 12)
The CBA's Defence of Britain project aims to record as many as possible of 20th-century military sites and structures. This is an illustrated handbook providing an introduction to the recognition and interpretation of Britain's wartime archaeology.

Those interested in historical aviation may be interested in joining the **Airfield Research Group**. Contact: John Nichols, 220 Woodland Avenue, Hutton, Brentwood, Essex CM13 1DA. A list of further societies with interests in various aspects of 20th-century military history can be found in the CBA's Defence of Britain newsletter, available online at:
http://britac3.britac.ac.uk/cba/projects/dob/
or contact the CBA for a paper version.

BAWSEY ST JAMES, NORFOLK

The Anglo-Saxons, edited by James Graham-Campbell (Penguin, 1991, paperback £16.00)
Three experts have collaborated to produce this complete, illustrated guide to the Anglo-Saxons, from their arrival in England to their conversion to Christianity and defence of Britain against Viking attacks.

An Archaeology of the Early Anglo-Saxon Kingdoms by C J Arnold (Routledge, new edition. 1997, paperback £17.99)
The key introduction to Anglo-Saxon studies and the polemics spurring research in this field. The book confronts the major questions concerning how Christian medieval England emerged from the chaotic and pagan Dark Ages.

Churches in the Landscape by Richard Morris (Phoenix, 1997, paperback £14.99)
Classic study of the development of the English parish church. The author shows how the placing of Christian churches was often affected by earlier pagan traditions.

Recording a Church: An illustrated glossary by Thomas Cocke *et al.* (Council for British Archaeology, 3rd edition. 1996, paperback £6.50)
An invaluable reference book, giving illustrated definitions of 500 terms used to describe church architecture and furniture.

The Stone Skeleton: Structural engineering of masonry architecture by Jacques Heyman (Cambridge University Press, 1995, paperback £19.95)
Explores in scientific detail the structural action of stone buildings, considering among other questions, how the flying buttress of a Gothic cathedral can transfer weight to the foundations and the effect of wind on a spire or bell-ringing on a tower.

The Vikings in Norfolk by Sue Margeson (Norfolk Museums Service, 1997, paperback £7.50)
A brief but well-presented and clearly expressed account of the Viking arrival in Norfolk and what they did once settled. Lots of good pictures; easy reading.

KEMERTON, WORCESTERSHIRE

Britain and the Celtic Iron Age by Simon James and Valerie Rigby (British Museum Press, 1997, paperback £9.99)
Excellent introduction to the Celts; marvellously illustrated with lots of pictures of sites and artefacts and chapters on people, economy, settlement, society, ritual and communications.

Bronze Age Britain by Michael Parker Pearson (Batsford, 1996, paperback £15.99)
Based on the prehistoric evidence, as well as current research and debate, this book examines how life in Britain changed during the period 4000–900 BC. Illustrated with lots of maps, plans, reconstructions and photographs.

Crickley Hill: The hillfort defences by Philip Dixon (Crickley Hill Trust, 1994, hardback £19.95)
Just across the valley from Bredon Hill is the huge Iron Age hillfort of Crickley. It shares more than just location, containing extensive evidence of earlier, ritual habitation just like Bredon. This is the first volume of excavation reports and describes the huge stone walls and ditches that defended the fort.

Farmers in Prehistoric Britain by Francis Pryor (Tempus, 1998, hardback £18.99)
Wearing both his hats as archaeologist and farmer, Pryor has produced an empathic work on the life and methods of prehistoric farmers. Often what survives is just a few cropmarks, but this work brings what is now obscure into vivid reality. The author appears in the TIME TEAM Kemerton programme.

Iron Age Britain by Barry Cunliffe (English Heritage, 1995, paperback £15.99)
Between 700 BC and the Roman conquest of Britain in AD 43, a number of important social changes took place. Still existing regional boundaries were established, hillforts such as those on Bredon Hill were built by warring chiefs and the first towns were founded. This well-illustrated book surveys the period.

TURKDEAN, GLOUCESTERSHIRE

The Landscape of Roman Britain by Ken and Petra Dark (Sutton Publishing, 1997, paperback £10.99)
A history of Roman Britain, considering the effects of human activity on the landscape, with particular attention paid to the Iron Age background.

Roman Britain by Martin Millett (English Heritage, 1995, paperback £15.99)
Making full use of the archaeological material available, this introductory study of four centuries of Roman presence in Britain explores the central themes of daily life, laying particular emphasis on the social, economic and cultural history.

Roman Gloucestershire by Alan McWhirr (Sutton Publishing, 1991, paperback £6.95)
A summary of the evidence for the Roman towns of Cirencester, Bath and Gloucester, as well as for the rich rural villas.

Roman Villas and the Countryside by Guy de la Bédoyère (English Heritage, 1993, paperback £15.99)
Places villas firmly in the context of the wider landscape and examines their place in the overall economy of Roman Britain.

Vitruvius: On Architecture, translated by Frank Granger (Harvard University Press, 1996, hardback £12.95)
Studied by architects from the Renaissance to the present, Vitruvius's book is an incredible DIY handbook ranging from recipes for plaster and paint to the aesthetic use of marble and the construction of siege engines. An invaluable reference for TIME TEAM cameos and a guide to the styles and means of construction of Roman buildings that survive today.

Women in Roman Britain by Lindsay Allason-Jones (British Museum Press, 1992, paperback £9.95)
Tombstones, writing tablets and curse tablets have revealed a great deal about the lives of Romano-British women, their social status, health, pastimes, dress, jewellery, hairstyles, homes and religion. The author, a TIME TEAM 'finds ' expert has produced a wide-ranging survey of the information.

NEVIS, WEST INDIES

An Archaeology of Social Space: Analysing coffee plantations in Jamaica's Blue Mountains by James A Delle (Plenum Press, 1998, hardback £29.95)
An archaeological study of the use of space in three coffee plantations, addressing various issues including negotiation of power within the context of a plantation, both before and after the abolition of slavery.

A Guide to Artifacts of Colonial America by Ivor Noel Hume (Vintage, new edition. 1991, paperback £12.95)
A clear and concise illustrated reference guide to Colonial-era artefacts ranging from Delftware and Wedgwood to clay tobacco pipes, cutlery and firearms.
Historical Archaeology: A brief introduction by C E Orser and B M Fagan (HarperCollins, 1995, paperback £8.99)
The archaeological study of people documented in recent history has expanded dramatically in the last few decades. This book describes the basic principles, theory and global applications.

Seeds of Change, edited by Herman J Viola and Carolyn Margolis (Smithsonian Institution Press, 1991, paperback £7.95)
Attractive and stimulating book about the exchange of plants, animals and disease between the Old and New Worlds.

Settlers on the Eastern Shore: British colonies in America 1607-1750, edited by John Scott (Facts on File, 1994, paperback £7.95)
A concise history of the British colonisation of North America.

Swords, Ships & Sugar: A history of Nevis to 1900 by Vincent K Hubbard (Premiere Editions International, 1997, paperback $14.95)
A history of the island of Nevis, documenting the lives of its earliest peoples and later settlers.

TIME TEAM THANKS

TIME TEAM would not be possible without the generous assistance and support of a large number of individuals and organisations.

The producers would like to express their sincere gratitude to all of them - too many, unfortunately, to name here, but omission from this list does not imply that your contribution has not been valued.

Dr Humphrey Welfare and the Royal Commission on the Historical Monuments of England, whose staff and vast library of aerial photographs are always at our disposal (*see* p113).

Andrew Lawson, Director of Wessex Archaeology.

Professor Richard Harrison and Dr Mark Horton of the Centre for the Study of the Historic Environment at the University of Bristol.

For the provision of maps for all the sites: Ordnance Survey (Romsey Road, Maybush, Southampton, SO16 4GU) and Landmark Information Group Ltd (7 Abbey Court, Eagle Way, Sowton, Exeter).

For the loan of artefacts for the filming of the title sequence: Bristol City Museum.

English Heritage, the Natural History Museum and the National Maritime Museum.

Airshelta Ltd, Scotts Pumps and Trenchshore Ltd.

GSB Prospection Ltd (The Old Sunday School, Kipping Lane, Thornton, Bradford) for their untiring geophysical work.

The county archaeologists and services and local archaeological trusts without whose support many programmes would not have been possible – especially Andrew Rogerson in Norfolk; Malcolm Atkin in Worcestershire; Neil Holbrook and the Cotswold Archaeological Trust; Bill Klemperer, city archaeologist, Stoke-on-Trent; Dr Keith Ray, CAO for Devon; and Mike McCarthy, city archaeologist for Carlisle.

And finally, all the landowners without whose permissions and cooperation there would be no series.

Published in 1999 by Channel 4 Television
124 Horseferry Road, London SW1P 2TX

Produced by Broadcasting Support Services to accompany TIME TEAM
(a VideoText/Picture House production for Channel 4),
first shown on Channel 4 in January-March 1999

Editor: Paula Snyder Editorial consultant: Nancy Duin Design: 9th Planet, London
Writer (Plympton and Bawsey St James): Steve Platt Writer (updates): Victoria Batten
Maps and illustrations: Nick Pearson
Computer reconstructions: Creative TV Facilities Printer: Windsor Print Production Ltd
Distributed by Broadcasting Support Services

bss

Broadcasting Support Services provides follow-up services for viewers and listeners and runs long-term helplines.

Channel 4 would like to thank the following for their assistance:
Stewart Ainsworth, Guy Apter, Malcolm Atkin, David Barker, Gaye Blake Roberts, Nigel Cameron, John Fuller, John Gater, Damien Goodburn, Karla Goodman, Jim Johnson, Bill Klemperer, Sue Ovenden, William Pinney, Ray, Chris, Reynolds, Andrew Rogerson, Jane Siddell, David Small, Sgt Paul Stratford, Mick Worthington.

To find out more about off-screen services for Channel 4 viewers

- telephone (0990) 44 66 99 for a free catalogue of booklets in print
- go to 4-Tel page 340
- visit the Channel 4 website at www.channel4.com

For further copies of this publication, please send a cheque or postal order (made payable to Channel 4 Television) for £7.95 (including postage & packing) to:
TIME TEAM 98, PO Box 4000, Manchester M60 3LL or Cardiff CF5 2XT
Alternatively, you can telephone 0990 44 66 99.

If you would like to find out about archaeology or history courses or other local learning opportunities, you can ring Learning Direct on (0800) 100 900. Lines are open from 9am to 9pm Monday to Friday and from 9am to noon on Saturday. All calls are free.